PRAISE FOR

Will Write for Food

"*Will Write for Food* is a great gift, not just for those who are new to food writing, but for those already ensconced in the business. Dianne's clarity, kind suggestions, and nudges and admonitions to work well are truly inspiring."

—Deborah Madison, author of *Vegetarian Cooking for Everyone*

"After writing a successful blog for over a decade, writing four books, and still expanding my business, I really do credit this book with giving me the hope I could do this."

—Shauna James Ahern, Gluten-Free Girl and the Chef

"I quite often recommend and give a copy of *Will Write for Food* to new authors . . . it's a terrific introduction to cookbook writing."

—Robert McCullough, Publisher Appetite by Random House

"Dianne Jacob has presented budding food writers with a clear blueprint on how to get started in the business."

—Michael Bauer, Executive Food and Wine Editor,
San Francisco Chronicle

"My only complaint about *Will Write for Food*—and it's a big one—is that it wasn't around when I started my career. If you're serious about becoming a food writer, save yourself years of banging your head against the wall in frustration and run to the checkout with this book now."

—David Leite, food writer and publisher
and editor of Leite's Culinaria

"Required reading for everyone interested in learning how to translate their passion for food into words. Dianne Jacob offers up a smorgasbord of practical advice for anyone who has ever aspired to write about food, and she shows how to make writing a tasty and lucrative pastime."

—Darra Goldstein, founding editor, *Gastronomica* magazine

"This book does a great job of covering the nuts and bolts of food writing, for sure, but Jacob delivers much more than the usual advice: She shoots straight about the realities of the business, provides loads of insider insights and practical exercises, and radiates enough genuine enthusiasm to get both beginning writers and seasoned pros up and at 'em."

—Martha Holmberg, cookbook author and former publisher,
Fine Cooking magazine

"You'll find everything you need to know about becoming a food writer in this indispensable information-packed book. And if you're already a food writer, this book will help you become a better one. Useful writing exercises concluding each chapter help sharpen your skills. If food writing is your passion, then grab a copy of *Will Write for Food* and get busy!"

—Greg Patent, author of *Baking in America*

Will
WRITE
for
FOOD

Will WRITE *for* FOOD

THIRD EDITION

the complete guide
to writing cookbooks,
blogs, memoir, recipes,
and more

DIANNE JACOB

Da Capo
LIFE
LONG

A Member of the Perseus Books Group

Copyright © 2005, 2010, 2015 by Dianne Jacob

All rights reserved. No part of this publication may be reproduced, stored in a retrieval system, or transmitted, in any form or by any means, electronic, mechanical, photocopying, recording, or otherwise, without the prior written permission of the publisher. Printed in the United States of America. For information, address Da Capo Press, 44 Farnsworth Street, 3rd Floor, Boston, MA 02210

Designed by Pauline Brown

Set in 11 point Goudy Oldstyle by the Perseus Books Group

Library of Congress Cataloging-in-Publication Data

Jacob, Dianne, 1955–

  Will write for food : the complete guide to writing cookbooks, blogs, memoir, recipes, and more / Dianne Jacob. — Third edition.

    pages cm

  Includes bibliographical references and index.

    ISBN 978-0-7382-1805-2 (paperback) — ISBN 978-0-7382-1806-9 (e-book) 1. Food writing. I. Title.

  TX644.J33 2015

  808.06'6641—dc23

                                                        2015003915

First published by Marlowe & Co, © 2005.

Da Capo Press 2015 edition

Published by Da Capo Press
A Member of the Perseus Books Group
dacapopress.com

Da Capo Press books are available at special discounts for bulk purchases in the U.S. by corporations, institutions, and other organizations. For more information, please contact the Special Markets Department at the Perseus Books Group, 2300 Chestnut Street, Suite 200, Philadelphia, PA, 19103, or call (800) 810-4145, ext. 5000, or e-mail special.markets@perseusbooks.com.

10 9 8 7 6 5 4 3 2 1

For my parents, who used food as a vehicle for memory
and identity, and who loved a good story

CONTENTS

INTRODUCTION

Welcome back, or if you are reading this book for the first time, welcome. This is the latest edition of a book I have been writing and updating since 2005, when the first edition of *Will Write for Food* appeared. A few years earlier, I had started teaching classes on food writing, and I couldn't find a reference book for my students. I decided to write it myself, packing it with sound guidance and wisdom from experts on all kinds of food writing, from memoir to blogging to cookbooks.

Much has changed since 2005, most notably the rise of blogging. Ten years ago bloggers had barely emerged, and the print world did not respect them. Since then, a national food magazine asked a food blogger to write a monthly column (Molly Wizenberg), a food blogger got a show on the Food Network (Ree Drummond), and the same food blogger sold the most cookbooks in the United States in 2013. More than a hundred food bloggers have book deals, and a few make a six-figure income. Learning good photography, social media skills, and self-promotion has become as important—maybe more so, if I'm being honest—than being an excellent writer. There's also been a decline in opportunities to write for magazines and newspapers, particularly restaurant reviewing, and more established cookbook authors have tried self-publishing.

These and other trends are reflected in this revised and updated edition. Within these pages I'd like to be your friendly guide, encouraging you with practical and realistic advice no matter what stage of development you're at:

- If you're just starting out and considering blogging or writing articles for fun or as a hobby, you'll find information and tools to give you a good foundation.

- If you hope to support yourself full-time as a food writer, you're in for a challenge, but some people do it, and you'll learn how. A new chapter on making money lists all kinds of exciting opportunities, from the traditional to new ideas that will surprise and inspire you.
- If you are already a food writer, congratulations! This book builds on your skills and shows you how to branch out to other types of food writing. And the new chapter on making money may tempt you to try some new sources of income.
- If you've already bought a previous version of *Will Write for Food*, Chapter 12 is new, and I have updated every chapter, filling in details about writing cookbooks, addressing the latest in social media trends, updating old information, including new voices and expertise, and adding new exercises. I hope you'll buy it once again. Fortunately, this is an inexpensive book.
- If you want to self-publish, you'll find detailed information in the publishing chapter, including advice on ebooks and apps.

Regardless of what stage you're at as a food writer, I hope this book will answer questions you've always wanted to ask, and will provide the tools to move forward. It will help you appreciate the effort that goes into writing, selling, and publishing food writing. *Will Write for Food* takes you inside the heads of some of America's most powerful food writers, bloggers, editors, and agents. Their wisdom, recommendations, and experiences appear in every chapter, along with stories of how successful food writers broke into the business. I've also packed the book with nitty-gritty tools, resources, and exercises designed to enrich your knowledge and skill level. Understanding the process behind food writing, the characteristics of those who succeed, and which tools are necessary will help lessen any anxieties you're bound to endure.

My own adventure with food writing began after graduating from journalism school in Vancouver, British Columbia, when I became the editor of a city restaurant magazine. I wrote features about restaurants and managed a staff of restaurant reviewers. Later in my career in California, I became a full-time magazine editor and freelance food writer, writing restaurant and cookbook reviews, recipe columns, cover stories, profiles, feature articles, advice-based essays, and opinion pieces for magazines and websites. In 2008 I coauthored my first cookbook, *Grilled Pizzas & Piadinas*, with Chicago chef Craig Priebe. In 2009 I started a blog on food writing, also called Will Write for Food, at diannej.com. In 2015 my second cookbook with Craig, *The United States of Pizza*, comes out, as does a *Cooking Light* cookbook I helped write, based on pantry items.

My career as an editor and writer for newspapers, magazines, books, and websites has spanned more than thirty years, giving me a valuable well of experience from which to draw. For more than a dozen years I've coached writers on how to freelance or get a book published. I've edited manuscripts for both individuals and book publishers, and I've judged cookbook awards for both the James Beard Foundation and the International Association of Culinary Professionals

Teaching remains a passion. Since the last edition of this book, I've taught food-writing workshops in Canada, Australia, Ireland, and the United Arab Emirates. In the past I've taught at the Smithsonian and at University of California Los Angeles Extension. I've been a guest speaker and workshop leader at many conferences, including International Association of Culinary Professionals, BlogHer and BlogHer Food, Food Bloggers of Canada, Food Blog South, and the International Food Blogger Conference. Teaching and presenting give me the opportunity to meet people like you and to get to know the kinds of issues today's food writers face.

The material in this book comes from my own experience, research, and interviews with established food writers, editors, and agents. Some writers have submitted essays on how they operate. Many quotes came from personal interviews. Occasionally I quote from previously published material that appeared in print or online, indicated by "said in an interview." I've also quoted a few times from speakers at conferences or on radio programs.

How to Use This Book

Will Write for Food is not a basic book on writing. Chapters such as those devoted to memoir or fiction focus on the use of food as a vehicle and do not address the entire subject of how to write in that form. Many excellent books will give you comprehensive information in those areas. You will find them listed within the chapters and in the bibliography.

You can read the chapters consecutively or open to whichever chapter interests you most. Each is designed to be as complete in itself as possible, but sometimes you will want information that lurks in other sections. I've provided page numbers to enable you to flip back and forth quickly.

Most chapters end with writing suggestions designed to put what you have learned to immediate use. The usefulness of any one exercise may not seem apparent, but if you complete at least one in each chapter, you will find new points of entry into writing. You'll uncover new material, open vaults of memory, and access your passion. If you already write, these exercises will expand the way you find and process material and maybe give you something new to try.

It's normal to have resistance to writing suggestions and to turn the page. Find it in yourself to examine your reasons not to write. The exercises are short, fun, and not very time consuming. The goal is to write, so why not do so? Trust yourself.

Food writing is a tough field with fierce competition, and it's extremely difficult to make a living at it. I aim not to frighten you but to inspire you to act on a lifelong dream, a passion for eating and cooking, or to move forward as a professional writer. You deserve inside inspiration, solid information, resources, and support. It's so much easier than moving forward all alone. Don't stop with my book. Find others who will guide you by joining industry groups or writing groups, or doing volunteer work. And most importantly, keep at it. Persistence is half the battle. Besides, you need written work to show the editors who are actively looking for you. Give them something to read.

Please let me know if this book has given you a place to begin or refocus. Write to me at dj@diannej.com, or comment on my weekly blog, Will Write for Food, at diannej.com. I look forward to hearing from you.

1: WHAT, EXACTLY, IS FOOD WRITING?

A recipe for fettuccine with prosciutto, cream, and nutmeg. The history of tea. A blog post about Toronto's Chinatown. A roundup on where to get the best deli sandwiches in New York. A guide to sustainable cooking. An exposé on fish labeling at grocery stores. Food writing wanders over dozens of subjects; the storytellers and their craft are what bring it together. Hundreds of people publish books and articles on food, some writing for the first time. One of them could be you. It's easier to choose what to write about if you understand why you want to write about food in the first place. Says writer David Leite of LeitesCulinaria .com, "People get this warm glow when they say, 'I want to become a food writer.' It becomes this romanticized overarching career." What's your reason to write about food?

- You'd like to tell your life story and pass down recipes to family members.
- You're a caterer, chef, or restaurateur whose customers have asked for recipes.
- You're fascinated by the history of a certain food and want to research it.
- You want to write a cookbook based on expertise you've developed.

- You can't find a blog that deals with your child's allergies, and you know other parents could use one.
- You want to capture the cuisine of a country and people you love.

Whatever motivates you, food writing has a requirement that makes it irresistible: you love food, and you get to eat and write about it. What's better than that? Today is a great time to be a food writer. While at its most basic, food writing covers recipes and restaurant reviews, just about any topic and form can be about food, including:

- blogging
- recipes
- restaurants, chefs, and farmers
- essays and memoir
- novels

- history
- politics
- news and trends
- travel
- science

This first chapter explores writing in blogs, newspapers, magazines, and books as a starting point to define food writing. I asked some of the most creative minds in the field to tell me what good food writing means to them. Is it simply good writing? Or is the most important element that it makes readers hungry, helps them experience pleasure, activates their senses, and evokes images of a certain place and time?

Good Writing Is the Essence

I believe good writing is the main determining factor of good food writing, and I set out to see what others had to say. *Saveur* magazine cofounder Colman Andrews, now editor at theDailyMeal.com, puts it bluntly: "If you're not capable of being a good writer, you can't be a good food writer. It's about clarity of expression, style, voice, accuracy, knowledge of structure, and rhythm of language. The idea that food writing is a separate discipline is false." Ruth Reichl, former editor of *Gourmet* magazine and author of several memoirs and a novel, is even more adamant.

She told me the term "food writer" is pejorative, like "woman writer." She's a writer, she says. That's it.

I'm a big admirer of Calvin Trillin, who has written about food for decades in the *New Yorker* magazine. He adamantly refuses to describe his work as food writing. He calls it "writing about eating" and doesn't distinguish it from any other nonfiction. He insists he is not a cook, has no culinary knowledge, and does not rate food. "It's probably fair to call me an amateur," he cracks.

To further make his case, Trillin told me he does not describe food in anything he writes. I found it hard to believe. How could someone write about food without adjectives? I dashed to my bookshelf and reviewed several of his essays. Here's an example from his book *American Fried: Adventures of a Happy Eater*: "Being in a traveling trade myself, I know the problem of asking someone in a strange city for the best restaurant in town and being led to some purple palace that serves 'Continental cuisine' and has as its chief creative employee a menu-writer rather than a chef. I have sat in those places, an innocent wayfarer, reading a three-paragraph description of what the trout is wrapped in, how long it has been sautéed, what province its sauce comes from, and what it is likely to sound like sizzling on my platter—a description lacking only the information that before the poor beast went through that process it had been frozen for eight and a half months."

For Trillin, the most important part of the craft is "careful writing, making sure every word is the right word." He says he learned from A. J. Liebling, a *New Yorker* writer and author of *Between Meals: An Appetite for Paris*, an acclaimed 1959 account of eating well in Paris.

Well then, if you're a writer whose subject is food, what constitutes that form? Leite explains: "While the best food writing is evocative, has an unmistakable voice and an immutable sense of place, it does all the things good writing can do. Some people can write about changing motor oil with as much sensuality as eating a peach. It's how you use the language, how you communicate."

"Food writing is a wonderful, weird passion," adds blogger and Beard-award-winning author Shauna James Ahern of GlutenFreeGirl .com. "You can drop artifice and pretensions and just start to write about what you love, even if it's what you had for breakfast. If you have a strong, distinctive voice and you've honed it well, readers will feel like they know you. You know you've succeeded when people will want to meet you."

As in other fine writing, there's lots of room for creativity, say two award-winning freelancers. Jeffrey Steingarten, a former columnist for *Vogue*, says his essays take the form of "flashbacks and flash forwards." GQ magazine contributing writer Alan Richman says food writing provides more opportunity for free expression than most other forms of journalism. "When it's a review or critique of food, the experience is subjective, so you can say whatever you want. You can be mean, funny, or profound," he explains. "When it's a piece about a head of lettuce or a new shop or a restaurant opening, you're writing about a subject that's been covered thousands of times, and you have the opportunity to seek out a new angle. The repetitive nature of food writing should encourage creativity, not stifle it."

What All Food Writing Has in Common

Some say there's something specific about food writing, that it must, at minimum, stimulate the senses and make you hungry. "The primary requisite for writing well about food is a good appetite," writes Liebling. "Without this, it is impossible to accumulate, within the allotted span, enough experience of eating to have anything worth setting down. Each day brings only two opportunities for fieldwork [meaning two meals at restaurants], and they are not to be wasted minimizing the intake of cholesterol."

And then there's the factor of overall pleasure and enjoyment. Says award-winning cookbook author Darra Goldstein, founder of the now-defunct *Gastronomica* magazine, "Some food writing is almost utopian. Communicating pleasure and enjoyment is a part of that."

Food writing often evokes a place or memory, or the immediacy of a moment. Judith Jones, a vice president and senior editor at Knopf who has edited such legends as Julia Child and James Beard, says food writing "describes taste, textures, flavors, and smells, and gives a food experience a larger context by writing about a more common experience, drawing on something universal that speaks to everyone." She points to an essay by M. F. K. Fisher, whom she also edited, titled "P Is for Peas," in which the author and her family pick peas in the vineyards of Switzerland. Here's a sentence: "I dashed up and down the steep terraces with the baskets, and my mother would groan and then hum happily when another one appeared, and below I could hear my father and our friends cursing just as happily at their wry backs and their aching thighs, while the peas came off their stems and into the baskets with a small sound audible in that still high air, so many hundred feet above the distant and completely silent Léman."

Yes, this is food writing, because peas are the subject. But there's so much more: a scene, a terrain, ambiance, and relationships, all vividly drawn. You are there with her on the hillside, watching the scene.

••

AN EDITOR WHO CULTIVATED BRILLIANT FOOD WRITERS

JUDITH JONES, vice president and senior editor at Knopf, has influenced American culinary culture for decades by publishing gifted food writers, including Julia Child, M. F. K. Fisher, Edna Lewis, and Laurie Colwin. When I asked Jones how she came to work with them, she said modestly, "You follow your instincts, the things that you love. If you feel strongly about a book, the rationalization is that there must be others like you who want it. I thought if I wanted to know that much about food, there were others like me."

Here's more about these iconic writers and how Jones became involved with them:
JULIA CHILD. In 1960, Jones received a manuscript for what would become *Mastering the Art of French Cooking.* "The first choice had been Houghton Mifflin, but when the editor there reviewed the manuscript, her reaction was: Why would any American want to know this much about French cooking?" Jones had recently returned from living in Paris for three and a half years, and Knopf had hired her as a French editor to deal with translations. She lobbied to become the editor of Child's book, and Alfred Knopf gave her a chance. The rest is history.
M. F. K. FISHER. Jones became friends with Fisher over years of mailing her galleys of Knopf books. Fisher was already known, and Jones wanted her to endorse Knopf books. In the 1960s, Jones visited California with her husband, Evan, a distinguished food writer in his own right. Fisher invited them to her home in St. Helena for lunch. "It was so hot we ate in the cellar," recalls Jones. Fisher made a "Provençal lunch, cold salads and other things. She owed one more book to her current publisher. Then we did a book together." *Among Friends* came first in 1971, followed by *A Considerable Town* in 1978, *Sister Age* in 1983, and *As They Were* in 1982.

W. H. Auden once said he could not think of anyone in the United States who wrote better prose than Fisher, but because she chose food as her subject, her audience was extremely limited. Perhaps, but she is one of America's best-known food writers now, with a continuing fan base that enjoys her sensuous, humorous, and beautifully sad voice.

Fisher's most quoted essay is the foreword to *The Gastronomical Me*, which begins: "People ask me: Why do you write about food, and eating and drinking? Why don't you write about the struggle for power and security, and about love, the way others do? . . . The easiest answer is to say that, like most other humans, I am hungry."

"I tell about myself, and how I ate bread on a lasting hillside, or drank red wine in a room now blown to bits, and it happens without my willing it that I am telling too much about the people with me then, and their other deeper needs for love and happiness."

EDNA LEWIS. In the 1970s, Lewis had a restaurant in New York frequented by the likes of Truman Capote and Tennessee Williams. Jones was intrigued. "I could see right away that she had a story about her whole relationship with food, her family, that she was part of the American experience," Jones remembers. "She had a beautiful way of talking about food. She was an instinctive cook. I said, 'Write your own book, your own experience, and let's do it together.'"

The result was the classic *The Taste of Country Cooking*, published in 1976. You'd never know Lewis owned a New York restaurant. This book celebrates how her family prepared and enjoyed American food in a rural Virginia town founded by freed slaves. Dignified and knowledgeable, she expresses her joy of fresh, natural tastes, capturing a simpler time of living off the land, where vegetables came from a garden, meat from a smokehouse, fruit from orchards, and canned jams and condiments from the previous summer.

In her foreword, Lewis explains why she wrote *The Taste of Country Cooking*: "Whenever I go back to visit my sisters and brothers, we relive old times, remembering the past. And when we share again in gathering wild strawberries, canning, rendering lard, finding walnuts, picking persimmons, making fruitcake, I realize how much the bond that held us had to do with food. Since we are the last of the original families, with no children to remember and carry on, I decided that I wanted to write down just exactly how we did things when I was growing up in Freetown that seemed to make life so rewarding."

LAURIE COLWIN. Primarily a fiction writer whose themes were love and family, Colwin attracted an ardent following by word of mouth. In her novels, her characters are domestic sensualists who like to cook humble but deeply satisfying dishes. She wrote two simple and unpretentious books about cooking and food: *Home Cooking: A Writer in the Kitchen* and *More Home Cooking: A Writer Returns to the Kitchen*. Reading her makes you feel as though she is your favorite bighearted, funny friend, instructing you with love on how to entertain, and confiding about how much it delights her to cook and eat with friends and family.

Jones was a fan. Over lunch with the editor of *Gourmet*, Jones suggested Laurie Colwin as a strong new voice for the magazine, writing about food. "I had read all her stories, and they always had food in them, so I said, 'I bet she would be good.'"

Colwin wrote *Home Cooking* and *More Home Cooking* with Jones as her editor. In *Home Cooking*, she writes about her cozy home in New York, where she fed people plain, old-fashioned food such as roast chicken, string beans, lemon cake, and coffee. "One of the delights of life is eating with friends; second to that is talking about eating," starts a passage in *Home Cooking*'s foreword. "And for an unsurpassed double whammy, there is talking about eating while you are eating with friends." Colwin died prematurely of heart failure in 1992. All her books remain in print.

Other award-winning authors Jones has edited are Lidia Bastianich, James Beard, Marion Cunningham, Marcella Hazan, Ken Horn, Madhur Jaffrey, Irene Kuo, Joan Nathan, and Claudia Roden.

....

Writing About the Senses

As you've read in some of the examples I've provided, food writing often focuses on the senses: touch, smell, sound, appearance, and taste. Many newcomers to the form focus on how food tastes and skimp on the other senses. When I hand out a list of adjectives (see page 146) to students in my classes, it always thrills them, but food writing isn't just about descriptions. It's about putting the food in context. Here's an erotic passage from Ruth Reichl in *Comfort Me with Apples*: "He kissed me and said, 'Close your eyes and open your mouth.' I sniffed the air; it smelled like a cross between violets and berries, with just a touch of citrus. My mouth closed around something very small and quite soft, the size of a little grape but with a scratchy surface. 'Do you like it?' he asked anxiously. I tasted spring. 'They're fraises des bois from France!' He slipped another one in my mouth." That's four sensory experiences in a few sentences.

Smell is the most important sense, because most of what you taste comes from smelling it first. That's why you can't taste food when you have a cold. Jean Anthelme Brillat-Savarin, a lawyer and gastronome, had figured it out when he wrote in his 1825 book, *The Physiology of Taste*: "For my part I am not only convinced that without the cooperation of smell there can be no complete degustation, but I am also tempted to believe that smell and taste are in fact but a single sense, whose laboratory is the mouth and whose chimney is the nose; or to be more precise, in which the mouth performs the degustation of tactile bodies, and the nose the degustation of gases." (Brillat-Savarin was the author of the famous comment, "Tell me what you eat, and I will tell you what you are.")

Smell can also induce emotions, feelings of nostalgia, and involuntary memories, known as the Proustian Effect. You've probably experienced it when a smell triggers a childhood taste memory, and a wave of emotion hits as hard as a punch to the gut.

Identifying odors and tastes is elusive, and writing about them is just as difficult. Writes Diane Ackerman in *A Natural History of the Senses*, "Smells coat us, swirl around us, enter our bodies, emanate from us. We live in a constant wash of them. Still, when we try to describe a smell, words fail us like the fabrications they are." Most writers convey a flavor or aroma by using analogy, where something is "like" something else. But it's tricky. "You could say basil tastes a little like mint," proposes Colman Andrews. "What if you've never tasted mint?"

And how do you describe how things taste? As I mentioned, there's way too much focus on taste, at the expense of other senses. Jennifer McLagan faced this problem head on in her cookbook, *Bitter*. "Bitter, while a positive taste in many cultures, is not well loved among Anglo-Saxons," she wrote. "It is hard to evoke a positive taste image for bitter. Astringent, pungent, bittersweet, bitter as gall (bile) or wormwood, acrid, caustic, tart, astringent, harsh and sharp are some of the words you find in a thesaurus when you look up bitter," she writes. "Not a very appetizing list."

At least the list is specific. That's what good writers go for, to avoid being reduced to words like "delicious," "yummy," and "amazing," which tell readers nothing other than you liked it. Specific writing is always preferable, because you want readers to imagine the food, and they can't without a word like "peppery" rather than just "tasty."

It's easy to get carried away with adjectives when writing about the senses because adjectives are a perfect way to describe them. Too many will weaken writing, making you sound sentimental. Do readers really need to know that a brownie was fudgy and decadent? Strive for more original writing, and don't string together a raft of several adjectives. I see this so often I sometimes think adjectives are the crack of food writers.

Darra Goldstein suggests reading M. F. K. Fisher, who uses "one perfect adjective that somehow manages to encompass a whole range of sensation, or something atmospheric that allows you to understand what the sensation was." She gives this example from a *New Yorker* essay: "It was reward enough to sit in the almost empty room, chaste rococo in the slanting June sunlight, with the generous tub of pure delight between us, Mother purring there, the vodka seeping slyly through our veins, and real wood strawberries to come, to make us feel like children again and not near-gods." Rococo is anything but chaste, says

Goldstein. "It's over the top, but Fisher manages to convey the sense of childlike innocence she goes on to describe in the sentence by means of this single adjective."

While taste and smell are critical to food writing, so is touch. Touch informs the reader about the ripeness of a cantaloupe, or how to judge a steak's doneness. "Each culture has its own appreciation of food," writes McLagan. "A comparative study of words used to describe food textures found that [the Japanese] have more than four hundred words to describe the texture of their food. The Chinese have around one hundred and forty-four while English speakers seem impoverished with a mere seventy-seven terms. Do we not care about texture, or is it just too much pudding and mushy peas? The French, whose cuisine is renowned for its sauces, have more than nineteen words just to describe the viscosity of a sauce."

Steingarten believes we should monitor other physical sensations as well, such as the sense of locomotion in stirring, where you detect physical changes and sensitivity to temperature as a sauce thickens. Chef and author Anthony Bourdain explores touch in *A Cook's Tour: In Search of the Perfect Meal*: "I had to learn to use bits of bread, pinching the food between the two—and only two—fingers and the thumb of the right hand, the digits protected by a layer of folded bread. . . . Abdul (was) tearing the white centers from each little triangle of bread, creating an ersatz pocket. . . . I called him on it, accused him playfully of cheating while I struggled with the thick, not easily folded hunks."

Then there's the visual aspect. Some writers excel at writing about the physical features of food using similes and metaphor rather than adjectives. Similes compare, using "like" and "as." Metaphor calls it something else. In *An Omelette and a Glass of Wine*, Elizabeth David describes sugar-coated coriander and caraway seeds, "bright as shiny tiddlywinks." That's a simile. In *Between Meals*, Liebling wrote that the haricots verts he was served "resembled decomposed whiskers from a theatrical costume beard." That's a simile as well. Now for metaphor. Nigella Lawson wrote this about chocolate raspberry tarts: "With their dark chocolate shells and their white-chocolate mascarpone filling, these look fancy enough, but when you eat them what strikes you is their cleanly balanced simplicity." Of course the tart crust is not a real shell, but it's deft way to keep from repeating the word "tart." While these examples instantly bring images to mind, note that two sound delectable while one does not. Food writing is not always about rhapsodizing.

David, a British writer who educated first England and then the world on Mediterranean food, writes in a sensuous, stimulating, and intellectual style. Here she focuses on sight, scent, and taste: "Now there are signs of autumn on the leaves of some of the almond trees. They have turned a frail, transparent auburn, and this morning when I awoke I devoured two of the very first tangerines of the season. In the dawn their scent was piercing and their taste was sharp."

Writers Jane and Michael Stern provide an elegant example combining touch and visual writing. Read how beautifully they describe the ultimate apple pie. You can see their minds going into slow motion to describe the experience: "The crust is as crunchy as a butter cookie, so brittle that it cracks audibly when you press it with your fork; grains of cinnamon sugar bounce off the surface as it shatters. The bottom crust is softer than the top, but browned and still breakable. Where the top and bottom meet, there's a knotty cord of dough that becomes impregnated with enough fruit filling to make it chewy. Inside is a dense apple pack of firm Ida Red crescents bound in syrupy juice." The specificity of the words, combined with active verbs such as "bounce," "crack," and "shatter," makes this description evocative. Note the use of simile as well, in "crunchy as a butter cookie," and metaphor in "knotty cord."

Some writers think the least important sense is sound. But consider how it enlivens the experience in Alan Richman's colorful *Bon Appétit* essay "The Great Texas Barbecue Secret": "Because the meat is seldom pricked during cooking, the fat accumulates, sizzling and bubbling. Slice, and the drama unfolds. Think of a bursting water pipe. Better yet, imagine a Brahman bull exploding from the gate at a rodeo."

Describing your perceptions is difficult to get right. Most beginning writers tend to overdo it. In the worst case, says *L. A. Times* food columnist Russ Parsons, descriptions can be cloying, gratuitous, and prurient. "The idea is not to be flashy but elegant. You want to use enough sensual language that you get across your pleasure and your involvement with the topic, but don't want to come across as overblown, which reads as cheap and unconvincing. Write it and keep going over it, taking out as much as you possibly can and leaving the essence."

Perhaps the best way to access the senses is not to take them for granted. I like the way Richman and the Sterns slow down to describe each moment as it unfolds. Editor Judith Jones advises writers to use the senses as a starting point, the evocative element, and then go on to the larger theme or context.

Getting Passion Across

Just like the senses, passion is an essential part of food writing but difficult to get across. Strong feelings can mislead. It's easier to tell readers about your enthusiasm by stating it outright than by revealing it through the words you choose. The classic writing rule of "show—don't tell" applies here, where your job is to show your devotion rather than to tell the reader about it. It's challenging. When you turn a camera on people to get to their passion, says Andrews, they freeze up, use big words, and become stilted, especially when they're very emotional about a subject. "You can't just open a vein and let it flow out. If you're very passionate about some wonderful dish, you have to tame your passion to write about it, [or] it will probably come across sounding stupid."

Intensity during writing comes and goes, like being in and out of love, says David Leite. "At times I'm on a holy tear," he admits. "It's just coming out. I'm channeling something. As quickly as it came, one day I wake up and it's gone. I have to accept that. The only way to get it back on a regular basis is to sit down and write every day." Sometimes he writes for six hours, and it's only the last sentence of the day that delights him, he says. But when that happens, "it's enough to float me, to give me energy to pick up and start writing again tomorrow." The bottom line about passion, he says, is to take advantage of it when it's there, because there's no regular way to get it.

Obsession can be a by-product, and many editors love writers who learn every single detail and fact about their subject, master it, and laugh at their own compulsiveness. But compulsiveness can also lead to being in love with your subject, which occasionally means including too much information. For more on how to edit your own work, see page 124 in Chapter 5.

The Role of Voice

Great writers, including food writers, spend years perfecting their voice. Voice combines writing style and point of view. It is also called style. *The Elements of Style*, an essential handbook for writers, refers to voice simply as "the sound a writer's words make on paper." It's what makes you authentic. It conveys your personality, flair, and originality. "Voice exists to make the piece more readable, to make it more enjoyable, to explain or illuminate difficult concepts without seeming dry," explains Andrews. "People can explain a difficult subject, and because they write conversationally, it comes across better."

You can't invent a voice, most say. I once asked a writing coach how I could write in a lyrical voice. He suggested an exercise in which I copy a writer's style by parodying it, which would give me insight into how she pulls it off. I did the exercise by analyzing a piece by Reichl. I found it sensuous, visual, evocative, poetic, and reflective. I also noticed her use of personification, alliteration, and even violence. Then I did a writing exercise by employing some of her techniques, and found the exercise liberating.

But editor Jones disagrees. "Woe unto a writer who tries to imitate another writer's voice," she cautions. "It's not something borrowed or imitated—it is you. It describes how you actually feel. It's what makes the writer individual."

Certainly, reading other writers can influence your work. When Molly Wizenberg started her blog, Orangette, she was reading Steingarten, Trillin, and M. F. K. Fisher. "I didn't actually do an imitation, but I noticed certain things, like Trillin had a plain sentence structure. He wasn't getting all flowery and poetic with it. Someone more lyrical tapped into emotions, like MFK. She wrote about some philosophical things, like about the way we link food with love. All of these things have come through in my writing." Trillin, she says, does an incredible job of "noticing the nuances that are often universal in our lives," such as his obsession with Kansas City barbeque. "Something in us becomes obsessed too," said Wizenberg. "I love his sense of humor, his ability to create his own pathological enthusiasm. He puts us immediately in his shoes. His details are vivid, visual, and play on the senses."

Voice helps readers form an image of you, the writer. To put it in modern business parlance, it's as though you are creating a brand. It's possible to write a story without using much voice, particularly in newspapers and magazines, where the writing conforms to certain conventions of the collective voice of a publication. When I wrote my first essay after years of news writing, I was startled by my own voice. I wondered if I was revealing too much of my personality.

But for readers to get the most out of a story, they should understand who you are, perhaps even trusting you more than liking you. Your voice gives the narrative unity and strength, says Goldstein. "Writers starting out are afraid to put their voice in there. They think, 'What if people criticize it or don't like it?' Without it, your writing can be a little pallid, and sounds like everyone else's writing. Voice makes you sound sure of yourself." So don't worry about being correct or "writerly," because it makes your work more serious and boring. Write the way you speak.

Your writing expresses your uniqueness. "Voice is the sound, rhythm, and point-of-view that unequivocally evokes the writer," wrote Leite on forums.egullet.org. "You know it when you read it. And more importantly, you can never confuse or interchange them. Bourdain is not Steingarten, who is not Trillin, who is not Reichl."

"Voice is often misunderstood," explains the L.A. Times' Russ Parsons. "People usually think they must reveal their inner secrets, and it's a deeply personal matter. But voice is not about you. It's the rhythm of language, writerly tricks, the choice of words."

Maybe the way to find your own voice is to exaggerate it, especially if you are writing a personal essay or memoir. Amanda Hesser, Food52 founder and author of the memoir *Looking for Mr. Latte: A Food Lover's Courtship, with Recipes*, said she exaggerated both her own characteristics and her boyfriend's to make their voices clearer, and she did so without worrying that the story was becoming fictional. "She was the bumbling, snobby food person who needed to be put in her place; he was muse and hero," she explained in an interview.

So capture the authentic emotion of the moment, the tone of what's going on at the time, and what you feel physically. If you have trouble finding your voice, consult the list of descriptions on page 15 as a starting point. Ask a few friends to describe your voice to you. Often they're better at it than you are, because you might think of your voice as "just you," and therefore not describable.

Other ways to make your voice stronger in writing include language and cultural references. Examine your word choices, and play with them. Do you use big words, for example, or references to pop culture, architecture, old movies, or rap music? Your voice can show age, geographic location, gender, or even your religious persuasion. Here's how restaurant critic Jonathan Gold opens a review: "If you grew up eating hot dogs in the swinging San Fernando Valley '70s, your family probably had allegiances to the Hot Dog Show or Flooky's or the Wiener Factory, which were as inarguable, as inevitable, as the question of Orthodox, Conservative or Reform." Without his ever explicitly saying so, you can assume he's Jewish, he grew up in Los Angeles, and he's probably in his forties. Without a strong voice, you risk becoming a superficial narrator.

• •

WRITERS DESCRIBE THEIR OWN VOICES

ALAN RICHMAN, contributing editor at *GQ* magazine. I'm a diffident, cranky, New York guy who walks into a restaurant and waits to see how he's going to be abused. I'm a passive-aggressive guy who gets the last word. I am someone to whom things happen. Writers should take a passive role so readers feel represented.

CLOTILDE DUSOULIER, author and blogger, ChocolateandZucchini.com. At first my voice was clear enthusiasm and joy for my subject. Those feelings have not left me, but I'm probably a little calmer now. You can't be emphatic all the time. After a while, if I kept being that bubbly, people were going to think I'm on something. I became a little understated. I feel more mature now. My way of writing is friendly, approachable, and relatable.

DAVID LEBOVITZ, author and blogger. Friendly, funny, approachable.

DAVID LEITE, author and publisher of LeitesCulinaria.com. I write the way I speak, influenced through a lifetime of hearing my mother's humor. I can be a little wicked at times. I turned to humor in adolescence. I developed that person, and it came out on the page.

CALVIN TRILLIN, author and freelance writer. Genial glutton.

MOLLY WIZENBERG, author and blogger. I like to think of my voice as somewhat playful or whimsical. It's very important to me to be honest.

MICHAEL RUHLMAN, author and blogger. Authoritative, as in I've studied this, I've been in culinary schools, I've worked with the best chefs in the country. I have opinions.

RUSS PARSONS, food columnist, *L.A. Times.* By nature I'm kind of a smart-ass. I try to score as many points off myself as other people when I'm writing in the first person.

It's important to be self-deprecating, not self-aggrandizing. I pay a lot of attention to rhythm, sentence length, and structure.
RUTH REICHL, author and editor. Forthright.

DESCRIBE YOUR OWN VOICE

Writing becomes stronger when you know who you are. If you decide you are sarcastic, for example, then you have a tool with which to assess your writing to ensure your voice comes across that way. Go through this list and pick the top five adjectives that you think describe you and your voice. If you have trouble, ask friends to select some adjectives for you:

approachable	friendly	mysterious
authoritative	funny	reassuring
believable	humble	relaxed
competent	knowing	self-deprecating
confessional	knowledgeable	vulnerable

Writing Exercises

1. This exercise will make your writing livelier. Write a long paragraph about eating a favorite meal, using all the senses. Include a simile and a metaphor. (A simile tells the reader what something is like, such as "The grapes shone like a string of black pearls." A metaphor directly compares one thing to another, as in "I tossed one of the sticky puffs into my mouth.") When you're done, go back over the paragraph, and look for generic nouns, substituting concrete ones for them. For example, you might replace the word "fruit" with "blueberry." It gives the reader an immediate visual, whereas "fruit" is hazier. Once you've made some replacements, go over your work once more, and look at your sentence structure. Are you in a rut, with sentences all of one length? Adjust them to make some short and some long. Right away, you'll see a stronger, more distinct voice emerge in your writing.

2. More ways to use simile and metaphor: Fill in the blanks by comparing the following foods to nonedible objects: The

cheese was as ripe as . . . The donut smelled stale, like a . . . The roast beef sandwich tasted as though . . . Try being outrageous, and then try it again and be sensuous.

3. Review prior writing to see if you use the techniques described in this chapter. Try rewriting a paragraph in a new way.

4. Develop your writing ability to show rather than tell. Choose a favorite food. Write two paragraphs explaining why you love it. Get your passion across without sentences starting with "I just can't get enough of . . ." If you love licorice, show your devotion by writing about the lengths to which you will go to procure it, for example, or how often you consume it. Readers can deduce that you adore it without you ever saying so specifically.

2: THE GASTRONOMICAL YOU

If you want to be a food writer, you're probably already passionate about food and eating, and perhaps cooking as well. That's where it begins. Almost all the writers interviewed for this book talked about their passion, or exuded passion, no matter how many years they had been on the job. If your friends think you're odd because you love to talk about food, take heart. You're on the right path.

Many food writers I've met are enthusiastic, intense, and energetic in an obsessive kind of way, and love nothing more than immersing themselves in research. And who can blame them? After all, if you get paid to write about a day in the life of a cherry farmer, the history of tres leches cakes, or a restaurant roundup in Rome, it's hard not to throw yourself into the task. I've made a list of characteristics of food writers and editors based on my interviews. Some play off each other. For example, it's easy to be a fastidious researcher when you're passionate about your subject. It's easy to be knowledgeable about your subject if you've done your research. It's easy to be energetic if you're passionate. See how these traits come together?

Some characteristics can be learned. When I studied newspaper reporting in journalism school, I learned how to research anything and how to persist until I got the interviews I needed for stories. Those skills have served me well all through my career.

Few writers have all the traits I've listed below. You don't need every single one to succeed. Some characteristics may predispose you to be good at certain types of food writing. Researchers like historical writing and longer stories. Skeptics make good restaurant reviewers. Attention to detail, persistence, and curiosity are terrific characteristics for any kind of food writing, but particularly for recipe developers.

As you read, consider how many of these describe you. (If you don't mind marking up book pages, check them off.) You need to see if you are suited to the task, just as some people become firefighters because it suits their personality, values, and interests. Some of these identifications may be no-brainers, but others will deserve more thought. There's no magic number to tick off. Only you can decide whether you have the skills and determination to write about food.

Passionate. People who love food are an eager, enthusiastic bunch, and it carries over when they write. They have an appetite for joy and appreciation.

"Passion is really a compulsion, conveyed in a sense of urgency," says Knopf cookbook editor Judith Jones. "This is what makes writing come alive." Passion usually involves the pleasure experienced by writers and readers, but not always.

Some of the best writers remain passionate despite years on the job. Alan Richman, contributing writer for GQ magazine, says when on an assignment to find and eat food, he becomes "crazy with happiness when things taste so good," perhaps in part because it's not that common. You'll learn more about restaurant reviewing in Chapter 6.

Enthusiastic about research. You can never have too much information on a subject before you begin writing about it. Food writers are always asking questions. As voracious readers and researchers, it's common to have an obsessive personality, and think every aspect of, say, a goat cheese producer's life, is fascinating. By the time you have done enough work on the subject to justify writing about it, you should be bursting with information. *L. A. Times* food columnist Russ Parsons admits, "When I'm researching a story, I go completely berserk. I may have 300 pages of research and photocopies for a 1,500-word article. I want to know everything, to have total saturation in every aspect of the subject."

Saturation is a starting point for the article. Your next job is to sift through the information and decide what's compelling and necessary. That depends on the angle of the story, who your readers are and what they want to read, your word count, and your structure. This is what makes the difference between Parsons, a multiple-award-winning writer, and beginners, who think everything they found out is fascinating. He knows how to shape and cut the story. More about this a bit later, when we get to the importance of focus later on this page.

Research doesn't necessarily mean spending hours in a dingy library poring over dusty tomes. Food writers are constantly on the go—traveling, finding familiar foods in new and unusual places, tasting the way people in another country prepare a familiar food. Cooking is another part of research. It's easier to write well about some subjects if you cook, as it helps you understand your subject and how the context of cooking works into your story.

In recipe writing, research might mean looking up the origin of a dish, understanding the chemistry of how it works, or comparing recipes to see how others made the dish.

Enthusiasm keeps you interested, keeps you asking questions, keeps you engaged and challenged.

Energetic. You can't be running around, transcribing notes, endlessly looking up information, and interviewing without being energetic. And as I mentioned earlier, passion is the best fuel for working long hours or pushing yourself to get the story, chapter, or recipe done. On days where you're so immersed in your work that the hours fly by, you know you've chosen a great profession.

Focused. When you find a topic endlessly fascinating, it gets hard to decide what to leave in and what to leave out. You need focus. Fortunately, word counts will rein you in. Outlines are a good tool as well. The thing to understand is that people don't have to know everything, just what's most important. The more you add, the larger the subject becomes, and soon it's about everything and nothing in particular. Put yourself in your readers' shoes, and figure out what they want to know. A story for a doctor's magazine will have a different slant than one for a vegan magazine, even if they are both about the same subject.

Skeptical. Research often includes the ability to approach information with healthy skepticism. Ernest Hemingway, who often wrote about food in his novels, said in a 1958 interview in the *Paris Review*, "The most essential gift for a good writer is a built-in, shockproof, shit detector. This is the writer's radar and all great writers have it." It's not that you have to spend months trying to verify information and sources, but you shouldn't just rely on what other people have written unless you know that they themselves are good sources or experts. Origins of customs or events are particularly suspect in food writing, says Darra Goldstein, founder of the now defunct *Gastronomica*, because even when wrong, they become myths perpetuated as common knowledge. This is particularly true on the web, so it cannot be your only source of information.

I have read in the food section of a daily paper, for example, that Julia Child dropped a chicken on the floor during a television show, picked it up, and said it was fine to serve because no one will know. I've seen that episode. What really happened is that she transferred a potato-based dish from the stove onto a plate and dropped some of it on the stovetop. No chickens were involved, but the writer took what she read somewhere and ran with it. She should have been suspicious of that outrageous-sounding story, finding a way to check it out. Mistakes like that make people think they can't trust you.

Editors and writers can tell when others don't do their homework. Parsons, *L.A. Times* food columnist, says there's lots of writing that wouldn't be regarded as research, such as the passing along of second-hand information. I once worked with an author who spent hours in the library verifying assertions famous people in our industry had made about themselves, such as "I was the first to" or "I won an award for." Most of the time, she discovered, these people had exaggerated.

Fearless. Eating requires fearlessness. It's easier to be fearless if you're so enthusiastic that you plunge into things. Food writers must "taste things they don't want to taste, talk to someone they don't want to talk to, and get themselves wedged into a situation to get the information, to learn," says Leite. Author and television host Anthony Bourdain was once the king of fearlessness. He traveled around the world for his book *A Cook's Tour* and for a television show, doing extreme eating, a term he disavows. "It's really important to be a good guest, because the table is the best reflection of a nation and fastest way into that culture," he counsels. "You have to be willing to put yourself in a situation and let things happen. You can't be squeamish or hesitant. It might require that you match your hosts shot for shot with vodka laced with bear bile. Now is not the time to say 'I'm a vegetarian' or 'I'm lactose intolerant.'"

"It's a common flaw to be contemptuous of the subject or afraid of the nasty bits like dirt, strange food, unfamiliar experiences, or to feel jaded," he continues. "Fear of the other makes a lot of food and travel writers bad writers. Get people to talk about eating in Mexico—they complain about the water, think they might get sick, and they don't want to eat raw vegetables."

Sometimes fearlessness is about getting up the nerve to contact people you hold in high esteem. I had that challenge writing this book. I had to contact authors I worshipped from afar. They turned out to be polite, accessible, prompt, and interested in helping me.

And sometimes fearlessness is about writing, where you do it even if you're scared that it might not be good. You keep going and eventually you hone it into a piece you like.

Here are three ways to get difficult tasks done. If you have to make a phone call or write something, do it first thing in the morning, as soon as you get to your desk. That way you won't stew over it all day long and keep procrastinating. Second is to act "as if." That means behaving as though you are a superconfident, warm, witty person who would be fun to talk with, even if you're nervous as hell and don't believe it. Third, ask yourself, "What's the worst that could happen?" Fear of what will happen is often blown out of proportion compared to the consequences.

Inquisitive. Food writers share endless curiosity and culinary adventurism. They like to wander around hoping to stumble on something curious or magnificent, such as finding four new kinds of melon at a French street market or meeting a master bread baker at a party and talking for hours. Richman says he has been called a culinary anthropologist because of the amount of research he unearths while working on his stories. If you're not curious enough, says Leite, "You're not going to discover the next thing to write about."

Persistent. Hand-in-hand with curiosity is the ability to be relentless. Former *New York Times* restaurant critic Mimi Sheraton writes in her memoir, *Eating My Words*, that she went to a restaurant twelve times until she was sure how she felt about it. Luckily, the *Times* picked up the bill. Even if the work seems tedious, such as poring through tons of information to find a few facts, or asking so many questions you run the risk of sounding dumb, the best food writers keep going until they get what they want.

Knowledgeable about the subject. When they're ready to write, the best food writers know the subject matter inside out. This strategy increases confidence and helps provide credibility if you're not an expert on a certain food or ingredient. If you're not an expert, suggests Colman Andrews, cofounder of *Saveur* and editor at theDailyMeal.com, "the next best thing is to learn about it and take the reader along with you as you go." This takes guts, because you must sound as if you know what you're talking about. Laura Werlin took this approach with her first book about cheese (see pages 160–161).

Don't try to be an expert on everything, which becomes overwhelming. Pick a subject that resonates with you, and learn it inside out. Take cooking classes, read books, and interview experts.

You might structure a story or blog post by playing the neophyte and taking the reader on a journey as you become more knowledgeable.

Professional. Beginning writers are sometimes perceived as lazy or as dabblers. People think there are special rules for food writing, that it's not as demanding as other kinds of writing, says Andrews. "Because food writing is kind of trivial or unimportant, they think they don't have to be as accurate, because they're not writing about the president—they're writing about Wolfgang Puck." I'm glad he's honest enough to say so. When I tell people outside the profession that I write and edit on the subject of food, I get a curious look, as in "Is that really a profession?" Some people also think food writing is a hobby and an excuse to eat and travel well. Close. It's actually a profession in which you get to eat and travel well, if you're doing it right.

The standards for being a professional food writer are not rocket science:

- Be polite in your transactions, particularly when asking for help, and thank people who have helped you.
- Be thorough and accurate, particularly when spelling names and stating titles. Fact-check your work to avoid embarrassment later.
- Make deadlines, and provide exactly what you've said you were going to write or what you've agreed to write; cooperate with your editor to the best of your ability.
- Avoid hissy fits or prima donna behavior if you want more work.

Good at telling stories. "On a very basic level, you have to be capable of transporting your reader somewhere else, just for a minute, and do that by showing them where you're taking them," explains blogger and author Molly Wizenberg. "Evocative, vivid writing that plays on the senses is crucial." Notice the nuances that readers can relate to, she says. The best writers can put us immediately in their shoes and remind of us ourselves.

Here's what Wizenberg said about storytelling at a blogging conference: "I love the shape food gives to my life—the stories it tells me about who I am, about the people close to me, about the city I live in, all of it. Food is a very sharp lens for looking at what matters to us, and suddenly, I wanted to find out what else it could show me. Those were the stories I wanted to tell.

"And that's what I've been trying to do ever since, both on my blog and in my books. I'm trying to tell the kind of stories that I like to read. My goal in everything, always—in my writing and in my photographs and in the restaurant that my husband and I now own, which is a whole other story—my goal is to do the work that I want to see done. I think that's the highest goal we can aim for, the hardest goal. It's the goal that really gets me fired up. I try to write what I want to read. We try to make the food that we want to eat. Sometimes I think I'm onto something. Sometimes I love what I'm making. Sometimes it works!"

Not stuck in nostalgia. When I wrote my first food-themed personal essay, it was about my mother and her cooking. I'm still proud of it, but I've realized it's where many people start. Eventually I learned I was not alone in writing about food and early memory. It's common to want to write about your family, particularly the person who taught you how to cook, or someone you admired. It's what you know. The information is easily accessible because it's right there in your brain.

When I teach, students tell me of their desire to write nostalgic memories. I've heard it so often I've decided it's a normal part of the process. Sure, start with your recollections. Create a riveting scene, write good dialogue, and put the story in context. If publishing is your goal, you must say something new. My essay about my mother was published in an international food magazine because it was unusual. It focused on her inability, as an immigrant, to master Western foods like sandwiches, spaghetti, and meat and potatoes. It was funny and bittersweet, but most important, it had an angle that made my story different from the same old thing editors see repeatedly: most editors don't see a lot of memoir pieces about an Iraqi Jew from China who cooked funny Western foods.

Editors see lots of nostalgic writing that turns them off. There's no shortage of sentimentality in food writing, for the good old days and things done by hand. If you want to write about the past, you might start in the present, to anchor your reader.

I'm not trying to dissuade you from writing about your family. If you know how to shape your writing, it's certainly viable. Take, for example, *In Nonna's Kitchen: Recipes and Traditions from Italy's Grandmothers*, by Carol Field, which succeeds for a couple of reasons. It's about Italian food, and Americans are obsessed with Italian cooking. Field is an accomplished cookbook writer, and it was not her first book. And it's about several grandmothers who have spent their lives guarding their culinary heritage, not just about one grandmother who cooked for Field. *Monsoon Diary: A Memoir with Recipes*, by Shoba Narayan, chronicles family rituals and love of food, but also discusses her trouble adjusting to an arranged marriage and shatters stereotypes of immigrant life. Her funny, sparkling narrative enlivens the story. It might have something to do with her master's in journalism from Columbia, where she was awarded a Pulitzer fellowship.

Ethical. Along the lines of persistent visits to restaurants (à la Mimi Sheraton) is the issue of ethics. Food writers must have a strong sense of who they are and whom they represent. They get offered many free things, particularly food and travel, and particularly if they are bloggers with big audiences. This may seem odd to you, but ethical writers pay their own way or, if they're lucky, a publication pays their way. Otherwise, a writer might feel indebted to a restaurant or tourist association, and the writing comes out more like promotion than anything else. Bloggers who write about free meals from restaurants are rarely honest. They rave about everything or snap gorgeous photos.

Inevitably, food writers get to know other people in the business, such as chefs and public relations people, and sticky situations can result. You owe it to your readers to be honest. You do not owe it to the restaurant, tourist board, or food company. Restaurant reviewer Richman explains that good food writing is "not press trips to Tuscany, not free meals at restaurants, and not the adoration of famous chefs where you sit around saying 'yum yum' to everything put in front of you." For more on ethics, see Chapter 4 on blogging.

Careful with language. When I asked experienced food writers what they dislike most about other food writing, the number one complaint was the use of too many adjectives, clichés, and flowery metaphors, in which, instead of crafting beautiful sentences, writers rely too much on strings of adverbs and adjectives to move the story along. That means avoiding writing sentences like "The huge green artichoke on the garnet dinner plate was a sage-colored flower, its leaves pointing skyward, concealing the hidden treasure within." While "a sage-colored flower" counts as a metaphor, it's not a good one because most readers already know artichokes are green and look like flowers. "Hidden treasure within" is a cliché because it's not original. Treasures are usually hidden. And while I'm critiquing, "was" does not carry the sentence forward with strength or interest.

Generic descriptions are just as bad as overwrought ones. Here's an example I found just now when I picked up a national food magazine and turned to a recipe: "These beans are fantastic served with grilled chicken and rice. And if you have some nice chicken stock on hand, you can use it instead of water to cook the beans."

Why are the beans fantastic? Do they complement the chicken and rice a certain way, and if so, how? Texture? Flavor? What is "nice" chicken stock? There's no way to know.

While vague language won't ruin the recipe, a more specific intro-duction helps the reader imagine making the dish and eating it. Suppose the beans, with their dark red color, provided colorful contrast to the white rice, or the stock was dark yellow with small globules of chicken fat floating on the surface. Use a synonym finder to find the right words, because you can only say "delicious" so many times.

And remember that writing about food isn't just about describing flavor and smell. Food may be the subject, but the point of the story can reside in recounting, reporting, and finding the right details, as well as in the history, associations, implications, and of course, the context of the story itself. Most importantly, good food writing is about telling a story well.

Not self-focused. All the writers interviewed here write in the first per-son, but they pull it off because of their experience, writing style, solid reporting, and research. They separate the narrator from themselves—the writer—so they are not building a story based on confession. They don't say "I" in every sentence. Even though the writing involves them, it's not about them. It's still about engaging their readers in a great story.

Good writing isn't about showing off. I've read lots of the self-satisfied kind of food writing, such as the "I'm-sitting here-eating-truffles-on-the-balcony-of-a-terribly-expensive-hotel-in-Piedmont-and-you're-not" approach. This type of writing implies that the writer thinks he's excruciatingly important—and his readers are not. Insulting your readers does not endear you to them. Plus, as a reader, you're not right there with him, savoring the moment. He's too busy trying to make you jealous that he can't pull you in.

Related to this focus is too much navel-gazing. When I was a mag-azine editor, I found many of my writers' first drafts filled with minutiae, particularly in the beginning of the article. I call this the "deep dive," in which writers move quickly into the small details. They get so involved in the story that they lose perspective.

I hope you've read this long list of credentials and recognized yourself in most of them. That's cause for celebration. If not, you know which areas need more investigation and development. Be kind to yourself, and don't try to master all these skills and characteristics at once. Doing so would take a lifetime.

Writing Exercises

1. Write a paragraph about your passion for a certain food. Remember to "show—don't tell": show your passion instead of telling readers ways that you are passionate. Showing would be: "Before I knew it, the bowl was empty, with a few shiny kernels rattling at the bottom." Telling would be: "I really love popcorn."

2. Write two paragraphs about your favorite dish using no adjectives. Don't just describe it, but give details of different ways you've made the dish, where you've eaten it, or who joined you at the table. At first the writing will look stark and spare. Now go back and add specific adjectives to make the story sparkle. Limit yourself to three.

3. Go back over your writing samples from exercise 2, and see if you can make one of them into a nonfiction story from your own experience or memory. Add context, where you focus on what the story means and how it is related or connected to the food. I know it sounds obvious, but make sure the story has a beginning, a middle, and an end.

3: THE FOOD WRITER'S MISE EN PLACE

If you've always wanted to write about food, you probably have lots of questions: How do I get started? What kind of writing should I do, and what kind of qualifications do I need? How do people move up the food chain to become food writers?

Fortunately, lots of answers exist. Above all, you must enjoy learning. That's what keeps the best food writers growing and moving forward. They're interested in homemade pasta, food politics, Indian street food, and kitchen gardens, not just their area of expertise. You probably have the same kind of enthusiasm about food, so the next step is to back it up with knowledge. If you're feeling intimidated about your qualifications, this chapter will show you how to pump up your background and skills. Credibility is an important part of writing and being taken seriously. The more you have to offer in terms of knowledge and experience, the more likely you are to succeed.

Most food writers start out as hobbyists, something they do in their spare time. They're not trying to make a living at it. Some also find they enjoy it so much they'd like to write full-time. To that end, I've described the types of work you can do, and I've invited a few successful colleagues to tell you about their lives at their desks and in the kitchen.

What Types of Work Can a Food Writer Do?

Food writers write all kinds of things: cookbooks, blogs, newsletters, news, feature articles, travel pieces, menu guides, recipes, product labels, and more. When I tell people I'm a food writer, their mouths water as they imagine my glorious life of eating. They imagine I hold court in expensive restaurants every night, open baskets of fine wines and pâtés delivered to my house, hold elaborate dinner parties, jet to Italy on assignment to do a story on pasta . . . Well, no. That's not my life. It could be someone else's in the food-writing world, though, if it was ratcheted down a notch—perhaps that of a top author or food personality who writes for the biggest, glossiest magazines with big budgets and expense accounts. There aren't many jobs like that, though, so if it's your fantasy, it might take you several years to get there.

No two food writers do exactly the same job. We are a tough bunch to categorize. Many people do a little of everything, as you'll see in the stories in this chapter. And what they do changes over time.

Here's a breakdown of the most common categories of food writing, so you can see what kind of work writers do and how much the jobs overlap:

Food blogger. Most food bloggers don't blog full-time. For some, it's the first time they've ever written about food, and it's a fun hobby. Blogging provides an easy way to try out food writing, particularly recipe development. Some people fall in love with food blogging and find that, as they build readership, they want a professional blog. Others use it as a portfolio to express themselves and promote their work. If you want to write a book, it is the best place to start.

It takes just a few minutes to set up a blog. What takes longer is keeping up the pace of posting regularly, learning photography, and dealing with comments. To learn more, read Chapter 4 on becoming a blogger.

••

A DAY IN THE LIFE OF A FOOD BLOGGER AND WRITER

STEPHANIE STIAVETTI started food blogging in 2006. Over the years she has written a cookbook, a blog, web content, and freelance articles. She has twenty years of experience in the tech world and also works as a culinary digital media consultant. She has completed many professional culinary programs in Chicago and San Francisco. Here's Stephanie on blogging:

"As the blogger of TheCulinaryLife.com, I create and share recipes. That means I spend time cooking and taking photos of food, though there's a lot more to this work than playing in the kitchen. Right now I make a living through my food writing, so I need to treat it the way I would any other business venture.

"I get a lot of email. Every day I sift through the monumental pile of pitches from public relations people with pitches for food products, cookbooks, cookware, and press trips. I also get pitches for all sorts of non–food-related items, like cars and computer equipment, which leaves me scratching my head. I very rarely reply unless I know the PR person directly or, occasionally, what they're pitching catches my eye. I don't do many reviews, so I like to save those slots for the products and cookbooks I'm really excited about.

"Next I check on any freelance proposals I've sent to magazine editors. I don't freelance as much as I used to, because the hustle of getting and keeping an editor's attention just doesn't appeal to me, but I do craft the occasional story idea and send it to one of the editors I've met personally through my involvement with the International Association of Culinary Professionals. I can credit this organization with the majority of my nonblogging professional contacts. While food writing and blogging is a wonderful community, it's much easier to connect once you boot yourself out of your office chair and get out of the house.

"Now comes the onslaught of social media. Lots of bloggers love this part, but I'd rather be in the kitchen. I use MeetEdgar.com to automate my posts on Facebook, Twitter, and other channels. Of course I still post fresh content daily, but Edgar makes it easier to batch my social post writing. I can sit down for an hour every month, write a bunch of posts, and then plug them into the tool. Edgar schedules and posts everything automatically, according to a calendar I set up ahead of time. All I have to do is hop on once or twice a day and answer replies.

"No day would be complete with the requisite tinkering on my blog's back end. This includes answering comments, updating plug-ins, solving technical problems, and just generally hitting WordPress with a lead pipe until it does what I need it to do. I'm lucky that I have a technical background and can take care of a lot of this part myself.

"And then there's email marketing. Writing a weekly newsletter sounds easy, but it requires a surprising amount of focus for such a small amount of prose. Managing my list also involves some administrative tinkering, such as ferreting out folks who don't read the newsletter and asking them personally if they still want to be onboard. I get charged for each and every subscriber, so it doesn't make sense to keep folks on the list if they haven't opened a newsletter in six months.

"By now it's four pm, and my butt is still in the chair at my desk. There's bookkeeping to do, web stats to check, launches to plan, informative business-related blog posts to read, culinary topics to research, and reader questions to answer. Really, there's never a dull moment in this business. Once a week, I have a two-hour Skype call with my project manager to discuss business strategies, what's working, what's not working, adjustments to social media campaigns, where I'm at with branding or the design of some ebook or web page.

"At this point it's six hours into my work day, and finally I may get a chance to write a blog post, a magazine article, or a section of my most recent book. I have always struggled with writing at set times, with no looming deadline. My muse is coy. Apparently I need to invest a little more effort toward beating her into submission.

"Later I get to the kitchen, where I test recipes, take photos, and film video snippets. This becomes a problem during winter, when the sun goes down at five P.M. and I'm in a panic chasing the last licks of daylight for a photo. Eventually I flip my schedule so that I'm cooking and shooting in the morning, roasting a full chicken dinner in time to catch the magical nine A.M. light.

"I try to not work after dinner, but many late evenings find me back at my desk, performing tasks I didn't get to during the day. It seems like the to-do list is always a step ahead of me. Thankfully I love what I do, so building my business rarely feels like a chore.

"Whenever someone tells me they think I must spend all day in the kitchen, dreaming up good things to eat, I have to chuckle. I wish cooking took up most of my time as a food writer and blogger! Sometimes I'm working full-time as an employee, and then I have to cram all this into the six-hour window between after work and bed. A lot of my fellow bloggers live a similar life, but we wouldn't have it any other way."

• •

Freelance writer. When you see stories in newspapers and magazines, the full-time employees—editors and assistants—have written some of them in addition to doing their regular jobs. They rely on freelancers or syndicated stories to fill in the rest. Some food writers fill the need by writing feature articles, personal essays, interviews, regular columns, and recipes for magazines, newspapers, and websites.

Most write as a sideline to something else because it's hard to make a decent living as a freelancer. Or they have other sources of income. They might also cater, work in restaurants, be private chefs, develop and test recipes for companies, take people on food tours, or teach cooking classes, for example.

Writing for corporations—such as press releases, website copy, or recipes and curricula for chefs—pays better, but those jobs are in high demand, and it's hard to break in.

Syndicated writer. This person writes a regular column that a syndication service sends to many newspapers around the country. Most freelancers, however, write a story that is published in one publication.

THE FREELANCER'S LIFE

MARGE PERRY is a full-time, award-winning freelance food writer and recipe developer for many national magazines, including *Cooking Light, Health,* and *Self.* She writes a weekly column for *Newsday,* teaches at the Institute of Culinary Education (ICE), and writes a daily blog for MyRecipes.com. Here's how she spends her days:

"I make a living as a food writer. Okay, I do a few other things, too—I teach, I make videos, I photograph, I speak—but they are all related.

"There are hard days, long days, and stressful days. But there has never, ever been a day that I have said, 'I don't like my job.' I feel incredibly fortunate to making a living doing something about which I am passionate.

"To be clear: to earn enough money (and we all have our own definition of that) requires that I work long days—longer than my friends who are lawyers, doctors, and bankers. But when your workday begins at seven A.M. with a stop at the market on the way home from the gym, and you get all dreamy gazing at the most beautiful tomatoes to photograph for your column, I'd say it is worth the extra hours.

"I got my start writing a column for a small local newspaper. I still write a newspaper column (now for a larger newspaper), and it is also part of my job to provide the accompanying photograph. Photography was a skill I acquired on the job, but one that has turned out to be important for my corporate work with a few companies whose cookware, tools, or food products I love.

"Every part of my business—the business of being a food writer—seems to feed into the other parts. I began teaching to establish my presence as a food writer, but discovered I loved cooking with students. While teaching at the Institute of Culinary Education in New York City, I love helping students gain the skills they need to feel really good about cooking. The students helped me be a better writer. They showed me what readers need to know.

"When I saw I was getting a lot of the same questions over and over from students, I developed a column for MyRecipes.com called 'Ask the Expert.' That, in turn, became the source of material for a video series.

"I share this freelance life with my husband, David Bonom (and two dogs, two cats, and two children), with whom I have a company called Vittles and Verbs. We are hired both separately and together, although in truth we bounce ideas off each other even when we are not working on the same project. We each have our own business, and our own professional strengths, but we spend about half our time working together.

"At the heart of it all, this is about doing two things I love most: writing and communicating about food and cooking. I still spend days in the kitchen cooking, long stretches of time writing at my desk, and hours capturing the visual story of food. When I've sat too long, I cook; when I've been cooking too long, I photograph. And when I need to escape the confines of my home (meaning my office, photography studio, and kitchen), I teach.

"My freelance career is greater than the sum of its components. I am a better writer because I teach, a better teacher because I develop recipes, a better photographer because I write. And it is a good thing, too, that these different components are so interwoven. It is the combination that keeps me financially stable, challenged, excited, and inspired."

• •

Cookbook author. While these self-employed writers concentrate on writing cookbooks, most also write freelance articles and might develop recipes for industry as well—for food retailers, food manufacturers, or any company that takes out an ad, produces a newsletter, magazine, or book, or puts recipes on its website. Some also consult for food manufacturers about their products.

Publishers give cookbook authors an advance to work on their books, which might take anywhere from one to six years, depending on how many recipes they develop, how much research they need to do, and where they travel to. Those who are well known with a significant fan base and publishing history may command an advance large enough to put off other jobs while writing the book, but this is rare. Almost all continue taking on other sorts of work, because the advance will not support them. (Self-published cookbook authors do not receive an advance.)

Chefs and business owners often work with ghostwriters and collaborators to write their cookbooks. See more on page 170 about how this works.

• •

WHAT IT'S LIKE TO BE A COOKBOOK AUTHOR

MOLLY STEVENS, based in Vermont, is a food writer, cookbook author, editor, and cooking teacher. She has won James Beard Foundation awards for her cookbooks *All About Roasting: A New Approach to a Classic Art* and *All About Braising: The Art of Uncomplicated Cooking.* Both books also received accolades from the International Association of Culinary Professionals (IACP). Molly's articles and recipes appear regularly in *Fine Cooking* magazine, where she is a contributing editor. She has contributed to *Saveur, Bon Appétit,* and *Eating Well* magazines, and her recipes and tips also have appeared in the *Wall Street Journal, Everyday with Rachael Ray,* and *Real Simple.* Classically trained in France, Molly has directed programs and taught at many prestigious cooking schools. She has been the Bon Appétit Cooking Teacher of the Year and IACP Cooking Teacher of the Year.

Here are her reflections on a long career:

"For me, like many cookbook authors, writing books is merely one element of a multifaceted professional and personal life. Yes, I write cookbooks, but I also work as a cooking teacher, a recipe developer, and a ghostwriter. In addition, I am a freelance editor, a magazine contributor, a consultant, a food stylist, a recipe tester, and a cook.

"In fact, I am always a little stumped by the simple question, What do you do? I suppose the most honest answer is that I do a lot of things, and that I like it that way. About twenty years ago I left a full-time job as a culinary instructor to pursue a freelance career with the simple goals of getting a few magazine articles published and becoming a better food writer and editor along the way. I learned very quickly the value of saying yes to any viable opportunity, especially those that felt beyond my reach. From the very start, my freelance career has been a roller coaster roaring from peaks of intense productivity to quiet lulls where I can find myself worrying if there will be more work ahead.

"When it comes to writing my cookbooks, I take my time writing them for a number of reasons. For starters, I am slow. Sure, I can crank when I need to, but my natural creative process requires time to sort things out. I used to beat myself up over my sluggish pace, but this only seemed to make it worse. Now I try to be kinder to myself and just keep at it.

"Second, my spirit flags when every meal I prepare is either recipe development or recipe testing. There are some evenings when all I want is a simple dinner for my husband and me without taking notes or having to be hypercritical to determine if a dish is 'cookbook worthy.' These nights off make me less prolific, I know, but they also remind me of the pleasures of the table.

"Third, I live in the woods in Vermont, and I can go a little stir-crazy when I spend too much time alone, so the notion of locking myself up to write a book for months on end is not healthy for me. To balance the solo lifestyle of a writer, I teach cooking classes, attend conferences, travel, study, volunteer in my community, and play. These 'breaks' slow down the cookbook progress, but they energize and inspire me. They also provide essential exposure. With no real platform (like a restaurant, a TV show, or a madly popular blog), getting out there, meeting people, and hand-selling books seem key to building my brand and therefore, ideally, selling books.

"And finally—and this one is a bit of a chicken-and-egg situation—I don't sustain myself financially as a cookbook author, so I need to take other work projects. As a result, I am always juggling multiple deadlines and projects. For instance, I am currently under contract for a new cookbook, so I am plugging away at that. Last week I submitted Thanksgiving recipes and text for a magazine assignment. This week I am finalizing recipes and making travel arrangements for an upcoming teaching tour. Earlier today, I answered students' questions from an online cooking class. Tomorrow I meet with the owners of a local café and educational space that hired me as a consultant.

"So to answer the question of what it's like to be a cookbook author, all I can say is what it is like to be me. I am happy to have made a life around my love of cooking, writing, and teaching. From early on, my goals have revolved not so much around money as around creating a purposeful life for myself. I don't draw strict lines between my work identity and my authentic self. I like being a cookbook author because it's an integral part of who I am and how I have chosen to live and work. I feel lucky."

Menu consultant, recipe developer, and tester. Menu consultants work directly for restaurants or public relations companies and usually have a background in the restaurant industry. They might be wordsmiths who write or check menus. Recipe developers and testers work for corporations that want recipes based on their product, such as food manufacturers, to put on their packaging. These jobs usually pay well and are held by freelance cookbook authors, dieticians, and nutritionists.

Restaurant reviewer. Restaurant reviewers at daily papers and websites can be full-time employees, but most publications rely on freelancers. Many blogs also include or focus on restaurant coverage. (For more on restaurant reviewing, see Chapter 6.)

Newspaper writer. Full-time staff writers often migrate from another section of the newspaper. Kim Severson, now an award-winning food reporter for the *New York Times*, moved into food from regular reporting. Other reporters migrate from the sports or business departments, or become restaurant reviewers after writing movie or book reviews. Former *New York Times* restaurant critic Frank Bruni previously headed the *Times'* European bureau office (and he's now an op-ed columnist for the *Times*). If you want to work on a newspaper as a full-time writer whose beat is food, you may have to become a journalist first, or a successful freelance writer.

What You Need to Break In

There are three ways to break into food writing. One is to have a background as a writer: someone who knows how to develop and write a story, and how to interview, research, and report. If you are already a published writer and choose to change your focus, it's easier to break in.

I started out as a general newspaper reporter and later edited magazines. I had learned how to write, research, interview, and get published, and any subject was game. Eventually I discovered that food was my true passion. The hard part was gaining enough knowledge to write about food, and earning credibility as a food writer.

The second is to have experience in a restaurant or food service. Many cookbook authors and restaurant reviewers spent time in a professional kitchen. Food52.com cofounder Amanda Hesser wrote her first book, *The Cook and the Gardener: A Year of Recipes and Writings from the French Countryside*, after cooking in France in a chateau with a live-in gardener. John Birdsall, a senior editor at Chow.com, worked in restaurants for fifteen years before becoming a restaurant critic. He's since gone on to write personal essays, wining a James Beard award for one published in *Lucky Peach* magazine.

Some think too much of a food background is a liability. "It's important to be open, to research, to not accept the norm, to explore and discover new findings and research thoroughly," says Knopf cookbook editor Judith Jones. "Sometimes if you think you know too much, it's limiting."

Many end up in food but don't start there. Jeffrey Steingarten was an attorney before becoming a food writer for *Vogue*. But more importantly, he was a funny guy, having honed his humor writing at the *Harvard Lampoon*. Among the mega bloggers, Ree Drummond (The PioneerWoman.com) had a background in marketing, David Lebovitz was a pastry chef, and Smitten Kitchen's Deb Perelman had been writing for a high-tech publication.

Aside from restaurant experience, you could also break into food writing based on your experience as a cooking teacher, dietician, nutritionist, food historian, culinary school graduate, food retailer, or food producer.

The easiest way, however, is to start a food blog. There are no qualifications other than access to a computer. Even having a camera is optional.

How to Get an Education

What if you're not already a writer or someone with a background in food? You can still succeed by getting an education. Even people with writing or food-industry credentials have to fill in the gaps. Studying, when it comes to food writing, is a pleasurable act. You like to eat, don't you? And you like to read good food writing, right? All you need to know is what to study, how to find classes, and how to network. So let's start at the beginning. One of the first things you need to know is how to become discriminating about food.

Taste, taste, taste. When I embarked on a food-writing career I felt intimidated by writers who seemed to know everything about food, including how it should taste. I wondered how I would learn this skill. The answer, fortunately, was to do more of something I did already anyway: eat, read, cook, and take cooking classes. Not just the same foods over and over, though. My job was to discover and understand.

"Eating a lot is the first thing," agrees *L.A. Times* food columnist Russ Parsons. But eat with an open mind. "People try to fit food into categories—it is this, it isn't that," he warns. "They compare it to how it fits their preconceptions. The point of view of the novice can be overdone. You can only play the fool so often until people ask themselves why they are reading your work."

Build your experiences. Here's Tamasin Day-Lewis writing in the A *Fork in the Road* anthology about tasting grouse: "It wasn't yet a memory. It was an experience. It led me to believe there must be other similar experiences that would hit me explosively and knock me off my culinary everyday feet. And in due course there were."

What if you don't like certain foods? That's fine, as long as you don't overreact. It's your opinion, after all, not a fact. Some restaurant reviewers announce their preferences in reviews, such as saying they don't like sweet sauces in savory dishes, for example.

In *The Man Who Ate Everything*, Jeffrey Steingarten decided to get rid of his food phobias—such as Korean food, anchovies, Indian desserts, and lard—by eating all the things he didn't like to see if his opinion might change. "Scientists tell us that aversions fade away when we eat moderate doses of the hated foods at moderate intervals, especially if the food is complex and new to us," he theorized at the beginning of his book. To his surprise, he liked almost everything except blue food. "In just six months," he writes, "I succeeded in purging myself of nearly all repulsions and preferences, in becoming a more perfect omnivore." He goes on to say that he eventually attained such a Zen-like state that all the food on the menu at a Parisian restaurant looked appetizing, making him unable to order dinner. You'll read more about developing the palate and how to approach individual tastes in Chapter 5.

• •

HOW SOME FOOD WRITERS GOT THEIR START

COLMAN ANDREWS. The cofounder of *Saveur* magazine used the pseudonym Persona to write restaurant reviews in Los Angeles for an underground newspaper called the Staff, and then moved on to the *Los Angeles Free Press.* "Persona was an imaginary person who wrote very flamboyantly, used food puns, and had been everywhere and done everything," he recalls.

AMANDA HESSER. Inspired by M. F. K. Fisher, the cofounder of Food52.com decided to become a food writer and began by studying cooking in Europe. Later she worked for La Varenne École de Cuisine in France for two years, testing dozens of recipes for a cookbook by Anne Willan. She met the school's gardener, who inspired her first book. In New York, she freelanced before being hired as an editor and writer for the *New York Times.*

RUSS PARSONS. He had been a sports writer at a newspaper for ten years and never thought about becoming a food writer, even though he loved to cook. Because the paper was small, he was able to branch out into general feature writing and music writing. One day he got an assignment to write about a woman who was named cooking teacher of the year by *Bon Appétit.* He took her class as part of his research for the story and found he enjoyed it. He became an "obnoxious hardcore foodie, read voraciously, took more classes, and went to bed with a stack of cookbooks." Friends let him work in their restaurants.

Parsons grew dissatisfied with the way the paper covered food, where editors took the "rip and read" approach, ripping stories with no local angle off the wire and running them. He told the editor he wanted to write about food and got a six-week tryout, editing and writing for the food section. He became the paper's restaurant critic after six months and led the *L. A. Time's* food section for decades. He is now a columnist.

RUTH REICHL. During her job as chef at the Swallow restaurant in Berkeley, she became a restaurant reviewer for a San Francisco magazine, a gig she got from a customer who was an editor at the publication. She went on to freelance stories for *New York* magazine and eventually was appointed food critic of the magazine's sibling, *New West,* a California regional magazine. From there she became the chief reviewer for the *New York Times* before landing at *Gourmet* magazine. Now self-employed, she has published memoirs and a novel, and she's at work on more books.

ALAN RICHMAN. The freelance writer started out as a newspaper news writer, sportswriter, feature writer, and columnist. Later he switched to magazines and got a staff job at *GQ* magazine, writing features, profiles, and a wine column on the side. "The editor in chief asked if I wanted to make it a food-and-wine column instead. I jumped at the chance, since I'd rather eat than drink." He became a freelancer for *GQ, Condé Nast Traveler,* and *Bon Appétit* magazines. He never worked in restaurants nor graduated from a cooking school, yet has won several national awards for his writing.

JEFFREY STEINGARTEN. A former attorney, he wrote satire and parodies for the Harvard Lampoon while a Harvard law student and tried out for a job at the *New*

Yorker before his appointment as food critic for *Vogue*. He met Anna Wintour in 1979 because he knew her husband a bit. When Wintour became editor of *Home and Garden* magazine, she asked several writers, including Steingarten, to try out for a new, more serious column about food. The assignment was microwaved fish, 800 to 1,200 words.

"I said I didn't even know how to microwave," he recalls. "She said, 'We'll get you a microwave.' I said I can't have just one, as there are several manufacturers, and different features and power levels. She said, 'How many did you need?' I said twelve. She paused. She said, 'Well, okay, we'll get you twelve microwaves.' In the end I only got three because the fuses started going." Steingarten turned in 4,200 words. The magazine printed about 4,000. "The pattern was set," he says. "I turned the assignment into a first-person adventure, not perfectly well, but that's what I've been doing ever since, making some jokes along the way." Later Wintour went to *Vogue*, and Steingarten followed shortly thereafter. Books based on his columns resulted.

Asked if there was a slight difference between an attorney's salary and a full-time columnist's, Steingarten admitted he should have saved more. When negotiating his salary, he asked if Wintour would pay him "as much as a New York plumber makes annually." He got it the next year.

MOLLY STEVENS. The cookbook author was an established cooking teacher with bachelor's and master's degrees in English literature. She wrote a few food-related stories for a local arts and entertainment paper, and did some commercial writing for a local cheese company. "My big break was with *Fine Cooking*," she explains. "I had met and briefly worked with [editor] Martha Holmberg while we were both in France at La Varenne [a cooking school]. Later when she became the editor at *Fine Cooking*, she called me and asked, 'Can you write?' Well, turns out I could. I wrote a story on rack of lamb in 1995. The rest, as they say, is history . . . or at least my history."

CALVIN TRILLIN. He was a successful freelance writer, working for national magazines, before he began writing about food for *Life* magazine in the early 1970s. Later Trillin traveled around the country for fifteen years for a *New Yorker* series called U.S. Journal, writing a three-thousand-word feature article every three weeks. When he got "worn down on reporting," he wrote lighter pieces for comic relief, covering topics such as Cincinnati residents arguing about chili or people making the rounds at the Breaux Bridge Crawfish Festival.

"I had neither the credentials for nor any interest in inspecting, say, a serving of Veal Orloff for the purpose of announcing to the world how it measured up to what dog-show types call the standards of the breed," he writes in his foreword to *The Tummy Trilogy*. "I wrote about eating rather than food, and I wrote as a reporter who was enjoying his work rather than as an expert."

As for me, after journalism school I became the editor of a fourteen-page women's section of a newspaper, filling it with recipes from the wire service, plus wedding and feature articles. The publisher of a city restaurant magazine hired me to be the editor. In this new job I visited restaurants and wrote features about chefs and restaurants. I went on to a career as a magazine editor, then became self-employed in my forties, and got back into food writing.

Even though it sounds daunting, if you can immerse yourself in tasting, reading about, and cooking food, it doesn't get any better than that. Doing so just fuels your passion.

"You will embark upon an educated journey," explains David Leite of LeitesCulinaria.com. "As you go along, there will come these aha moments where you put together all these bits and you can talk intelligently about a rack of lamb or two types of apple. You realize you've moved to another level."

So read for knowledge, not just pleasure. This process takes time, kind of like practicing meditation or painting—you never stop learning and trying to improve. Here are specific suggestions on what to read:

Read the classics. If you don't like to read, you will find it difficult to write. Below is a list of books compiled from recommendations from people I've interviewed for this book, plus my own suggestions. It reflects the work of authors who are primarily literary nonfiction food writers, not recipe writers (see more about great cookbook writers in Chapter 7). I have not included books by anyone interviewed for this book. Please assume that whatever they've written is magnificent or I wouldn't have bothered.

The list below is of classic narrative food writing, which I'm defining as an American love affair with French cooking, mostly. Some of these books are hard to find, and some are out of print. You may have to special-order from bookstores, contact libraries, and peruse used book sites or used bookstores. But it will be worth your time. You can cook from these books, but they offer so much more than just the subjects of food and cooking. You'll find beautifully drawn portraits of people's lives and times.

- *The Art of Eating* condenses M. F. K. Fisher's first five books from 1937 to 1949 into one volume. It includes *How to Cook a Wolf*, *Consider the Oyster*, and *The Gastronomical Me*. She wrote narratives about food as a metaphor for life, with an exacting, sensuous vocabulary and sharp wit. Her style was new in a United States accustomed to recipes and instruction.
- *Auberge of the Flowering Hearth*, by Roy Andries De Groot. A 1937 adventure about his visit to a mysterious French inn in a hidden valley. Also see *In Search of the Perfect Meal: A*

Collection of the Best Food Writing of Roy Andries de Groot, a collection of essays by this gifted writer and gourmand.

- *Between Meals: An Appetite for Paris*, by A. J. Liebling. A *New Yorker* writer reports on eating in the now-vanished Paris of the 1930s.
- *On Food and Cooking: The Science and Lore of the Kitchen*, by Harold McGee. So much more than a reference book, combining culinary lore with scientific explanations.
- *Blue Trout and Black Truffles: The Peregrinations of an Epicure*, by Joseph Wechsberg. Writing devoted to the eating places and vineyards of France.
- *Clementine in the Kitchen*, by Samuel Chamberlain. A cook introduces Americans to the charms of French cooking.
- *Delights and Prejudices*, by James Beard. An erudite memoir with recipes from a great American gastronome.
- *Eating in America: A History*, by Waverly Root. With Richard de Rochemont, this former journalist chronicles an erudite and fresh history of American food and eating customs.
- *Home Cooking: A Writer in the Kitchen* and *More Home Cooking: A Writer Returns to the Kitchen*, by Laurie Colwin. Novelist Colwin, who died in 1992, wrote two memoirs that are a mix of warm conversations, practical advice, and recipes.
- *The Physiology of Taste: Or Meditations on Transcendental Gastronomy*, by Jean Anthelme Brillat-Savarin. Lively and amusing meditations, examinations, and discussions on food, cooking, and eating. Try to find the version translated by M. F. K. Fisher.
- *South Wind Through the Kitchen: The Best of Elizabeth David*, by Elizabeth David. A collection of her best writing and recipes compiled from nine books written between 1955 and 1977. You'll find long sentences and sensuous depth and detail about food and ingredients.
- *The Taste of Country Cooking*, by Edna Lewis. A joyful and evocative memoir of American country cooking from the granddaughter of a slave.
- *The Unprejudiced Palate: Classic Thoughts on Food and the Good Life*, by Angelo Pellegrini. A charming look at the good life

of food, wine, and cooking from a passionate Italian American cook and gardener.

If you prefer to sample many authors and styles of food writing at once, here's a list of suggested compilations:

- *The Best Food Writing* is an annual anthology featuring many of the writers interviewed for this book.
- *Endless Feasts: Sixty Years of Writing from "Gourmet."* Ruth Reichl introduces a banquet of food and travel writing, profiles and memories.
- *The Penguin Book of Food and Drink* celebrates a century of gastronomic writing, including humorist S. J. Perelman's "Farewell, My Lovely Appetizer." (Many food writers revere Perelman's writing style, most of which is not directly about food.)
- *Through the Kitchen Window: Women Explore the Intimate Meanings of Food and Cooking.* One of my favorite anthologies, because of the wide range of topics, including living on food stamps.
- *The Wilder Shores of Gastronomy: Twenty Years of the Best Food Writing from the Journal "Petits Propos Culinaires."* A collection of essays that includes many written by writers in this chapter. The journal began in 1979 and has been out of print for many years.

Read great magazines and newspapers. Read the national food magazines, such as *Food & Wine*, *Cook's Illustrated*, *Fine Cooking*, *Cooking Light*, and *Saveur* to keep up on trends and as a continuing form of education. Don't be a snob: pick up the celebrity food magazines and *Taste of Home* too. Read newspaper food sections, particularly those in the *New York Times*, *Washington Post*, *San Francisco Chronicle*, and *Chicago Tribune*—all available online.

Read food blogs. Subscribe to several so that they arrive in your email or on your browser's home page by RSS feed. You'll want to devour blogs on the local scene, big and small bloggers, and those who cover your favorite subject, whether it's baking, gluten-free cooking, or pizzas. See Chapter 4 on blogs to learn more.

Follow food writers on Facebook and Twitter. Most food writers have discovered social media, so it's an easy way keep up with them and possibly to develop relationships.

Study cooking. Take cooking lessons through adult education classes, a community college, retail stores, or privately. Many professional cooking schools hold weekend classes for the public. Cookbook writers sometimes hold private cooking classes in their homes.

Cooking classes can be revealing. I took many classes on French technique that helped me as a restaurant reviewer, particularly on classic sauces. I've also taken lots of cooking classes in different kinds of cuisine. As a result, I'm better at picking out the ingredients of a dish I've eaten that I would like to create at home.

Or work in a restaurant for a while. Russ Parsons, as a general newspaper reporter, wrote a story on a cooking teacher, and by taking her class realized he wanted to learn more. He took more classes and began assisting her, and then friends let him work in their restaurants at no pay. "After I really immersed myself, I felt comfortable writing about food," he says. Working in restaurants isn't for everyone, but you'll get to see chefs in action, see how the back of the restaurant functions, and learn techniques and tricks cooks use to get dishes to the table on time. Perhaps a restaurant would let you watch, rather than cook.

You don't even have to leave the house to study cooking and food. You can learn a tremendous amount from television today. Watch cooking shows and shows about food. My favorites are the classics—Jacques Pépin, Julia Child, and Martin Yan.

Cook more often, and take more risks. It takes a commitment to start making foods you've never made before, including foods that are time consuming or use new techniques or ingredients. That means you'll be going to specialty food stores, which are also part of your education.

Study food writing, or just writing. Go to food-writing classes and blogging conferences. Find food writing and freelance writing classes in your city or online, such as those at MediaBistro.com. Continuing education classes sharpen your writing skills. Look for classes in your community on nonfiction writing, memoir, and personal essay. (See the Appendix for more suggestions.)

Get a degree in food studies, writing, or journalism. Get a degree in food studies from New York University, Boston University, or the University of Adelaide in Australia. Most universities take a more interdisciplinary approach to food studies and offer classes through departments that include anthropology, psychology, and nutrition. Journalism programs are offered at universities around the country. Find a master's of fine arts in writing that focuses on nonfiction. The master's degree in journalism program at University of California, Berkeley, offers the added attraction of Professor Michael Pollan.

Internships are one of the big benefits of studying at a college or university. Freelancer Mary Margaret Pack worked as an intern at the *San Francisco Chronicle* while a student at the California Culinary Academy. By the time she graduated, she had a handful of feature stories to show as credentials for future freelancing queries. As a result she has written for years for the *Austin Chronicle*.

During college studies in journalism, *The Cake Mix Doctor* author Anne Byrn interned at her hometown newspaper every summer and winter break. She formed relationships with people in the food section. Her coup at the paper was scooping the story of Elvis's death. Living in the South, that was a big deal. She was a junior in college. "It was a Sunday night," she recalls. "That was my shift. There was no one else to write the story."

Travel. Experience firsthand how food tastes and how people make dishes in their own countries. Watch food preparers in markets and on the street. If possible, meet home cooks, and watch them in the kitchen. Visit the night markets of Asia and farmers' markets in Europe. Rent a place with a kitchen, and try cooking something unfamiliar. Go on food tours in other cities. Go to big and small restaurants to try a range of dishes, and order dishes you've never had before. Take culinary vacations led by experienced cooks and chefs, and get to know them. Buy cookbooks about the food of places you've visited.

Network. If you are a cooking teacher, entrepreneur, or other food professional, join the International Association of Culinary Professionals so you can attend its annual conference and access its membership directory. Attend food-based events in your community. If you are a food blogger, join BlogHer.com, or attend other blogging conferences to learn or meet other food writers like yourself.

Byrn says she can't emphasize enough how networking has aided her career. While in college she majored in home economics in addition to journalism. When she graduated she heard about a job from a home economics networking group she had joined. Some of its members were food writers. The opening was for a food writer at the *Atlanta Journal*. She got the job in 1978 and worked there until 1993, when she became the section editor.

Believe you will move forward, and be patient. "Sometimes when you throw yourself into the moment you find out you are more learned than you think," says Leite. "Past experience can suddenly coalesce, and you know more than you thought you did." Persevere, and most likely it will pay off in the end.

Writing Exercises

1. Make a plan of five things you can do to move your knowledge base forward and get closer to writing about food. For example, subscribe to a magazine, take a cooking class, join a forum, or choose a blogging conference. What are the things you need to do to succeed? Give yourself a deadline for accomplishing these five tasks.
2. Find five of your favorite food writers on social media, and follow them to keep up with their work.
3. Read one of the books listed on pages 41–43. Choose a style of book you might like to write. Write a 250-word book report on what you enjoyed about the book most. Evaluate the author's writing technique, subject matter, and structure, and whether the book held your interest.

4: ON FOOD AND BLOGGING

Food blogs began as online journals and have evolved to be everything from amateur recipe listings to sophisticated marketing machines. The best have a strong personal voice and message, as well as excellent photography. They're meant to be spontaneous, based on events in the blogger's life or what they cooked recently. They engage and develop a loyal community of readers.

Blogging is the most exciting area of food writing today. Food bloggers are pushing boundaries, writing about food in ways that print can't. They write about their own lives, about current events and cooking, and about new restaurants and travel. There's immediacy to their writing, a kinship among fellow bloggers, and exhilaration in saying whatever they want, unfettered by editors.

After initially ignoring food blogs, some publications have embraced them. *Gourmet* experimented with blogs before its demise and the online version of Saveur has a regular section dedicated to "sites we love." Wizenberg of Orangette.blogspot.com was the first food blogger to have a regular column in *Bon Appétit*. Everyone blogs now, including newspaper food writers and cookbook authors.

Book editors and literary agents read blogs, always on the lookout for the next talented blogger worthy of a book contract. Hundreds of food bloggers have published cookbooks.

In this chapter, you'll learn about why to start a blog, how to begin, what to write about, how to develop your voice, how to post good photographs, get noticed, ethics of accepting free products, and what's involved in turning a blog into a book. I've interviewed and referenced the best and most exciting food bloggers, who will encourage and guide you. Whether you're a beginning blogger or an experienced one, there's something new for you. Since most people blog as a hobby, that is the focus. If you'd like to make an income from your blog, read Chapter 12.

Now, settle in. This is a long chapter. You'll find lots to think about in terms of finding a subject, developing your voice and content, improving your photography, and keeping up the energy to post. Get your pen out. I hope you'll be generating new ideas for blog posts as you read.

Why Blog?

Quite simply, it's the easiest way to explore being a food writer because you can start now. Jump in and publish your first post within an hour, once you've chosen your software platform (page 51).

More importantly, there are no gatekeepers. In the diminishing world of newspaper and magazine food writing, it's harder than ever to get your foot in the door. Editors seem to ignore email queries for story ideas, budgets are small, space is tight, and competition is fierce. Even if you do succeed in print, your piece will be reviewed by an editor and may be edited or even rewritten. Having coached beginning writers who want to freelance, and seeing how hard it is, I now suggest they start a blog.

I started a blog myself, in 2008, to see what it's all about, as a way to continue the work of this book, and to keep up with readers on current events and things of interest to them. If you haven't been there, see diannej.com/b. It's been so much fun to write whatever I like, and satisfying to get a response. When I'm done, I press a button, and there's my work, published on the web. I've been delighted and amazed by the response and my online community.

Cookbook author, freelancer writer, and blogger Dorie Greenspan is just as enthusiastic. "When I started a blog, I wanted everyone to start a blog," she explains. "Now I feel like everybody has a blog. I would say start it because you have something you want to say, you have something to share, and because it would be fun." (Her blog is doriegreenspan.com.)

"I respect connoisseurship and expertise. I love that there are experts in every field, and I love seeing their work. But I also think there's a place for people who are learning, for people who want to share it, and every blog finds its own readership."

These are all great reasons to blog. Here are some others:

Blogging is all about you. Who wouldn't love that? Not what you ate for breakfast, necessarily, but a conversation with readers about food, events, and ideas that interest you. It's all about what turns you on—what you cook, taste, discover, learn, and share. Writing about your own life is so much easier than writing about anything else, because you are the expert on your own experience. What used to be niche has become more mainstream, such as paleo blogs from Michelle Tam of NomNomPaleo.com and Melissa Joulwan of ClothesMakeTheGirl.com, and Angela Liddon's vegan blog, OhSheGlows.com. All have a wide and dedicated audience who value the writer's personal stories.

Writing a blog means writing regularly. If you want a writing practice, there's nothing better. The point of a blog is to write often. Once you establish a schedule, it becomes easier to produce.

You'll write and publish immediately. There's no turnaround time. "I was in Paris and went to a new pastry shop, where the pastry chef was turning classics around and making them in new ways," says Greenspan. "I'm no longer an active freelancer, but here I could write about it immediately. It's so instant."

You can write about whatever you want. When Heidi Swanson started 101Cookbooks.com, she did so to cook from the cookbooks she had gathered and never used. Now she writes her own recipes and adds stories about travel. "My site is really simple," she told me. "It's my life where it intersects recipes. I can weave in travel, day-to-day tasks, whatever I like. I love to cook and always find something inspiring."

It gives you a way to build a platform immediately as a writer. A platform is your visibility to readers, and it's important if you want to move forward in your career. It shows editors and agents that you have a following, and it creates a springboard to other opportunities. If you want to freelance, now you have writing samples to show an editor. If you want to write a book, the content in your blog gives you a good starting point, and its readership shows that people are interested. And if you want to start a food business, a successful blog creates an audience.

You'll have readers. What I love most about blogging is the community of writers and thinkers who leave comments both on my blog and in social media. I spend a lot of time alone at my desk, and the willingness of others to post their comments and insights makes me feel that I'm part of something larger. The camaraderie among other bloggers is another terrific part of blogging. I've helped others, and they've helped me, particularly with the technical issues.

Here's what a longtime food blogger, Adam Roberts of Amateur Gourmet.com, wrote about the benefits of blogging: "Aside from the fact that lots of people will read what you write on a daily basis (which is always exciting), you get to act as your own editor, producer, director, publisher and secretary. You can make money from ads (though not enough to act as a super incentive). You can find a way to channel your creative energies (hence all my films and songs and EXTREMELY LONG posts like this one). And, best of all, you have a great reason to really explore the world of food: both in the kitchen and out in the world. If I didn't have a food blog, I doubt I'd cook all the stuff I cook or eat at as many places as I do. I do most of it so I can sit down later and process everything that I just experienced, for better or for worse. And over time you've created this gigantic record of your journey. If you click my archives and read the posts I posted my first couple of weeks as food blogger, I think you'll detect a marked difference in my competence level, my knowledge and my confidence both as a writer and as a chef. Food blogging pays off."

For some people, their blog is their life story. David Lebovitz (davidlebovitz.com), whose tagline is "Living the Sweet Life in Paris," says he doesn't think of himself as a food writer but as someone writing about his life. "That's how you keep readers," he advises. "You never know what people are going to respond to. It's being personal, talking about something engaging, having a conversation."

The thing about blogging is that you're not just the writer. You're also the publisher of your blog, so you need all kinds of skills. You are the photographer, the designer, the marketer, the subscription manager, and the complaints department. So there's a learning curve, but it's not difficult.

Regardless of all these reasons, it's a good idea to ask yourself why you want a blog. Even if it's just for fun, and you don't care if anyone reads it, sooner or later you will want readers and some kind of return on your investment. If you are doing it to make money, unless you have huge readership, you'll be disappointed. Most food blogs are hobby blogs, and it's difficult to make money. (For more on that, see Chapter 12).

Speaking as someone who's had a blog for several years now, blogging has given me a platform, business opportunities, new relationships, and a reason to write every week. That might be your biggest challenge. Here's some tough advice from the blog From Away, in a post called "How to Start a Food Blog": "This constant demand for new content, this constant churn, can be challenging. It requires a lot of time, as well as the ability to not become emotionally attached to a post that requires an emotional attachment in order to make it compelling. Tough, right? Your writing has to be good, but it can't be precious. It has to be important enough for you to work on each day, but not important enough that you will be crushed if it doesn't receive a huge response (or worse, if it receives negative criticism) and is gone from the front page of your site the next day. You have to care about your site more than anything else, and somehow manage to not care about it at all. It's a challenging balancing act."

Choosing a Software Service

If you're not scared off by that last quote, good. Before you begin writing, you need to know some technical basics of getting your blog started. You'll have to decide which blogging software service to use and on whose server. Each service has different templates to fill in, customizable by you. Here are the platforms bloggers use most:

WordPress.com. You can have a free blog with an address that ends in wordpress.com, or register a domain name and host it on a server of your choice for a fee. WordPress is robust, offering the freedom to grow and experiment with customization, and it is probably the most-used content management system in the world.

Blogger.com. Blogger, the oldest blogging platform, is owned by Google, which launched it in 1999. It's a good starter service because it's easy to use. However, it lacks the ability to customize with widgets and plug-ins such as those available on WordPress. Note that your web address will end with blogspot.com because this is a free service.

Tumblr.com. This is another free option, but you can pay for premium themes. It's considered a microblogging platform: the goal is to follow other blogs, like others' posts, or get your own posts liked or reblogged. It's sleek and minimalist.

Typepad.com. While Typepad will host your blog, it is not free because the target customers are businesses, not individuals. Some say the interface is easier to use than WordPress. There are beautiful design templates, too.

As I mentioned, the downside of these blogging platforms is that their names (blogspot, typepad, wordpress, etc.) will appear as part of the address of your blog name, unless you pay to move the software to a host service company. Doing so means choosing your own domain name, which does away with the name of the software host. Most bloggers recommend you get your own domain name immediately, as it makes you seem more professional. When I started my blog, for example, the address was diannejacob.wordpress.com. After a few months, I moved my blog to the company that hosts my website, and now the address is part of my website, diannej.com. Registering for a domain name is inexpensive, and some web hosts and Internet service providers offer free registration for the first year. Next, find a company to host your website. That costs anywhere from $10–$150 per year, depending on which service you choose. Many food bloggers like Bluehost, which offers a free domain name. I have used GoDaddy and Siteground. Research your options online.

No matter which service you use, most blog templates have standard design elements. A header appears on every page of your blog and shows people the blog name, like a newspaper masthead. Customize yours with colors, fonts, illustrations, or photographs. The templates make it easy. Below the header, each post begins with a title. Under each post, readers are invited to comment. On the side, the widgets you install create items such as buttons that link to social media, or a list of links to favorite sites, called a "blog roll." Most blogs include a bio section, often called the "About" page (see page 54).

Widgets or plug-ins offer ways to make your blog more efficient. I use Akismet, for example, to help protect it from spam, and comment reply notification, which automatically sends an email to a commenter when I respond. To figure out which plug-ins you want, search online. You'll find plenty of recommendations from bloggers.

If you're not tech savvy, ask technical friends to help you set up your blog. Or you might hire a professional website developer to help you launch. You will need a written post and at least one good photo to start.

When you're ready for the next version of your site, you may choose to hire a designer. Make sure the designer understands the blogging software you use, and be prepared to shell out anywhere from five hundred to a few thousand dollars, depending on the scope of the project. To find a designer, get recommendations from others, shop around, and obtain a few bids to compare prices. You can also check on blogs whose design you like, as sometimes the designer will be listed with a link.

Come Up with a Title

Blog names are usually more personal than book titles and make a statement about the person or the spirit of the blog. Avoid inside jokes and titles only you can understand. Also avoid difficult words to spell. You don't want people to continually mistype your blog's name into their web browsers. This is your brand: you want it be catchy, distinct, and easy to remember.

Some titles are evocative or literary, such as:

- Orangette
- Chocolate & Zucchini

Many are autobiographical:

- The Amateur Gourmet
- Cooking with Amy
- Gluten-Free Girl

- Homesick Texan
- Hunter Angler Gardener Cook
- The Paupered Chef

And many are clever or funny:

- Accidental Hedonist
- Blog Appétit
- Cake Wrecks
- Smitten Kitchen

The best way to find out if your title ideas work is to try them out on friends. If you get a blank stare, keep brainstorming.

Create an "About" Page or Section

An "About" section or page explains who you are, why you started your blog, and what you hope to achieve. If people like reading your blog, they'll go there to find out about you. Grab their attention by explaining your blog's philosophy in a sound-bite–sized sentence. At Smitten Kitchen.com, it's "Fearless cooking from a tiny kitchen in New York City." At SteamyKitchen.com, it's "Fast, fresh and simple for tonight's supper."

I hope you'll post a photo of yourself and state your name and where you live. When I'm reading a blog post in which the writer refers to herself only as "I," I want to know who it is. Say how to contact you, and consider including an email address. Some people use [at] instead of @ to discourage spam. If you're worried about online harassment and bullying, only you can decide how much contact information to divulge. Know that professionals in your field will want to contact you, including companies looking for product reviews, or those who want to invite you to an event or perhaps even hire you. (For more on privacy, see page 61.)

Post enough content to let your readers get to know you. It will make them more likely to connect and comment. The "About" page is not meant to be your life story, however. A few paragraphs are sufficient. Stick to the subject of your blog and let your personality shine through. If you're funny, self-deprecating humor works well. Here are three examples of "About" pages, in which the voice and personality of the bloggers come through clearly:

Deb Perelman of SmittenKitchen.com. Perelman has a long page of text broken up with categories: Contact, Logistics, Photos, Recipes and Cooking, Kitchen Stuff, Blogging, Book, and Etceteras. Even though the headers might seem mundane, the content is anything but. Here's a sample from Kitchen Stuff: "The first thing I need to tell you is that the idea of anyone, anywhere mistaking me for a neat/clean freak is hilarious. I have my moments of obsessiveness (cough), but for the most part, I storm out of the kitchen when I'm done cooking and cross my fingers that this will be the day that it up and cleans itself. Eventually, someone caves."

Clotilde Dusoulier of ChocolateandZucchini.com. "Chocolate & Zucchini is a blog written by Clotilde Dusoulier, a French food writer based in Paris who shares her passion for all things food-related. Her focus is on fresh, colorful, and seasonal foods, making room for both wholesome, nourishing dishes and sweet treats. Here you'll find recipe ideas and cooking inspiration, plus musings on quirky ingredients, cookbook acquisitions, nifty tools, and restaurant experiences. The blog was created in September of 2003, and soon allowed Dusoulier to become a full-time food writer. She writes food and travel articles for magazines in English and in French, writes and edits cookbooks, and works as a recipe developer, public speaker, and food trend consultant."

Michael Procopio of FoodfortheThoughtless.com. "My full name is Michael Clinton Procopio. My middle name has nothing to do with politics and has everything to do with the fact that I was born exactly 60 years to the day after my late grandfather, Clinton Beeson Moore, who himself was named for the two doctors who popped him into a warm oven upon his birth to revive him. It was just like that scene in *101 Dalmatians*, but without puppies."

The only thing I'd change about some of these "About" pages is that they are written in the third person. The rest of the blog is written in first person, so it seems inconsistent. I understand why people do it. It feels uncomfortable to write what "I" did, kind of like bragging. "Sally cooks a mean pot of curry" sounds less egotistical than "I cook a mean pot of curry." But since you write your blog in the first person, try writing your "About" page in first person too.

When you're done with the text, I'd recommend adding a good quality headshot. It doesn't have to be a professional photo, but you don't want a selfie that's blurry or low resolution, shows extraneous details in the background, or has little contrast (for more about photography, see pages 75–81). Your photo is part of your online persona and helps people connect with you.

Other pages you might consider adding, once your blog gets going, are a policy page about accepting products (see pages 81–85) and a list of rules if you plan to give away products. Start a Frequently Asked Questions (FAQ) page if people keep contacting you about the same topics. Readers of Lebovitz's blog often want Paris restaurant recommendations and information about living in France, so his FAQ provides this information, saving him from answering the same questions individually in emails. At the bottom of your blog page, add a copyright notice—that everything on the site belongs to the author, and any reprints are only by permission of the author.

What to Write About

One of the top reasons people start blogs is to write about their life and experiences. Food blogging can be just about that, because there's no end of topics based on your food-loving life. You might write about a restaurant, a kitchen tool you can't live without, a trip abroad, mastering a challenging recipe, a school lunch program, or a new cookbook. It seems that most food blogs are recipe-based, but if that's not your thing, don't feel obligated to go that route.

When you begin a blog, you might not have much of a focus. You just want to express your knowledge, joy, and passion. That's fine. I hope that eventually you'll determine what you're passionate about. Otherwise, a broad theme, such as "I love food," can feel overwhelming or vague. Try to distill your interests. Carve out your niche. Don't worry about a tight focus. Said Josh Ozersky in a *Time* magazine essay, "There is no room for somebody whose subject is 'food.' The subject is broad and so generic that it is necessarily colorless and dull. And anyway, nobody can know enough about 'food' to have anything worth reading. Get a niche. Indian food. Weird street food. Barbecue. Insects. Foraged and fermented weeds. Whatever. Then, when an editor wants something on that subject, they will have a reason to reach for you."

Dusoulier of ChocolateandZucchini.com has a general blog about food but tries to keep the focus on her life in Paris. She says she writes about "new things, things I've not written about before, or haven't cooked before, to keep myself and readers interested. I'm that way in general in life. I don't like to rehash things. I don't watch movies several times. I'm most excited about a recipe when I've recently overcome something, when I've tried something new and it turned out well. I want to share it."

"None of us blog exclusively for ourselves, otherwise we'd just keep diaries," she said in an interview with *Food & Wine*. "But I think it's important to want to blog primarily for the sake of it—the documenting, the sharing, the sense of purpose—before worrying about traffic and recognition, because in the current blogging environment, that can take a while. But if you focus on expressing your passion and your perspective through great-quality content that brings real value to your readers—because you're informative, inspiring, entertaining, or better yet, all of the above—I firmly believe they will find their way to you. But patience, persistence and experimentation are definitely part of the process."

Whatever you find yourself thinking and talking about most could be the focus of your blog. To figure it out, pay attention to which magazine articles catch your eye, which food shows you watch most, which books attract you, which cuisines you cook most, or what you're doing when you lose track of time. If you still can't figure it out, ask your friends to tell you what you obsess about most when it comes to food.

You don't have to worry about whether you're a gourmet cook. Two bloggers who started their blogs for a creative outlet started writing about their situation and their beliefs and investigations, which led to compelling others to take action. Jack Monroe, a single mother in England, started a blog called AGirlCalledJack.com in 2012 that morphed into advice on budget food on just ten pounds a week. A post called "Hunger Hurts" spread widely and led to two books, an Oxfam ambassadorship, and a weekly recipe column in the *Guardian* newspaper.

"Poverty is the sinking feeling when your small boy finishes his one Weetabix and says, 'More, Mummy, bread and jam please, Mummy,' she wrote, "as you're wondering whether to take the TV or the guitar to the pawn shop first, and how to tell him that there is no bread or jam."

Another example is Vani Hari, who has a blog called FoodBabe.com. She started it in 2011 to share her healthy lifestyle, which is a pretty standard approach. But then she began investigating harmful ingredients in processed food. Her activism has included getting Chick-fil-A to remove additives from its chicken, Chipotle to stop serving genetically modified food, and Kraft to remove harmful dyes from its mac and cheese. Her activism has led to appearances on television shows, keynote speeches, and a post as food expert on CNN. Her blog also led to a book, *The Food Babe Way*.

So if possible, pick a theme. One of the best reasons to do so is just to rein yourself in. In one of the early food blogs and easily the most famous, the Julie/Julia project, Julie Powell decided to cook her way through Julia Child's *Mastering the Art of French Cooking*, and posted about her trials with herself, her husband, her job, and blog readers. She gave herself a challenge, and you could do the same. Blog to discover, explore, or master a new subject. Blog to cope with a crisis or to reflect. Strike a balance, and look for topics that connect with your readers.

How to Make People Care

At this point you're probably thinking, Why should anyone care about what I have to say? Good question, and a valid one. If all you want to do is document what you ate, probably few people will. For some bloggers, that's enough. They write as a form of self-expression, or to create a journal, but they don't care if anyone reads it.

Others want to be read. If you do, it helps to understand who your readers are, what they want to read about, and how to relate to your readers and gain their trust. I'm always surprised when bloggers tell me they have no idea who reads their blog. If you can't visualize a reader when you start out, make up your ideal reader, and write to them.

Above all, tell stories. Food blogging is about more than your performance in the kitchen or a list of the dishes you ate at a restaurant. Develop your storytelling skills so readers keep coming back. Use humor, self-deprecation, confession, guilt, and suspense. Your posts must draw readers in. They want to relate to your experience. You want to elicit emotions and remind readers of events in their own lives.

One way to write about food is to approach your material in a new way, says Lebovitz. "What do you say about vanilla ice cream that hasn't been said before?" he asks. Ask what's interesting about your subject, or figure out a quirky approach. Even when he posted about his classic vanilla ice cream recipe, he educated readers on common types of vanilla beans and how to evaluate them based on smell and taste. He also covered how to choose vanilla beans and how to use them after the casings are spent.

Conflict always gets people going, if you can be entertaining at the same time. "People love when I'm butting up against the bureaucracy of France or a nasty salesperson, but nobody wants to read a six-page rant," says Lebovitz. Author and blogger Michael Ruhlman (blog.ruhlman.com) likes conflict as well: "My most successful posts tend to be rants where I fly off on something, and get hundreds of comments."

What is a good rant? You need a subject on people's minds, where they want to know more and to be entertained and relate to your opinion— or get irate about your opinion. Either is fine. The most important thing is to get an emotional reaction and to not go on and on.

Even recipe blogs are not just about what someone made in the kitchen that day. Three of the biggest and most successful food bloggers—Elise Bauer of SimplyRecipes.com, Ree Drummond of The Pioneer Woman Cooks (thepioneerwoman.com/cooking), and Heidi Swanson of 101Cookbooks.com—have built huge databases of recipes, and perhaps that's how new readers find them initially, when searching a recipe for a particular dish. But what makes readers stay or return?

Here's Drummond's recipe for acorn squash roasted with lots of brown sugar and butter: "But the holidays are approaching. And the holidays are a time for celebration, not restraint. I wonder how many consecutive years I'll tell myself that before I can no longer fit through the door of my house? Oh well. I'll cross that bridge when I come to it."

Drummond reveals her vulnerabilities and writes as though she's talking to a sibling or a best friend, even though you don't know her. She also tells you to go ahead and enjoy yourself, and who doesn't love that message?

Bauer is close to her parents and often writes about them in her recipe headnotes. Here's an example from the headnote of Spicy Vegetarian

Chili: "Those of you who have been reading *Simply Recipes* for a while probably sense (rightly) that my father is a committed carnivore. Thus you may appreciate that dad, spending an afternoon making this vegetarian chili with vegetables he bought at the farmers market that morning, would only put so much care into a meat-free chili, his dinner, if that chili were darn good. . . . Of course my mother did have to convince dad that no, we didn't need steak in addition to the chili, [because] the beans were full of protein." Ostensibly, the piece is about chili, but it's really about her family members, their dynamics, and her contentment with the arrangement.

Swanson's post on pineapple rice is up to almost one hundred comments. Read her lead, and see if you can figure out why: "I've been to Hawaii two times. Once when I was sixteen, and again when I was twenty. Once to Maui, once to Kona. I remember it being lush and vibrant, achingly beautiful. The more miles you put between yourself and the resort areas, the better it got. I think I'd like to go back at some point, so when I realized there was an Edible Hawaiian Islands publication I subscribed to it with the hope that I'd discover farms, producers, markets and restaurants to seek out when we finally get around to going. The latest issue arrived in the mail the other night, and while flipping through it, I came across a recipe for a pineapple rice salad. I rarely cook with Hawaiian flavor profiles, but this looked too good to pass up."

Suddenly it's not about the rice. It's about being young again, traveling, remembering the beauty of a place, and subscribing to a magazine to be reminded of your experience. These themes are what draw us in.

In each case, these bloggers tell stories from their own lives. They are experts at engaging your emotions and making you react. They present ideal scenarios, such as deserving a rich holiday dish, or living happily with parents, or memories of a trip.

The best bloggers know how to make you identify with them. "My hook, as you all know, is that I'm an incompetent louse who really wants to learn about food," jokes Roberts on AmateurGourmet.com. "Hence my blog details my adventures making mistakes and learning the ropes."

Jaden Hair attributes some of her chatty style on SteamyKitchen .com to dictation software with a headset. Once Stephanie Stiavetti of TheCulinaryLife.com tried the software, she said it changed the way she wrote, because it made her language so much more conversational.

Each of these bloggers has a strong voice; their personality comes across on the screen. They can be goofy, nostalgic, witty, scholarly—whatever their temperament, they know how to get it across.

Blogging is different from writing in a journal, which no one sees. At first readers might be your family and circle of friends, but eventually strangers will come to your site. Try to figure out why they care about your posts, what makes them comment, and write a thoughtful reply. Blogging is about reaching out with a story you want to share. Universal themes, the kind of subjects everyone understands, are always good, such as love, failure, curiosity, and loss. No doubt your readers have also made a dish that went horribly wrong, or tried a new ingredient and learned from it, or fretted about growing older. And that means deciding about how personal to get, a subject of some anxiety among bloggers.

How Personal Should You Be?

What all good blogging has in common is the ability to evoke emotion from the reader. To do that, you have to get personal.

As in the samples of recipe headnotes I mentioned earlier, evoking emotion means getting in touch with your vulnerability and letting readers identify with your situation. That requires honesty and, to some extent, courage. "Believe it or not, people want to know things about you," explains Roberts on AmateurGourmet.com. "People want you to air your dirty laundry. People want to know if you're happily married, if you like your job. People want to know if you're dyslexic, if you used to be bulimic, if you're a recovering Republican. People really want to know if you're gay (believe me). Tell us who you're dating, tell us who broke your heart, but do it in the context of food. Remember this is a food blog, not a confessional."

You may not be comfortable with divulging this level of information, but if you are, pouring your heart out can make a difference to your readers. Consider what Charity Lynne Burggraaf, a food photographer, says in an interview: "What I have found to be the most important thing to put into a blog is your heart. Which was something I tried to separate from my writing for a long time on my blog (might sound strange, but I didn't want to get too emotional—as it is my work). But I was amazed at the amount of support I got when I decided to open myself up a bit and talk about my mom and her battle with breast cancer this past year. Come to find out that my most popular posts often don't have to do with food at all!

"I've found that people are interested in my life, and not just my work. Heck, if they wanted to see my work they could visit my Website! I'm learning that by opening myself up, it in turn creates a sense of community and a great support system of foodies and photographers—something I've often heard about and been a part of on the outside—but I'm still in awe of it happening on my own little blog. And I'm grateful for it."

Ruhlman believes the personal part adds value, and he's not paranoid about it. "I'm not concerned that someone's going to kidnap my kid because they're reading my blog. If that was going to happen it's not because I'm writing about it. This is all so new, but if you don't feel comfortable, don't write about it," he advises. Criticizing people is off limits, he has learned. "You risk alienating people when you don't have to. Why alienate readers when you can bring them in? I can't afford to lose a single reader."

Dusoulier, on the other hand, doesn't feel comfortable with private matters. "I see some bloggers who talk about their relationship to their mother, or a marital situation or break up, or a struggle on an emotional level. I don't do that on my blog.

"It's not that I think it's wrong. I'm in a very happy place, so there's not a lot of turmoil to discuss. If it doesn't have anything to do with food, it doesn't come up. I'm very careful about my friends and family members' privacy as well. I don't reveal things about them they wouldn't like to read about online, and I'm vague about who I'm with. I don't reveal about people anything they haven't expressly told me it's okay to share." Instead, says Dusoulier, she gets personal in tone. "It's chatty enough. I try to draw people in as if they were guests at my table. If I met them in person, I would probably be the same way as I write."

Another person who's known for getting personal is Lebovitz. "I have broader boundaries than most people," he admits. Years ago, I asked him whether any of his posts might have been too personal. He pointed me to one with photos of a huge meringue he tried to flush down his toilet. Three days later, he wrote a second post, accompanied by a photo, because the meringue was still there. This post still makes me laugh. I love that he's willing to not take himself too seriously.

Regardless of how much you share with readers, a big part of writing is trusting yourself, believing what you write is worthwhile and valuable. Particularly if you're going to be vulnerable, you can't move forward if a negative voice in your head pops up. This voice makes unhelpful pronouncements, such as "You're no good at this," or "Why would anyone want to read this junk?" Some people call it the "internal editor" or "internal critic."

Everyone has one. You wouldn't believe how many top bloggers I interview who tell me they are not very good writers. But they don't let that voice stop them, and neither should you. Nor can you get rid of it. It's a part of you. I've dealt with this voice since I began writing professionally in 1975.

"It's the editor voice that stops you from writing," confirms Shauna Ahern of GlutenFreeGirl.com. "I think of a cramped librarian with a bun, yelling at me for putting my feet up on the desk. The more you can gently tell the editor to go get a cup of coffee and come back, the more you can trust your instincts. You want to be wild and funny and vulnerable and very much yourself. Then she can come back later and make it into a better piece of writing."

That's when the internal editor has value. Invite her back to help you edit. Personify the voice, and tell her, when she arrives, that there's a purpose to her comments and you value them, but to please help only when you need it.

Develop Your Voice

Related to the topics of evoking emotion and not taking yourself too seriously is your voice. While I've discussed voice in another part of this book (see pages 12–14), nowhere is it more important than in a blog. "Blogs are dependent on the voice—they live or die based on it," says Ruhlman. It's because people go there to read about you: what you think, how your day went. You need a conversational voice, less formal than a book, and more personal than a magazine or newspaper article. The key is to make it memorable and uniquely yours, so people could know it's you just by reading a few sentences.

"More important than a concept, more important than anything, really, is that quality that makes all great writing worth reading and that's your voice," advises Roberts on his website. "Bring yourself into your food blogging and everything else will follow. When I first started, I wrote a ridiculous food song every Thursday night and sang it for no good reason. . . . Do [the songs] really have anything to do with food? Of course not. But they give you a sense of what I'm about."

In one of my first blog posts, I wrote about what makes a great food blog. The number one characteristic was a strong personality. The bloggers I read are fun, intelligent, opinionated, and creative. They make me think and make me learn. Sometimes they just delight and surprise me. No matter what they're writing about, I want them to be passionate and well informed.

The actual subject matters less if you're a strong writer with strong opinions. "When I started my blog, I wrote about anything I felt like writing about, and I still more or less do, and that's what makes my voice unique," says Ruhlman.

But writing with a strong voice does not happen right away. "It takes a while to find your voice, to have an aura, sense of who you are," says Dusoulier. "Keep at it, and don't expect much initially. Try to craft it."

••

FIFTEEN WAYS TO WRITE YOUR LIFE THROUGH FOOD

SHAUNA JAMES AHERN, a former high school English teacher, writes in a strong, happy, and irrepressible voice on GlutenFreeGirl.com. You don't need food allergies to read about life with her chef husband and her passion for cooking. Here's Ahern's suggestion list of how to write about life and food, culled from a class she gave about voice:

- Read avidly, at least ten blogs, and more than one magazine. Be voracious. Gobble up the information.
- Eat well. You probably eat better now than before you started reading about food writing anyway.
- Pay attention to everything. We rush through our days, and we miss most everything. Take notes. Ask yourself what food reminds you of. It's amazing how much we filter out.
- Write. A lot. Write every day.
- Allow yourself to write lousy first drafts. We have so much anxiety about writing, so many bad teachers who taught us writing was about spelling and grammar. (But remember, first drafts don't get published, even on a blog.)

- Write to connect, not to impress. It kills good writing to think it has to be amazing every time. You don't think that when cooking.
- Play.
- Figure out what fascinates you about food.
- Avoid the passive voice. Use strong verbs, rather than "was," "have," "going," "being." Make your writing vivid.
- Avoid adjectives, if possible. Focus on dynamic verbs instead to make your subject sing.
- Think film. Show people your world and how you see it. Think like a camera, pulling back, getting the close-ups, and doing flashbacks like you see in films.
- Forget taste. Listen instead, and describe the sounds.
- Point sideways. Allow yourself to go down trails and expand on what you find, and then see where you end up.
- Think about how you construct sentences.
- Remember to give yourself in every word. Choose each word consciously, to create sentences that are your own. No one else could write the sentences I write because no one else is in my head, with my experiences and memories and expectations. The more we reveal ourselves, the more other people will connect.

Writing Your Post

Now that you've learned the basics of starting a blog and contemplated what to say and how to say it, it's time to write a post. Your biggest challenge might not be what you think: writing a blog is a commitment. To be successful, post at least once a week. It keeps you engaged and keeps you connected to your readership. Some people post more often than that. Dusoulier says she posted twice a day for a year when she started ChocolateandZucchini.com, on top of a full-time job.

Set up a schedule of which days of the week to post, or start a few drafts for those days when your brain turns to mush. While Lebovitz says he has no schedule, and posts whenever he likes, he also confessed that he might have as many as forty drafts going at one time, some that will never be published.

It might help to make a list of ten potential ideas for posts, even if they're just a sentence long. That way you'll frame the subject of your blog and keep on topic. If you're really organized, write extra posts on timeless subjects, and save them in drafts.

It's one thing to think up subjects for your blog, but another to figure out how to frame or develop them. Here are a few suggestions:

Start a conversation. Bring up a topic, tell a story about it, and ask what others think.

Hook onto the news of the day. Have an opinion about the latest survey on junk food, or on a winning chef contestant on television, or discuss a newspaper story with your own spin. Get your post up quickly so people can find it when they search on the news event.

Make an argument. You believe donuts are unfairly maligned or coriander is the world's most versatile spice. Speak your passion, and voice an opinion. It's also effective to be a contrarian sometimes, when everyone else is busy agreeing.

Tell a story. Did you talk with a memorable character at the farmer's market? Did a pie become a colossal flop? Look for moments like these to make a larger point about your life, moments everyone can relate to, when they think, "That's what I would do," or "I've been there," or even "I would never do that."

Talk about a book, movie, or product. They don't even have to be new. Perhaps you looked through your cookbook collection and became inspired to try a recipe, or you thought about a treasured utensil you can't live without.

Give away a product. Giveaways are a terrific way to boost visibility of your blog. Most bloggers just announce a giveaway, with no strings attached, and then pick a commenter at random and mail off the item. If it's a product given to you for free, and you promote it, however, different rules apply. More on that later (see pages 81–85).

Hook on to an upcoming event. Add a twist to stand out, such as "Ten Vegan No-Fail Dishes for Thanksgiving."

Surprise your readers. Write something unexpected, or spin a well-worn story and give it an unusual twist.

How Much Should You Write?

You'll also need to think about length, structure, and organization of your content. As for length, usually the idea is to keep it short, but even that notion is in question. When I first started blogging years ago, I read on several sites that the maximum word count for a post is 250 words. That seems hard, and I always write at least twice that much. People typically skim posts and don't read them closely, so you might want to be mercifully brief. Make your point, and get out. Blog readers only expect to spend a minute or two on your site.

On the other hand, many successful food bloggers write long posts of more than a thousand words, contradicting this conventional wisdom. "A couple years ago, longer content was frowned upon," says a story on *PR Newswire*. "Audiences are showing increased willingness (and even desire) to consume longer posts." Additionally, the author says, Google is placing a premium on the long form, in terms of search results.

Lebovitz points out that, more than other types of writing, blog posts that go on too long can be boring and cause readers to click away. "Most people are reading on small screens " he points out. "I suggest people go back and tighten up the post, removing anything that isn't helpful, compelling, or vital. It's likely readers won't miss those things either, and that will give them a chance to concentrate on what is important and interesting."

Once you've determined your content, learn how to structure a blog post. Writers, particularly journalists, use a system to keep people reading. Readers decide at every step of the way whether to keep going: like you, they're busy and want to know if their investment of time is worth it. Here are ways to keep them on the page:

Start with a good title or headline. This is your first point of entry for readers, so work hard on a good one. I've read that only two out of ten readers will get past the headline and into your post. Study headlines to see what captures your attention, and before you publish yours, put it into one of many headline analyzers available free online. When brainstorming titles, try one based on these ideas:

- Ask a provocative question, such as: "Are You Making These Three Mistakes with Smoothies?"
- Be intriguing: "Why I Would Spend $200 on Dinner."
- Make people curious: "Ten Dishes You Must Make This Fall."
- Provide expert guidance: "The Coffee Meister Talks Coffee Filters."
- Make a list: "Four Chocolate Questions Answered."
- Reassure readers, as in: "Freezer Jam: A Baby Step to Canning."
- Take a stand: "In Defense of Michael Pollan and a Civil Food Debate."
- Go for humor, especially with a potentially dull subject: "Dude Food."
- Make the description irresistible: "Baked, Buttered Corn."
- Be a little outrageous: "Blowtorch Prime Rib."

According to Copyblogger.com, several types of blog headlines include:

- titles that give it to you straight, such as a recipe title
- an indirect title that uses curiosity to raise a question in the readers mind
- a news headline, if you make announcements on your blog
- a how-to headline, which lends itself beautifully to food writing, such as "How to Make Your Own Sauerkraut"
- a question headline, such as "Are You Afraid of Butter?"
- a command headline that tells your readers what to do, such as "Make a Biscuit Mix and Save Money"
- a "reason why" title that tells people about your list, such as "Eight Ways to Top a Cupcake"
- a quote headline that has some of the copy in quotes, such as "'I Can't Stand Cookies,' Admits Martha Stewart"

You can be catchy by using a number followed by an effective adjective, such as "effortless," "essential," "strange," and "fun."

You can also refer to tricks, secrets, or ways. Make a promise, but you have to deliver it in the text, such as "Why I Love Stinky Tofu" or "How to Make Cassoulet in Just an Hour."

Follow with a lead paragraph. A compelling introduction reels people in with just enough detail to keep them interested and willing to continue. Tell a story, recite an intriguing statistic, or use the same techniques outlined for writing a headline. A good lead restates and expands on the headline.

Set up your story. Learn to repeat. Tell people what you're going to tell them (headline and lead paragraph), then tell them (body), and then at the end, tell them what you just told them (conclusion). It makes readers feel comfortable that they know what the story is about and that it's worth continuing to read.

Make one key point per blog post. Use the body of the post to expand on your title and lead. Engage readers' emotions, and connect with them.

Know your audience. As mentioned previously, it's easier to engage readers if you know who they are. Decide on whom you're talking to and what they want to know, and then give it to them. What keeps them up at night? What makes them laugh? What are they obsessed about? What do they fear when cooking?

Also remember that readers only come for a few seconds. If they don't like what they see, they hit the back button. Adam Roberts knows what people want to find on his site. "Spending time on a blog is like spending time with a person," he explains. "Imagine yourself at a party surrounded by people all of whom care about food. Would you rather talk to the sullen person with the digital camera who's standing near the cheese and crackers and mumbling about the levels of flavor in raw milk cheese? Or would you rather stand next to the high-spirited, highly animated talker who's telling a harrowing tale of a near-death experience with caramel? I know where I'd be."

On the other hand, don't pander to your readers and write just what you think people want to read. "There are things I could do to dial up my readership," admits David Lebovitz. "Everybody wants recipes. If I just did chocolate recipes three times a week, that would work." But he'd be bored out of his mind, and soon, writing his blog would stop being fun. Strive for a balance of what you enjoy and what readers want.

Own your topic. Write your own opinion, but offer value. Interview an expert for background information, or read up about your subject to make sure you know what you're talking about. Offer fascinating facts based on food history or cooking technique, or contextual information about the place you visited. Flesh out your story to add telling details.

Try not to assume that everyone knows what you know, especially if you're a fanatic on French chocolate or passionate about Peruvian food. Make sure you're talking to readers at the right level. Back up and explain. Hold their hands if you think they need it. Fill in details they might not know.

"Remember that your reader may never have made a scone before, or never deseeded a jalapeno, or doesn't know what a good cheddar is," says Ahern. "I want to encourage people to move into the kitchen, to invite them to the table."

Don't try to be the end authority on every topic, on the other hand. Said Drummond in an interview: "Now, if you have a specialized blog about baking and you're a trained pastry chef, then go ahead! Be an expert! But if you're merely imparting what you believe and understand about parenting, politics, religion, or current events, just keep in mind that at least 50 percent of your readers will have a legitimate opinion that's often diametrically opposed to yours. And that doesn't make them necessarily wrong. Not that you have to compromise what you believe; but always consider that others won't agree with you, and leave a little wiggle room for healthy, intelligent discussion."

Add links. Connect to other blogs and websites to give your site more depth and richness, particularly if you're referring to information on another website. I love using links because they let me keep my posts shorter but provide depth for those readers who want it.

Part of adding value is doing the research so your readers don't have to. It's a way to pack your post with more details without making it longer. Plus, the people you link to will find out and might link back to you, which increases your exposure. (For more on this, see pages 85–90.)

You'll also want to link back to an earlier post, whenever possible, to keep readers on your site.

Lebovitz cautions linking to sites that aren't reputable or those that may disappear over time. A reader contacted him once about a site he'd linked to, Filthy France, about dirty streets. It had become an explicit porn site, and she was surprised to find it on his blog.

Write a close or conclusion. Tell them what you just told them, or circle back to the theme of the lead and restate it.

Review your text for density. Before you post, make sure you've created a variety of short sentences and short paragraphs. People are in a hurry. Break up your text with subheads and links, which usually appear in a different color.

Review your text for errors. Before you click that "publish" button, check for typos, spelling mistakes, grammatical errors, and other faux pas that make your blog post look unprofessional. Unlike print, where your writing typically goes through a copyeditor and possibly a proofreader, you're on your own here to catch all mistakes. Read over your text and headline several times, including in "preview" mode. If you can, let it rest for at least twenty-four hours. Poring over your post with fresh eyes is a great way to catch mistakes.

As Deb Perelman said in a website interview, "When I see a site just swamped with errors and obvious spelling mistakes that could have been easily picked up by a spell-checker, I lose interest. If this person doesn't care enough about their readers to put their best site forward, why should I spend my time there? I like it when people seem like they really care about what they're doing."

A Word About Recipes—Text and Photos

It seems as though most food blogs are recipe blogs. If you're writing your own recipes, please read Chapter 8 on the subject of developing, testing, and writing recipes. Otherwise, here are few issues to think about for your blog: using photos, adding links, giving credit, and using other people's recipes.

Because blogs are such a visual medium, it's helpful to include photos of more than just the finished dish. Some bloggers, like Drummond, are all about the process, posting up to fifty photos for one recipe. You don't have to include that many, but it's useful to show your readers what a sauce looked like before and after you reduced it, or how finely you chopped the onions, or what the inside of the pie looks like, in addition to the top.

The key is to post photos that add value. A shot of you pouring olive oil into an empty sauté pan doesn't tell the reader anything, nor does a photo of an orange on a countertop. A photo of *mise en place* (prepped ingredients ready for cooking), on the other hand, is popular and effective.

And of course, regarding photos, they have to be good enough to drive people to your post. For more on that subject, see pages 75–81.

As another way to add value, build in links within your recipe whenever relevant. A recipe Dorie Greenspan posted required making caramel. "I was able to refer people to an incredible link on David Lebovitz's site about making perfect caramel," says Greenspan. "Before I would filter the info, and now I can send readers off, and it more than doubles the information."

When readers have questions about your method or ingredients, refine your recipe immediately. That's the beauty of writing online. In print, you'd have to wait for the next printing or edition.

If you're using other writers' recipes, it's essential that you give credit. Whatever you do, don't post a recipe exactly the way it appears and claim it as your own. If your Aunt Helen handwrote a recipe for angel food cake on an index card and doesn't remember where she got it, do an online search to see if you can determine the original author. Aside from that, all you can do is tell people about Aunt Helen and her recipe, so no one thinks you've stolen it. Besides, now you've got a unique story to tell as a creative headnote.

If you're reviewing a cookbook or want to use a published recipe, you have two options. Either adapt the recipe and explain how you have changed it in the headnote, or ask the publisher for permission to print it exactly as it appears. Most publishers provide contact information for reprint permission on their websites.

If You Want to Write Book Reviews

If you're an avid reader, you might review cookbooks and other kinds of food books on your blog. Start with books from your library, and eventually you could build enough credibility to get on publishers' lists of reviewers. If you make it, you will receive complimentary books with the expectation of a review, but it's not mandated.

Most food bloggers I know who do reviews have a policy: if they don't love the book, they don't review it. I'm not a fan of this kind of thinking, and I believe it leads to mediocre reviews that are always raves. After a while, readers don't need to read your reviews because you will always rave about the book. The best reviews are balanced opinions. They are mostly positive, but also point out weaknesses in structure, clarity, voice, accuracy, and other issues. On the other hand, there's not a lot of point to a purely negative review.

So don't go for either extreme in your writing. Pure raves are boring, and there are few reasons to trash. Instead, be positive and constructive. Include what you didn't like and what could be done better. Reviews are opinions, so you are allowed to have some that are not all positive. Your reviews will be more interesting as a result, and you will have done a service for the reader. When you are done, imagine you are the book's author, and read your review from his or her perspective. I bring this up because the Internet sometimes lacks civility, and chances are good that the author will eventually see what you wrote. That doesn't mean you should follow "if you don't have anything nice to say, don't say it." There is a way to criticize.

Here's an example of constructive criticism from Nora Ephron on Food52.com: "There are a lot of tomato recipes in Canal House Cooking; after all, it's a summer cookbook. One is for a tomato sandwich. I love tomato sandwiches. I had one every day last summer until the tomato blight. There's nothing wrong with having a recipe for a tomato sandwich in a cookbook, but it's not singing to me because I already know the song. There's also a recipe for stuffed baked tomatoes served over pasta. This sounds good. But oddly enough, the recipe says that it takes ninety minutes to bake the tomatoes. I don't understand this. I've been baking stuffed tomatoes for years. Who needs ninety minutes to bake a tomato? (This reminds me, by the way, that one of the recipes in Canal House Cooking is for a pork loin cooked in milk. We all remember this recipe—we learned to make it when Marcella Hazan put it into her first cookbook. The recipe in the Canal House book is almost exactly the same as Marcella's, except for one thing: it takes 60–90 minutes longer, to reduce the milk. This seems weird.)"

Notice that Ephron is specific in her criticisms and limits herself to three items. Many critics use a sandwich technique, where they praise at the beginning and end, and insert the criticism in the middle.

To write a serious book review:

- Read the whole book, even if you skim parts of it.
- Look up the competition as a point of comparison.
- Read about the author and familiarize yourself with his or her previous work, so you will have a context in which to review.
- Imagine the book's target reader. If it is not you, consider whether it's appropriate and useful for that reader.
- For cookbooks, make at least three of the recipes so you know whether they work. Now you can say how you liked them with authority. As explained above in the recipe section, if you want to include recipes from the book, you cannot type in published recipes without the publisher's permission, unless you adapt the recipe and explain how you did so in the headnote.
- If you loved the book, explain why, and remember to "show—don't tell." Show readers why with examples, rather than just writing, "I loved it."

Many book reviewers also do giveaways at the end of their review as a way to build blog traffic. Sometimes they give away an extra copy from the publisher. If you want to do this, define the parameters of your giveaway. Since anyone anywhere in the world can read your blog post, you may not be happy about filling out customs forms and spending half the cost of the book on postage.

....

HOW TO EDIT YOUR BLOG POST

Writing is rewriting, as the saying goes. And while it's true, do you know what to look for when you read your first draft, or how to improve it? Here's what I look for when I edit both my own posts and the work of others:

KEEP YOUR FOCUS. Do you start by moaning about a cold, move to the merits of a new smoothie you made for breakfast, and end with a recipe for chocolate cake?

You're all over the place! Stick to a central idea. Make sure your title, lead sentence, and body copy reinforce a specific topic.

REVIEW THE STRUCTURE. Are you throat clearing, which means that the true start of your story is three paragraphs down? Your readers may never get there. Make sure your post's subjects flow in a logical order. You may need to move around paragraphs as a result.

REFINE AND TIGHTEN. Think about what you've left out or what needs to be fleshed out so vague writing does not confuse readers. This is particularly true of adjectives when describing food. Be specific, and avoid overused words. Get rid of repetition of ideas, inconsistencies, overstatement (especially too many exclamation points), and disproportionate emphasis.

CHECK THE RHYTHM OF YOUR SENTENCES. Is every sentence the same length? Or are they all super short, so that after a while it sounds as if you're on too much caffeine? Go for a mix of sizes and rhythms.

READ YOUR WORK OUT LOUD to see if it sounds natural. If you're gasping for air, that's a clue to break up your sentences.

SWEAT THE SMALL STUFF. Check facts whenever possible, especially names and dates. You don't want emails pointing out errors. Put commas in the right places, and banish typos. Use exclamation points, ALL CAPS, italics, and ellipses (. . .) very sparingly—or better yet, concentrate on writing without those gimmicks.

GET CURRENT. You might look for ties to current events, trends, or subjects that you know are on your readers' minds. I like to insert current links that add value and weight to my post.

CHECK YOUR RECIPES. If you include a recipe, make sure you've listed all the ingredients, and that they are listed in the order used. Don't even get me started on all the other things that can go wrong, but this one is number one. For more on proper recipe structure, see Chapter 8.

• •

Good Photos Are a Must

It sounds obvious, but good photos of food are critical on a food blog. "Unlike political or music blogs that focus on things that rarely have a visual component, food is something tangible, something you can hold, and something you want to see before you taste," writes Adam Roberts on AmateurGourmet.com. "And the fact that you see food before you taste it—the fact that how the food looks often affects whether or not you want to taste it—makes photography an integral part of food blogging. Any food blogger can write on and on and on and on about a piece of pie or a fish eyeball they ate at elBulli, but more than in any other form of blog (and maybe I'm overstating) when it comes to food blogging, a picture's worth 1,000 words."

Matt Armendariz of MattBites.com concurs. "A food shot is special when the photographer or stylist (or even blogger) has a real connection to the food," he says in an interview. "This appreciation and love really shows in the final frame; you simply can't fake it. I've never met a successful food photographer that wasn't also a foodie. There's a reason for this.

"When buying photography or art directing a shoot I look for two factors: my emotional reaction and the technical factor. Does the food photo wow me? Do I want to reach in and take a bite? And is the photo high quality, unique, and technically well executed? I'm willing to forsake one side if the other side excels."

Now you may have no idea how to get photos like that. You have a few choices. You can buy food-specific photos on stock photo sites helpful to bloggers, such as iStockPhoto or Veer, which cost a few dollars per photo. They are sister sites of Getty Images and Corbis, both of which are aimed at corporate clients. Some sites, such as StockVault.com and FreeDigitalPhotos.net, offer free photos. It takes a lot of searching, however, to find the right photo for your post, particularly those large enough and good enough to feature. Donna Turner Ruhlman, a professional photographer, offers some free medium resolution photos for food blogs at RuhlmanPhotography.com.

You can't just take an image from the web and insert it into your blog. "Many bloggers and readers have a tenacious memory and will alert the original copyright holder about possible copyright infringement. So if you intend to use a photo, podcast, etc., from another blog, ask for permission, and host it on your own web space, giving proper credit with a link back to the original source," says Nicole Stich of Delicious Days.com.

Your best choice, and the one that will serve both you and your blog best, is to become an excellent photographer. This will take work on your part, obviously. Try not to avoid it. You may take photos now that are acceptable but not good, and they pull down not only the quality of your blog but your page views. Besides, so many of the sites that drive readers to food blogs, such as Pinterest, FoodGawker, and TasteSpotting, focus on photography, so it's in your best interest to improve.

You might resist this idea of becoming an excellent photographer because you see yourself as a writer. But food blogs are very visual; plain text won't cut it. Besides, if your blog is based on cooking, you'll want photos of your own dishes and baked goods. And if you want to write about trips to restaurants, farmer's markets, or events, you'll have to take your own photos to show where you've been. So it's inevitable!

For this section, I've talked with great photographers and researched the websites of the best food photographers thoroughly to guide you as you develop your own style. Here are their tips:

Always carry a camera. You never know when you'll be inspired. It might be at a market, a restaurant, a grocery store, a farm, or just driving down the street, spying a neighborhood tree loaded with ripe persimmons.

Get a decent one. Your phone is sufficient for casual photos, and a small point-and-shoot camera is fine for when you're on the road. But if you can afford to, you may want to take the route of many serious food blog photographers. They use a digital single lens reflex (dSLR) in AV (aperture priority) or manual mode, so they can shoot in low light without a flash. Lebovitz has said that getting a digital SLR camera was "the single most important thing" he did to improve his blog, and that an SLR camera makes taking a great photo much easier.

Whichever camera you choose, get one with macro mode, so you can get in close, and one with high ISO spreads. The last one is important if you shoot indoors at night.

Take lots of photos. You don't want to take just a few and then discover they're blurry or the contrast is too low. Lebovitz says he takes twenty-five to fifty photos for each published shot.

Lauren Ulm of VeganYumYum.com says she averages around a hundred photos per recipe, which she whittles down to a handful for each post. "Buy a large memory card for your camera to make sure you have enough space for all those photos," she advises on her website.

"I try overhead, straight on, close up, environment shots, and many different angles. My photographs start out boring and move towards interesting as I shoot. It's hard to explain how I plate or frame, but it involves a lot of photos and looking at each photo and saying, 'Hmm, the image looks too bare,' or 'I need to figure out how to emphasize this particular quality of the dish.' As I said before, the more photos you take, the better chance you have of getting that perfect shot."

Study your composition and props. As Deb Perelman has advised on SmittenKitchen.com, "Try as best as you can to identify what you like about what is before you, and find ways to make that the very essence of the picture. That's why photography is an art and not a science—you're letting your image tell a story about something. Look at the picture—is this what you wanted? How can you make the part that charmed you speak louder? Take it again. And again."

Look at food magazines and cookbooks to see how food stylists do it. Clip photos that appeal to you, and study them to figure out why. Most food is brown, so use a splash of color to make the shot more interesting, such as a garnish, a colored plate, or a pretty tablecloth under a white plate. Says Perelman, "A little food styling can go a long way. I'm not really into props or overly composed food. It's not a pinafore—it's dinner. I think plate smears and lightly rusted spatulas are honest, and I find that warmly appealing, but much of this comes down to personal taste. That said, white plates (as opposed to our sage green ones that seemed such a good idea at the time) that are not too patterned and a little garnish or a fork propped just so can add a lot to a picture."

Ulm offers these tips on props: "White will always, always work. Square dishes always look classy. Smaller is better—small dishes are easier to fill up with food, which prevents your plate from looking bare."

Beware of busy backgrounds. Look for a solid color instead. Some food bloggers buy inexpensive foam-core boards and paint them different colors to use for solid color backgrounds. Elise Bauer of SimplyRecipes.com recommends using wooden cutting boards. "The wood is warm and works well to show off the food," she writes on her site.

"I believe background is just as important as the subject, and that's led to some interesting discoveries," says Armendariz. "Because the background is usually thrown out of focus in food shots it's not so much what the actual surface is as the color of the surface. Plain corrugated cardboard becomes a beautiful tan color when blurred; cheap art paper is handy; napkins and fabrics do wonders, too. Just make sure your object is large enough. Other than that, use anything. You'll be surprised how pleasant everyday items can be."

Work quickly. Food must look fresh. Salads wilt; sauces congeal; ice cream melts. Besides, if you're eating it for dinner, you'll be hungry and wanting to eat.

Shoot in natural light. Here's Ulm again: "When using natural lighting, don't place your food in a sunbeam. You want ambient, diffuse light. Things shot directly in the sun usually look too harsh, but again, it can sometimes work depending on the shot. The 'safest' set up is diffuse side-lighting coming from a nearby window." Buy vellum or tissue paper, and tape it to your window to diffuse the light.

Lebovitz takes most photos by the window with a tripod to keep the focus sharp. He also uses "a piece of Styrofoam propped up by a malted milk powder jar to fill in the dark areas." In warmer weather, he takes photos outside.

If you must use a flash because it's too dark, point the light straight up to get fill-in flash, rather than dead-on flash, which will cause too many shadows and bleach out your colors.

If you're cooking or baking, take photos during prep. "Don't get hung up on capturing the quintessential 'final shot,'" advised Heidi Swanson in *Food & Wine* magazine. "There are all sorts of great details that emerge throughout the cooking process."

Compose. Keep in mind the photography rule of thirds, where the photo is divided into nine equal parts (two vertical lines and two horizontal lines). Place the most important compositional elements along these lines or intersections. You can also use leading lines to bring a reader's eye to part of a photo. Put your saucepan or finished dish off-center whenever possible, for a more interesting photo. Use symmetry and patterns for eye-catching compositions, or break them in some way to introduce tension. Change the point of view so your photos don't appear to be too similar within a blog post.

Get in close. A macro lens or setting allows you to get as close as you want, to capture the drop of water on a freshly washed raspberry, or the crispy crust of a baked macaroni and cheese. You want your readers to feel as though they can taste the food through the photo.

Steady yourself. If you don't have a tripod, use the top of a water glass as a makeshift tripod. Ulm suggests a can of tomatoes or a pile of books for the same purpose. You'll want to use a tripod when doing macro photography particularly, advises Stephanie Stiavetti, because the movement of your hands while you press the shutter button will cause blur.

Edit your photos. Adjust them by cropping, editing, and other techniques. Lebovitz downloads his shots into Apple's iPhoto and runs them through Photoshop. He posts them to his Flickr page first and then pastes them onto his site.

Approach photography as storytelling. You have two ways to tell a story: through your writing and with your photos. Some bloggers excel at this notion of storytelling through photos, where context is just as much a part of the story as the food itself. Here's an explanation from Tara Brady of SevenSpoons.net, interviewed on GreatFoodPhotos.com: "I hope to capture a sense of the food as it was, in the setting it was in on the day I made it, or the day we ate it. I don't mind that you can tell if it was cloudy and stormy, or the difference between summer light and winter light—if that's how things looked, then so be it. I appreciate the context of that."

I also like the way she talks about what to photograph: "I'm not always trying to represent a schematic of a recipe. If, say, it's the texture of the pastry that makes a pie exceptional, then I'm happy to concentrate on a corner where the crust shattered. There will be a shot of the whole pie, but it's that crumbly bit that I hope you'll remember."

• •

FOOD PHOTOGRAPHY REFERENCE BOOKS, CLASSES, AND WEBSITES

Almost all the bloggers I interviewed in this section have comprehensive pages on their blogs about food photography. A good one is Lauren Ulm's discussion at VeganYumYum.com/2008/09/food-photography-for-bloggers. Also see photography tips at TaylorTakesaTaste.com/food-photography-tips-tricks-and-tutorials, and these books and resources.

BOOKS

- *Focus on Food Photography for Bloggers*, by Matt Armendariz. Written specifically for food bloggers in a warm and cheerful voice, this book includes all the basics plus helpful graphics and sample photos.
- *Food Photography: From Snapshots to Great Shots*, by Nicole S. Young. A full-time photographer, Young creates stock images for her portfolios on Getty Images. This book covers the same mechanics and aesthetics as the others, in addition to post-processing (using software such as Photoshop, for example).
- *Food Styling for Photographers: A Guide to Creating Your Own Appetizing Art*, by Linda Bellingham and Jean Ann Bybee. Bellingham has photographed for Baskin Robbins Ice Cream, Harry & David, and more. The book covers setups, lighting, and before, during, and final photos.
- *Plate to Pixel: Digital Food Photography & Styling*, by Hélène Dujardin. Dujardin is the blogger behind Tartletteblog.com and now the senior photographer for Oxmoor House, a cookbook publisher. Her book features gorgeous photos with lots of basic information on the things you need to learn: aperture, exposure, and light.
- *The Food Stylist's Handbook*, by Denise Vivaldo. Part of being a great photographer includes how to get the food to look its best. Vivaldo explains the tricks of the trade, how to create a styling kit, and how to do food styling as a business.

PHOTOGRAPHY WORKSHOPS

Many food bloggers have fallen in love with photography, branching out to well-paid gigs for magazines, cookbooks, grocery stores, food manufacturers, restaurants, and more. Some of those I've quoted in this section list advice on food photography on their blogs. For more, see this list at nikas-culinaria.com/food-photo-101.

Some bloggers hold private photography workshops and teach at food blogging conferences. See the sites of some of the people mentioned in this section for more:

- CulinaryEntrepreneurship.com holds classes including ones on food styling and photography techniques around the world.
- For post-production, take classes at Lynda.com to learn Photoshop and Photoshop Lightroom. "Photoshop is a professional tool, with a steep learning curve," Bauer on has said on her blog. "Years ago I subscribed to the tutorials at Lynda.com to learn this software. Lynda.com's tutorials are self paced and very well done. For $25 per month you have access to a library of thousands of tutorial videos, and many are provided free, just so you can see how useful they really are. Lynda.com also has tutorials for Photoshop Elements, a more basic photo editing tool."

•••

Accepting and Reviewing Free Products

As you build readership on your blog, you're also building a target market for companies that want to get their cookbooks, kitchen equipment, and other products in front of your readers. Companies use blogs as an inexpensive way to get publicity, offering free products for both you and sometimes your readers in exchange for reviews or mentions in posts. And it's big business. Within a few months of creating my blog, I received offers for a gift card, free products for giveaways, and a chance to win a vacation if I created recipes about butter.

Many bloggers have no problem taking free stuff. I've done it too, if it is of little value. I never promise to write about it, however. At a BlogHer conference, Liberty Mutual surveyed 175 bloggers on responsible blogging and found 98 percent believed it is acceptable to receive a free product, and 87 percent believed it is fine to write company-sponsored posts. At least most mentioned transparency, disclosure, and honesty as key caveats to receiving free products and writing sponsored posts.

Should you plug free products, books, restaurants, hotels, and trips? There are several considerations. The first is to evaluate whether the freebie is within your blog's focus. Always consider your readers first when choosing to write about a product or service, not the company that gave you the money or freebie. Readers can smell a compromised post a mile away, otherwise. When you get a freebie, keep in mind that it's simply a form of payment. You don't want to lose your readers' trust, something you've worked hard to build, so it's best to disclose you were paid in kind. In fact, in the United States, it's the law.

Some bloggers go overboard when they receive a small freebie. They think they owe the company lots of promotion for taking a box of crackers or a free meal, as if there is an implied contract. There isn't, although it's unethical to keep taking products if you have no intention of writing about them. Just don't devote a whole post to a pack of gum. I can't see how that's a reader service. Your posts have value, and your readers will get confused if you suddenly write hype about an everyday product you have never mentioned before.

Actually, you might like the idea of endorsing products, but readers don't. In a survey conducted by Contently, two-thirds of respondents said they felt deceived when they realized an article was sponsored (paid for) by a brand. More than half said they didn't trust branded content, regardless of what was discussed. And many weren't even sure what "sponsored content" meant. Half thought the sponsor paid for and influenced the article. Eighteen percent thought the sponsor paid for its name to be next to the article, and 13 percent thought it meant the sponsor actually wrote the article. This is probably because most people don't write sponsored posts well, but either way, readers are suspicious.

To address this issue, the Federal Trade Commission requires American bloggers to disclose payment in kind when they endorse a product, place, or service, including free meals, hotel stays, and trips. This includes when you write a recipe with product given to you for free, or when you take a trip sponsored by a tourist board, but not when given a bag of free products when you attend a conference.

If you want to write about freebies, create a policy about how you handle free products and services from marketers. You have only your reputation, and having a policy makes you appear ethical, upstanding, and transparent to your readers. You might lay out your philosophy on posts about products in a friendly, straightforward manner on your "About" page with copy like this:

- I try to write about products and services that I feel fit into the theme of my blog.
- I always disclose when the product or service was given to me as a sample.
- I will not write a good review about a product simply because it was free. My reviews are always my own.
- I do not accept payment to write good things about a product. If I like something, I really do like it. And I'm not afraid to say if I don't.
- I believe firmly in keeping the integrity of my blog and would never compromise my beliefs and standards for the sake of a payment.

If you want to address marketers directly, you could add: "If you wish to send me a product, if I do accept it, I may or may not write about it on the site. I appreciate your understanding that this is my personal blog. I don't allow others to influence what gets published here. I don't accept products in exchange for a positive review or placement."

Here are recommendations on handling and endorsing freebies:

Don't be greedy. Take only what is relevant and appropriate for your blog. If you don't write about kitchen appliances, don't take them. Yes, some marketers are eternally hopeful and will keep sending products, but it seems greedy to keep accepting them. Also, food bloggers are a small community, and people will gossip. Be careful about the value of a freebie. At some newspapers, reporters are not allowed to accept anything worth more than $25. Would you feel right about taking free coffee for a year, if you had no intention of writing about it? I wouldn't. What should the coffee company expect in return? You don't want to be beholden because of a costly gift.

Do not take products to impress your friends, give as gifts, or sell. Return expensive products, unless the marketer says to keep them. With food blogging, it's easy to take things not because you want to write about them but because you want to cook with them, eat them, or enjoy them as a consumer. Watch out for that impulse. Be aware that the company is giving you this product because you are a blogger and it hopes you will endorse or mention it.

Don't promise endorsements of the product, service, or experience. Most marketers know not to demand a testimonial when they give you a product, but it won't stop others from trying. Don't agree to write about a product before using it, or at all. This also applies to giveaways. You can reserve the right to write about it if you want to. It is not an obligation.

Here's what a top blogger told me about guaranteeing coverage: "I always say that I will not guarantee that I will mention the product on my site and also do not want to be contacted afterwards if I will mention it on my site. In that respect, I only try to deal with companies that 'get it,' who don't have PR flaks who just want to hassle me endlessly. Most quality companies either have good PR teams or I deal with the owners themselves."

Evaluate why to take a free trip. Don't go if it is not relevant to your blog, but do go if it's something you want to learn more about. If you're only going because you feel honored to be asked, evaluate whether that's a good enough reason.

Don't always love everything. Many bloggers feel they should only tell readers about the products and places they love. I get it: life is short, and you only want to tell readers about the good stuff. But it's more interesting reading a balanced post. Plus, raving about products and places reads like promotional material and makes readers suspicious. Instead, strive for some nuance when you tell readers why they might be interested in that gluten-free flour or sous vide appliance.

For reviewing, see Chapter 6 on reviewing restaurants and page 72 for book reviews. Also see the Food Blog Code of Ethics, which tackles the ethics of restaurant reviews, at FoodEthics.wordpress.com. And keep in mind that if you like to dine at restaurants for free, you'll need to write mostly positive reviews to stay on invitation lists.

Disclose. I saw a post about a product and company in which the blogger said the company was a "client and sponsor." She gets my respect. Writers who endorse products represent their readers, not just themselves, and certainly not the companies they cover. They are guides to tell readers whether it's worth their money and time. Protect and respect your readers by being transparent about the products and services you write about. Disclose prominently—preferably at the beginning of a post. Without your readers, no marketer would be interested in you.

If you'd like to be paid in cash rather than freebies to write about products and services on your blog, see Chapter 12.

How to Get Noticed and Increase Your Views

When you start a blog, you'll wonder who's reading it. The answer, initially, is no one, unless you tell people about it. So you start with a few friends, your mother, your coworkers, and maybe they tell others. Little by little, your readership grows.

But it won't grow that much. Your next step is to build your blog readership. Building readership creates community and buzz, both essential to a good blog. The standard advice is that you need good content to increase your views. Here are additional suggestions:

Improve your photography. Since the web is such a visual place, this is the single best way to increase views. Of course it isn't easy, but having terrific photos can propel a food blog to stardom.

Put your blog photos on photo-driven sites, with a link to your blog. There's nothing like driving traffic to your blog with Instagram, which is climbing in popularity, or by repins on Pinterest. All it takes is for one big pinner to repin your images, or to have an image go viral, and people will come to your site in droves. Often there's no way to know why your photo of stuffed mushrooms went viral, so don't try to figure it out. Enjoy it! Obviously, pinning photos tied to holidays and seasons, especially those that evoke emotion, will work well. Be sure to put a "Pin It!" button on your blog photos to make it easy for people.

Also submit your photos to other aggregate sites, like FoodGawker .com and TasteSpotting.com. Get to know what works best for each site first, as they have specific aesthetic guidelines for submission. Be selective.

Offer subscriptions. Make it easy for people to read every post. Install an RSS feed. When readers subscribe, your posts show up automatically as a link on their blog aggregator. My favorite way to subscribe is through email. Google's Feedburner offers a free service that lets people sign up to receive your new posts in their email. Either way, people are more likely to read your posts when they're delivered, rather than remembering to visit your blog occasionally to catch up.

Comment on other food blogs. Drive traffic to your blog by commenting on other people's blogs, but put some thought into it. Many bloggers say they can tell when commenters do it simply to draw attention. Try for a comment more thoughtful than "looks delicious!" Building a dialogue with other bloggers will lead them to read your blog because of the great content it offers. It's not considered good etiquette to ask for a link, so don't ask for one. It's better to let it happen organically.

Seek out other bloggers on Twitter and Facebook as well, and get involved in their conversations.

Alert your communities when you post. You've got your Facebook following, your Twitter followers, Google+, Instagram, Pinterest, and perhaps the folks who receive your monthly newsletter. Or create a custom list of friends and colleagues to alert by email, and encourage them to share your posts with others. On social media, it's considered too promotional to only announce new posts, so make sure you do so between your regular comments.

Put the word out. People like to know when others write about them or write on a subject that interests them. They might also want to link to your post, through their site or through social media. If you think a particular blogger might enjoy your post, send an email with a link, explaining why they'd want to read it. They might even link to it, driving traffic to your site.

Respond to comments. When people take the time to type in their opinion or response, reply to their comment. I enjoy writing back to people, letting them know I've read their comment and appreciate it. Don't just reply to reply, though. Be thoughtful.

Join food blogging group events. Join a group like Tuesdays with Dorie, a blog where people bake from Greenspan's book. Once you get the hang of it, try hosting an online event. It's a great way to get to know other bloggers who might link to you.

Guest blog on other sites, and use guests on yours. It's a good way to exchange links, take a break, get someone else's perspective on your site, and perhaps reach a new or larger audience. Make sure the blogger's style, content, and size of post fits your blog. Show him or her your edits before posting. As Elise Bauer of SimplyRecipes.com explained FoodBlog Alliance.com, "Mostly I invite guest authors whom I know personally, and know well, whom I trust, and whose voice on the site I think my readers would like. The one thing that is challenging is photos. Either the guest author has to include gorgeous photos, or I have to photograph them myself. Two of my guest authors live close by, so it's easy for me to shoot the dishes they are doing."

Post about what's trending. Use social media like Twitter and Google to see which food topics are trending. You can go to google.com/trends and enter a generic term like "kale" or "fried chicken." Look for a button called "Rising" that will show you a list or related terms trending in the last thirty days.

Hand out business cards with your blog name on it. Inexpensive, online vendors like VistaPrint and Modern Postcard can print colorful cards to hand out at events and conferences. Hello.moo.com is another good option, where you can use your own Flickr images.

Improve your SEO techniques and focus on keywords. A study from Searchmetrics found that web pages with more pictures ranked higher in search results. Otherwise, many of the techniques listed above will affect how high your name, or your blog's name, comes up in a search engine like Google. They are called search engine optimization (SEO) techniques, to help you place highly on search engine rankings. Readers will come to your blog from many sources. Some type your name in a search engine, so you don't want your blog name, or your name, to appear too far down on the list. Most will come to your site when they search for specific food or recipe keywords, such as "best mushroom pizza," and you want them to find your post on the subject.

Start using keywords in your title and text. Keywords are the terms people search on to find information. After you've written a post, use a free keyword tool, such as freekeywords.wordtracker.com, to determine which words people might use to find your post. Make sure the exact phrase appears in:

- the title
- the first sentence
- one main header within the post.

If your keyword is two words or less, use it five to eight times in the post; if it's three words or more, do not use it more than a few times, or the search engine will see it as "keyword stuffing." Somehow, with all this strategy, you've got to make your writing appear natural. Crowding a post with keywords doesn't work and may be detrimental to your search engine credibility.

Check your readership. Soon you'll want to see how many people come to your site, how many come back, where they come from, what they read, and how long they stay. Install software that gives you a report. One of the most popular is Google Analytics (google.com/analytics). It's free for the first five million page views, once you set up a Google account. One valuable part is the traffic section, which tells you where people came from to get to your blog. Here's where you find out what percentage of readers found you through a search engine or through links on other sites. It's fascinating to discover which sites drive the most traffic to you and to discover new links you didn't know about.

Roberts of AmateurGourmet.com says it's the accumulation of content that matters. "The more you update, the more content you create; the more content you create, the more Googleable you become," he explains on his website.

"I've learned this watching my statistics: I get the large majority of my hits from Google searches for strange things that have nothing to do with food, only because there's some obscure word in the title. Clotilde [Dusoulier of ChocolateandZucchini.com] explained to me once that Google has an algorithm that dictates how Googleable you are. It's based, I think, on how many people link to you and how often you update. So updating frequently has its rewards.

"But also, and more obviously, the more you update the more often people will check back to your site. The blogs I check most often are the ones I know will have new content every day. The more regular the new content, the more regular my visitation. I'm sure you can relate as a blog reader."

Keep in mind that Google changes its algorithms regularly and rarely explains its methods. Try not to get too obsessed with the numbers. It doesn't do any good to check them every day. Over time, you'll get better at deciphering what they mean and whether to take action. Likewise, don't get obsessed with the number of comments. I admit I was a mess when my posts were met with silence, when I first started blogging. I begged friends to comment. Then, once people discovered the blog and engaged in a discussion, I could relax.

While the advice I've given you here is practical and market-driven, there's also another part of blogging: The human side, where friendships and respect grow from being part of a community. Many famous early bloggers I've interviewed point to Elise Bauer of SimplyRecipes.com as the one person who helped them understand their blogs and move forward. Later she launched FoodBlogAlliance.com as a way to spread the knowledge around to the thousands more who started food blogs. She sent me an email that sums up her graciousness: "If there is one thing I would say to an aspiring food blogger, it would be to come at food blogging from a spirit of generosity. Be generous with acknowledgments, be generous with your expertise, and be generous with showering attention on and links to fellow food bloggers. Pay attention to others and eventually some of them will pay attention back to you. This, I believe, is the super-secret-sauce to success."

Going from Blog to Book

Once you've been blogging for a while and have created a body of work, you might wonder whether the blog could be a springboard for a book. It's possible, but writing a book is not a cut-and-paste process where you repurpose copy from your blog. If that were true, readers would find little reason to cough up $30 for a print version when all the content still lives free online.

Books launched from blogs have lives of their own, with new content. They must be thought of as their own product, separate from the blog. Plus, books are not usually made up of little bits like blog posts. Readers want a narrative that hangs together, with a beginning, middle, and end, and that takes craft and time to produce.

Some publishing companies contact bloggers directly when they think a book would succeed. Jaden Hair was only six months into Steamy Kitchen.com when Tuttle Publishing contacted her with a cookbook proposition. That's unusual, however. Tuttle could see that she was an excellent promoter who knew how to engage with her readers. You'd have to have a measure of success first to attract a publisher. (To read more about developing a platform that would interest a publisher, see page 243.)

Typically books that spring from blogs fall into two categories: cookbooks and food memoir. Heidi Swanson of 101Cookbooks.com has written several cookbooks since beginning her blog. Ten Speed Press senior vice president Aaron Wehner says he met Swanson at an International Association of Culinary Professionals annual conference in 2005. "We figured out we were neighbors, and we've become good friends. She's the gold standard of food bloggers, in terms of how well she's grown her site without changing the integrity of it." Swanson points out that while a blog is ongoing, a book is a separate creative process with a beginning, middle, and end. Even her culinary point of view is different in her books.

On her blog, she writes that an idea for a book can't be rushed: "Not long after submitting the manuscript for *Super Natural Cooking*, I started setting aside photos I loved, and continued to keep notebooks of my favorite recipes, ideas, and inspirations. I wasn't sure what I would do with them, or what would emerge over time, but I had a hunch something might. Or not. Either way, I don't like the idea of rushing these sorts of things. I've come to believe you can't really rush inspiration, it comes on its own schedule, emerging and intersecting my life when it sees fit. I just try to keep my eyes open."

Lisa Leake launched 100DaysofRealFood.com in 2010 to share her newfound knowledge about organic and nonpackaged food. Her cookbook came out four years later and hit the *New York Times* best-seller list shortly after publication. "Leake admits that her site wasn't an immediate hit," says a story in *Publishers Weekly*, "but after some local press, attention on Food Inc.'s Facebook page and the Yahoo homepage, as well as Leake posting a meal plan on her own Facebook page, the blog found a large, consistent readership. 100 Days of Real Food now gets four million monthly page views."

Leake thought that her first book would be about the same subject: her family's hundred-day pledge. Instead, it's divided into two parts, with the first devoted to planning, such as how to shop, getting your family to buy in, budgeting, and meal plans. The second part is one hundred recipes, 70 percent of which are new.

The other category of book that evolves from a blog is memoir. (Read more about the genre at the beginning of Chapter 9.) While your blog may be about you and your experiences, they don't necessarily translate into a book. Lebovitz says he only used two stories from his blog in his memoir *The Sweet Life in Paris* "because they fit and I liked them." The rest of the book, he said, was inspired by his move to Paris and the backstory readers asked about.

Besides, blog posts are short, and you can't just tack them together to make a book. "Even when a blog post is long, it's pretty short," says Molly Wizenberg of Orangette.blogspot.com, author of *A Homemade Life*, the first memoir from a food blogger to sell well. "The book has a process of immersion, where I had to be comfortable with not always knowing where a story was going. I had to slow myself down. The biggest thing was finding a narrative arc. I didn't know how to write a continuous long narrative."

She began by making a list of all the recipes she wanted to include, and then thought about the stories the recipes were attached to and whether they had a place in the book. She wrote the stories out of order because it felt easiest and then tried to put the book in order and smooth out the gaps.

"I cut stories from the blog, pasted them into Word, then rewrote them," she explains. "Some parts are closely related to the blog, but in most cases I had to do a decent amount of rewriting or add details to make that story hang together with the rest of the book."

She compared a blog to a series of TV shows, and a memoir to a movie. "A series of cooking shows does not make a movie, just as blog posts don't make a book," says Wizenberg. "A movie has a plot, gets us invested in a character and a story line, and transports us somewhere else.

"The book was a place to write about things that felt too big for the blog. For example, I wrote about my dad twice in five and a half years. There wasn't space to tell the story comfortably. Sitting down to write a book makes a commitment longer than writing a blog post, and it gave me space to expand upon things I'd written, in service to a longer story I was trying to tell."

When it comes to photos, if your book will have them, you'll have to be a professional-quality photographer to get a publisher to want to use your photos. It's an accomplishment, as a food blogger, to have a publisher accept your photos. Usually cookbook publishers use a professional photographer and stylist. As Jaden Hair explains about her first cookbook, "They rejected the idea to begin with, so for six months I practiced and practiced. I would send them pictures; they would print, review, and critique. They were very supportive of the idea, and then finally I got to the point where they felt my photography was good enough to publish."

In memoirs, photos are not as essential as they are in cookbooks. Lebovitz included some of his own black and white photos, but many have no photos at all. Clarify the costs for photos up front, and see Chapter 11 for more information.

Keep Posting

Whether you're thrilled about self-expression, hoping for a book deal, or honing your photography skills, the secret to blogging is to feel continually inspired enough to keep going, week after week, month after month, regardless of the response. If you have the stamina, perseverance, and capacity for entertainment and information delivery, you are likely to succeed. Lebovitz writes bluntly on his blog about how much work it is to blog and how much he loves it:

"After writing, editing, proofreading, translating terms, adding foreign accents (sometimes by hand-coding each one), writing the recipe (it's fourteen keystrokes just to type oven temperatures—no wonder my wrists are a mess!), formatting text in internet code, taking pictures, deciding which pictures look best, eating the leftovers because I can't stand to wait any more, editing pictures, uploading pictures, and placing the pictures in the post—which is a challenge because the whole document looks like a jumble of code, rather than the pictures and text that you see here—then re-reading and proofing, and finally, publishing the post, it can take me a couple of days to get it all together.

"Add to that, I love blogging and have so many things that I want to share, that I always seem to have five posts in the pipeline that I want to put up on the site as soon as possible. And I can't wait to jump into the next one."

I've taken his advice, and I try now to have a few posts as drafts. Some days, though, I have no ideas for my next post, and other days writing comes so easily I have no idea why I was concerned. Some days my posts land with a thud, while other days the comments fly in.

"Do not expect an easy ride when you blog," confirms Sudeep DeSousa on Problogger.net. "You can put in a lot of hard work and then realize that nobody is commenting on your post and on the other hand you will write a one-liner and you will have the whole world talking about it. You will have days when you will be banging your head against the wall wondering what to post about and then there will be days you have so many ideas in your head that you don't know where to start. So be ready to enjoy the ride.

"Since all this hard work is going to use up your time, you have to be prepared to give up something. For those that have a full time job—your personal life or work life is going to take a hit. Maybe some of your other hobbies or interests will get affected. So you need to decide carefully on the things in life that you are ready to forego in order to become successful as a blogger."

The best bloggers have a positive attitude about making their blogs part of their lives. When I interviewed Swanson, I asked her if she thought she would be blogging ten years from now. "I hope so," she said with a smile.

Another super-successful blogger concurs. "The blog is a part of who I am. It's become like a limb. I have to feed it all the time. I think of it as an engine that propelled me forward," says Dusoulier of Chocolateand Zucchini.com.

"I look at the world through my blogger struggles. When I go anywhere, I wonder if it's blogger material. I experience things more intensely because I'm asking myself more questions, not just living in the moment, so that I can talk to my readers afterwards. When I've found my groove and I'm not hung up on traffic and number of comments and whether I'm going to quit, it's so gratifying. It brings me so much in terms of interaction and feedback and ideas and inspiration. It's really worth every ounce of energy I pour into it. It has grown with me. It's really the key to everything else that I do."

The bottom line is that blogging can be hard work and time consuming, but it's also fun and worth it—however you define that—most of the time. Don't take it too seriously, and don't compare yourself to the food bloggers who have been doing it for years. Sit back, have a good time, and see what develops from your efforts.

HOW TO KEEP BLOGGING

It's easy to get out of the habit. You get sidetracked, a big project comes along, or you go on vacation. Or you can't think of anything to say! Here are a few tips to keep you on track:

- Set up an editorial calendar. Make a list of what you plan to cover and when you will post it.
- Blog by theme. Write two- or three-part series on topics, such as weekend projects or starting a special diet.
- Whenever you have an idea for a post, start one. Write the first sentence, or include links that inspired you. Write the rest later.

- Pick an event or topic in the news, and put your own spin on it.
- Go to an event, take photos, and blog about it.
- Write about a book that inspired you, or write a cookbook review.

GENERAL RESOURCES ON BLOGGING

While this chapter focuses on food blogging, many sources show you how to be a better blogger all around, covering dozens of topics in approachable language. Here are some of the most trusted sources:

PROBLOGGER.NET: dedicated to helping bloggers learn the skills of blogging, share their own experiences, and promote the blogging medium.

COPYBLOGGER.COM: a free website to help you improve your online writing.

Writing Exercises

1. Maybe you didn't try to flush meringue down the toilet à la David Lebovitz, but surely you have stories about food that readers would enjoy. I just thought of the time my sister put whiskey and blue food coloring into her cake icing during a high school party at our house. None of her underage friends would touch the cake, even though imbibing alcohol was a priority. Do you have a story like this to flesh out for a blog post?

2. Write a short post about a dish you hated when you were a kid and how you've come to love it today. Provide the recipe, if appropriate.

3. Write about the cookbook you used most when you first discovered cooking. Find links to information about the cookbook or its author, and include them.

5: GOING SOLO AS A FREELANCE WRITER

Writing for newspapers, magazines, websites, and clients satisfies many desires. It's a way to entertain and inform while unleashing your creativity and passion onto the page. It's also a great way to gain credibility in a subject, particularly if you want to write a book about it.

Best of all, it's such a thrill to see your own work published. I'm still not tired of it, even though it's been over thirty years since my first piece ran in a daily newspaper.

Writing articles can be a long and frustrating process if you don't know how to get to a published story. Months can pass—even a year sometimes—before a story you've pitched to an editor appears. Editors are busier than ever, sorting through dozens and even hundreds of story idea queries per month. Your job is to come up with a story idea an editor can't resist, get the go ahead, write the story, get paid, and then do it all over again. I'm going to tell you how. As a former newspaper and magazine editor, I've evaluated pitches from writers for most of my career. Since 1996, I've been on the other side as a freelance writer as well.

In this chapter I'll give you insider information on different kinds of freelancing—mostly for publications but also for corporate clients. You'll learn how editors assess a story. Editors and award-winning food writers offer advice on how to come up with, shape, position, pitch, pursue, and write your story idea, no matter what kind of publication or website you target or what type of writing you prefer. You can decide whether to stay in a niche you're comfortable in or target the big-league national magazines. There's no right answer, but if you choose the latter, I'll cover what it takes to get there.

While this chapter does not cover restaurant reviewing specifically (discussed in Chapter 6), it will provide valuable information on how to target and pitch a publication.

How to Come Up with Story Ideas

Make some time in your schedule to come up with story ideas, because work isn't going to fall in your lap. You have to go out and get it or be tapped into a network that will give you ideas. Let's start with what you should write about. Your brain should be constantly generating ideas based on what's going on in your life, what interests you, and what you read. "You've got to be like a lint brush," says writer Barry Estabrook, a former contributing editor for *Gourmet* and founding editor of *Eating Well* magazine. "Ideas are cheap. Execution is harder. People tend to get too attached to a single idea. Come up with so many that you don't get obsessed with any one."

Notice he didn't say to write one story and then find a home for it. Many beginning writers take this path and don't succeed, unless they're writing for literary journals, which is a different kind of writing. The problem is that every mainstream publication and website wants a story written just for them. Since yours was written for you, you'll have to convince an editor that it's right for the publication's specific style, voice, and readers. That's why editors reject almost 95 percent of ideas and stories.

So back up and give your brain fodder for ideas. Here's how:

- Read food sections of newspapers. Keep a pen and paper handy, and write down any ideas that come into your head. Tear out articles typical of those you'd like to write, either in subject or format.
- Do the same with food magazines, general magazines, and trade publications. This time, check writers' bylines against the mastheads of magazines (the list of who works there,

at the front of the publication) to see what kinds of stories freelancers write for each publication (see the Appendix for a list).

- Keep up with trends on social media, local websites, and national websites that interest you (see the Appendix for a list).
- Visit bookstores to find new magazines that take freelanced articles, and look online for new magazine-like websites that take freelance work.
- Notice trends in restaurants and food shops.
- Watch food shows on television.
- Visit farmers' markets and specialty food markets and producers to see what's new and to come up with trends.
- Spend an hour with your cookbooks, looking for subjects that inspire you.
- Look at your own life for ideas. If you just went through pastry school, or you're planning a trip to Morocco, you might have a story.
- Figure out what kind of pieces you're best at writing, based on your personality. For example, I'm a practical person who loves to explain how something works, or to help people get better at a task, so I'm attracted to service or how-to stories.

"If you want to find interesting things to write about, you have to crowbar yourself into interesting situations and circumstances," wrote J. Kenji Lopez-Alt, managing culinary director of SeriousEats.com. "If you're just doing the same thing or visiting the same restaurants that everyone else is going to and blogging about, chances are, you won't have much interesting to say about it. You should always think about your angle of attack and put yourself in a unique position."

If you are a blogger, you have an additional reason to write freelance articles. If you want to write a book, it's best to have some experience writing for the outside world first, not just your blog. Publishers want your book to be read by people beyond your blog readers. They might find out about you from a newspaper or magazine article you've written.

I call this process "preapproval." It means that a book publisher will be more interested in you as an author if editors of magazines, newspapers, or websites have already preapproved you for their readers. And in the best circumstances, those readers are potential readers of your book. So target publications strategically.

For any publication or website, you must put yourself in the shoes of readers and editors. What can you make with those yellow premade logs of polenta in the supermarket, and are they actually edible? I wondered. That led to a story and recipes for a "Busy Cook" column in an international supermarket magazine, followed by wondering what to do with a can of tuna besides make a sandwich, and what to do with a box of frozen spinach. Next came how-to stories based on answering other questions I had, like how to plan a great buffet, how to order wine at a restaurant, and how to plan a cheese course for a dinner party.

Freelance writing tends to fall into two categories: general writing and specialized writing. General writing covers all aspects of food. If you find everything about food exciting, from cooking to farming to travel to history, you're probably a generalist. Specialists, on the other hand, write mostly about one subject in many incarnations. Kirstin Jackson, for example, a cheese fanatic, started a blog, ItsNotYouItsBrie.com, She then wrote articles on cheese for the *L. A. Times* and NPR's *Kitchen Window*, and published a book about cheese. She also teaches classes on cheese and has started a monthly cheese club, thus increasing her desirability as a cheese expert. Writing as a specialist can be a strategic way to build your business.

What Kind of Story Should You Write?

Coming up with story ideas is the first step. Shaping them into certain article conventions is the second. Here are some of the most popular for freelance writing:

Recipes. For many consumer food-based publications, recipe-based stories are a huge focus. *Cooking Light,* for example, prints around eighty recipes per issue. Most of these stories comprise a short introduction followed by three to five recipes. The feature article might include small bits of side information on technique, a guide to choosing an unfamiliar ingredient, and information about its history, where to buy it, or how to serve it.

If you want to write recipe-based stories, find magazines that take them from freelancers, and read several stories to see what each publication wants. Think of a theme that helps readers plan, such as low-effort or low-fat dinners; or one that inspires them, such as Greek food for a party or slow-roasted stews for winter nights.

In the case of *Cooking Light*, for example, you would want to avoid esoteric ingredients and keep the method straightforward. Before you submit a piece that includes recipes, familiarize yourself with the publication's editorial style. Don't call for asafetida, for example, if you don't see esoteric ingredients in any recipes.

For national food magazines, recipes need personality and confidence to appeal to an editor, something different from what readers can find free online. And the bigger newspapers and magazines will test your recipes and may ask you to make changes if they don't like the result. Often editors can judge recipes just from looking at your story idea. If you read Chapter 8 on recipe writing, you'll be in good shape.

To write about seasonal cooking, keep in mind that national magazines have long lead times. Some publications have a one-year lead time, and editors form their own story ideas during monthly meetings. For most national magazines, you might have to pitch a story more than six months in advance, so a story on indoor grilling during winter would be pitched in late summer. Newspapers, on the other hand, think a few weeks ahead, unless it's a major holiday like Thanksgiving. In that case, even seven weeks ahead is probably not too early.

Most people don't break into national magazines as recipe writers until later in their career. It's best to start by developing a recipe story for a smaller newspaper or local magazine or website, which might lead to a regular column.

Trend. Usually articles on trends are reported, meaning you interview and quote experts and sources, and come to conclusions based on their expertise. Some include statistics from research firms. Trends from other print sources sometimes lead to great queries for food-based publications. If you subscribe to nutrition and health newsletters, for example, you might reshape the trend stories and pitch them to food publications with a health focus. If you see positive research on ginger as a defense against colds and flu, for example, dream up recipes and send a query to a health-oriented publication such as *Delicious Living* or *Health* magazine in time for fall.

Some people have trouble identifying trends because they're already participating in them. If you are an early adopter, that's a great qualification for freelance writing. The challenge is to identify the trend early enough, such as the craze for kale. If you pitch kale stories now, you'll have more competition, the publication may have recently done a story, and the editors might worry the kale trend is waning.

Guide. Here you'll educate readers on how to make choices about a particular subject, such as how to buy organic, organize their pantries, or discover the best restaurants. Travel guides help readers find restaurants and specialty foods in a region.

News. In news reporting, you would interview several people and piece together their comments for an article on a breaking development. Most news reporting appears in newspapers or websites rather than magazines, because it requires specialized skills in journalism and because with a magazine's long lead time, it may not be news by the time the story surfaces. Examples of news stories would be breaking news about mercury levels in fish or a state's new law taxing soda.

Personality profile. Based on an interview with one person, such as a chef, restaurateur, food producer, retailer, or food personality, the focus is on an interviewee who has achieved recognition, made a significant contribution, or performs unusual work. You may need to include their recipes, tested by you.

Interview. Similar to a personality profile, interviews take the form of questions and answers that follow an introduction and brief biography of the interviewee. Interviews can also use a question and answer format.

Roundup. Usually a comparison or list, roundups help readers choose from a group, such as five kinds of Indian spices or ten great Italian restaurants. If you're attracted to the idea of a roundup, find a publication with "Ten Best" kinds of titles.

How-to. Teach readers how to solve a problem or do something better. These articles can be technique-based, such as how to make great mashed potatoes, how to find vegan restaurants when traveling, or how to choose the right kitchen equipment. How-to or service stories are organized in a logical, instructional order, anticipating how readers think about a given task and the questions they might ask while thinking about it.

Human interest. These are stories about warmhearted people who do good deeds, such as soup kitchen cooks who feed 350 homeless people every day or someone who sells baked goods for a cause.

Historical background. Pique an editor's interest by combining food history with other forms listed here, such as destination or service writing. It's difficult to pitch pure historical stories without an anchor to current times.

Cookbook review. If your target publication or website includes reviews, find out how it assigns them. A magazine might get dozens of books every month from publishers, choose which ones to review, and hand them out to reviewers. If you find a small publication that publishes reviews, you could try writing one based on a cookbook you've purchased and submit it. Use previously published reviews as models for how to shape your story. Be careful how you criticize—very few cookbooks are all good or all bad, and publishers are more likely to publish mostly positive reviews than puff pieces or negative ones.

Destination and travel. Food-based travel pieces might take you to a food festival, a region known for artisan foods, or a city famous for its restaurants. You don't even have to go anywhere, says *L. A. Times* food columnist Russ Parsons. "Write about what's going on in your backyard. Don't be embarrassed by your limitations." He quotes a songwriter friend who wrote, "Some people can go around the world and not see anything; other people can go around the block and see the whole world."

For newspapers, try the travel section first, instead of the food section. Many freelancers find it easier to be published there.

What defines great travel writing? Deborah Needleman, the editor of the *New York Times'* *T* magazine, explains: "Travel journalism often falls into one of two camps—the highly didactic and servicey piece, 'go here, stay there, see that,' or the long-winded narrative in which the writer has the experience and we are meant to be satisfied by the first-person blow-by-blow he or she has brought back for us. . . . The type we favor at T is a hybrid . . . , in which great writing and personal narrative is done in the service of not just traipsing along with the writer who got to go on an amazing journey that we didn't, but bringing you back a new understanding of a place that is enlightening and satisfying regardless of whether you ever plan to visit."

· ·

HOW TO FIND A STORY IN A PLACE

ROBYN EKHARDT is a contributing writer at *Travel + Leisure Southeast Asia,* and freelances for the *New York Times, Saveur,* and *Food & Wine.* She has lived in Asia for more than fifteen years with her husband and frequent collaborator, professional photographer David Hagerman. Here's how she researches a travel story about food:

"When I travel to write, I allow my obsessions to lead me to a culinary story of a place. I keep my predeparture research to a minimum. I make a note of dishes and ingredients common to the cuisine, especially those that are unfamiliar. I try to find the names of a few better-known dishes and ingredients in the local language (cookbooks can be a great resource). What I don't do is read published culinary travel articles, or scour blogs related to where I'm going. I don't want to be influenced.

"Once I'm on the ground, I allow my obsessions to take over. I love markets anywhere in the world—a food market is the first place I go. I give myself plenty of time to stroll its aisles and poke around in its corners, and then to retrace my steps slowly, making note of whatever pops for me: the fish that every shopper seems to be buying, the shrines hung above every stall, the room occupied entirely by vendors selling suckling pig. By the time I leave I've got a few culinary nuggets about this place that interest me.

"Guided by ingredients, street food, home cooking, and the backstory of beloved dishes, I formulate possible angles. Might there be a story in those shrines, and what they mean to people who sell food in this place? What is that fish, and how do locals prepare it at home or on the street? What is the history behind that suckling pig?

"Next I talk to anyone and everyone who may have something to say about my topic or have a contact to offer. This includes hotel and restaurant personnel, taxi drivers, street food vendors, wait staff, the guy sitting next to me at the lunch counter, and the cashier ringing me up at the drugstore. I may return to the market and talk to vendors and shoppers.

"I also reach out to others. Bloggers, writers, and journalists are more likely to help when approached with a targeted request ('I'm curious about this fish and how it's prepared. Are you available to chat over coffee?') rather than a general ask ('I'm coming to town to write a food story. I'd love to pick your brain'). History, culture, and ethnographic museum staff can be troves of information and may refer you to other experts. If I don't speak the local language, I'll hire a fixer or guide, making sure our research is the focus of our forays.

"Find the angle that truly excites you, follow with determined research and you'll return from every journey with a compelling and unique story."

••

First-person essay. Personal stories are the top choice of many writers but not the priority of most publications and websites. Editors are flooded with personal experience articles. Usually they don't publish more than one article per issue, if they publish any at all.

That doesn't mean it's impossible to get published, just that you have lots of competitors. Increase your chance of success by writing about an experience that relates to readers and their lives. What themes resonate for them? If it's just about what happened to you, then the response from editors can be "So what?" The best personal stories convey a universal interest in a unique way, or with a unique angle. If you tell the story that only you can tell, your chances of success will improve.

When it comes to subject matter in personal essays, you have lots of choices. Perhaps you:

- achieved a goal, such as graduating from cooking school or cooking a special feast
- just returned from a fabulous food-based vacation (in a sidebar, give readers ideas on how to duplicate it)
- had a funny cooking, eating, or traveling experience, or one that should be avoided
- had a life-changing or inspirational experience that will help readers cope with a challenge in their lives
- did something for the first time, such as served as an apprentice in a restaurant
- went to an event, such as a wine auction, a family reunion with amazing food, or a food festival
- are obsessed with a favorite food or have a favorite story about food
- cook unusual holiday dishes
- volunteer in the food world
- like to garden, hunt, or camp or have some other hobby that could involve food.

A few places that take first-person essays are the *New York Times Sunday Magazine*, *Woman's Day*, and *Family Circle*. *Lucky Peach* publishes first-person stories. Magazines particular to niche-related subjects, such as camping, travel, or gardening, might be good prospects.

Regardless of the style or topic of your story, you must have a clear and imaginative focus, a fresh angle based on your own discoveries, and a slant appropriate to the publication. News and trends are always good. Sometimes it's enough to put a fresh take on a nonoriginal idea. Jeanne McManus, former food editor of the *Washington Post*, says, "I like pieces that broaden the discussion about food, that surprise you in that they take something—an ingredient, a technique—something that we think we all know about, and slightly change forever the way I, the reader, think about it."

If you're not finding success pitching essays to mainstream consumer publications, try literary magazines. Many of them take food writing, and personal essays are common. Search them out on the web and research what they've published in the past to get an idea of what stories will succeed. Some also have an editorial calendar so you can tailor a story to fit. Some only read submissions during a certain time; it may take a while for them to get back to you.

How to Target and Position Your Story

Your next step is critical, and one that many freelance writers fail to do: zoom in on a publication or website that's most likely to publish your story. Targeting means systematically finding the most realistic and appropriate place. Let's say I'd like to write a local story about the growing Vietnamese food scene in my town. Notice that my story idea is not a topic, but a trend. "Magazines are really of the moment, not a compendium or a definitive thing like a book or encyclopedia," said Martha Holmberg, former editor in chief and publisher of *Fine Cooking*, during an International Association of Culinary Professionals annual conference. "We don't want the whole thing; we want a slice. Not the topic. It's what you do with that topic."

The topic of the story would be "Vietnamese food." If that's as far as I got, an editor would be likely to say, "What about it?" A subject is not specific or intrinsically interesting by itself. If I change it to say that many markets and restaurants have opened in a particular neighborhood, however, now I have a trend story, one with news value that could be published.

The next question I'd ask myself is, "Who cares about this story?" The newspaper for that neighborhood might care, as might an alternative weekly, the daily newspaper, and local websites. All are local, a key point. A national magazine may not want the story, because it focuses on a small region, unless it's targeted as a travel piece or a cool new neighborhood for foodies to explore. And typically, for a national publication, you'd have to write about Vietnamese food markets in several cities, not just yours.

The person who has to care most about the story is you. You should be obsessed with the neighborhood, Vietnamese food, and other subjects relevant to the piece. You need to do research to come up with enough information to convince an editor that you understand the story, that it's relevant, and why it's urgent people read about it now. By the time you write the piece, you will be an expert on the subject.

"Great writing turns an interesting topic into a must-read story, one that makes a unique claim or argument matter to readers," wrote *Serious Eats* national editor Max Falkowitz. "If a publication reaches a national audience like *Serious Eats* does, then that writing also has to transcend its local interest and matter to people a thousand miles away. So put your story in context and ask yourself, 'Why does this matter?' Even if you know the answer, the line you tell yourself should probably make its way into your pitch."

The other part of targeting involves identifying an audience. This sounds obvious, but I can't tell you how many story ideas I rejected when I was an editor because the writers didn't understand the magazine's reader base. If you want to write about food for children, target magazines aimed at parents. I know that sounds obvious, but somehow it's not. If you like exotic, expensive vacations, focus on magazines and websites with upper-income, traveling readers. It's not hard to figure out who reads the magazine if you review the content in a few issues, especially the ads. Sometimes a magazine's website will list reader demographics under advertising information. Which publications interest you and share your values? In many cases you are the target audience and would therefore be good at coming up with appropriate story ideas.

Once you identify a possible place for your story, find up to a year's worth of issues and search for stories similar to your idea. This is harder than it seems, as some publications are not available in libraries and don't put their content online. Also, many industry magazines are free to qualified subscribers, which might not be you. Canvass friends and others who might keep the publications you need to review. Visit big newsstands. Respond to free offers for sample issues. If you're lucky, you can find tons of content online, on the publications' websites. If so, read all prior stories in the category and subject matter that interests you.

In the case of the Vietnamese food story, you'd look through the neighborhood newspaper or *Edible* publication to see whether it has published stories on food-based businesses and, if so, what kind. If you find none, you'd move to the weekly alternative paper and focus on restaurants because the readership is more likely to eat out than cook. For a daily, review past issues to see how they cover local food trends, and reshape your story as necessary. Perhaps there's a first-person essay on searching for the best takeout roast chicken. If so, a story about the best takeout Vietnamese might be too obscure. Follow this same reasoning with any other publication.

You're probably wondering whether to pitch a story to one publication or website at a time, or whether to send the same query to several at once. Speaking as an editor, I can't advise you to send custom pitches on the same subject to various publications simultaneously, unless they have wildly different readers. An airline magazine and a food magazine are different enough. But pitching a neighborhood story to three publications that cover the city is dangerous, because what if more than one publication wants it? You'd be safe with different angles for an airline magazine and a food magazine, but not for magazines fighting for similar readers. It's best to start with one publication and move on to the others if it's rejected.

Be realistic about which publication you target. If you've never been published, don't bother starting with *Bon Appétit* or the *Washington Post*. Find the smallest publications in your area, or a new website or small newsletter. They may not pay or may pay next to nothing. At this point, you shouldn't care too much, because you need clips to establish your credibility, as stepping stones to stories in a bigger publication.

Review each publication thoroughly. Check the masthead or contributor's list for freelanced material. Sometimes editors give small stories to beginning or new freelancers, to see if they can pull them off. That might be where you start. Estimate the length of features by doing word counts of stories. Examine which stories are text-driven and which are recipe-driven. Examine the structure of stories, such as how many sidebars (boxed smaller stories or lists) they use. If they have submission guidelines, read them carefully. This could help you figure out what an editor wants. Some websites expect you to provide your own images, and some want an estimate for a research budget.

Once you feel confident your story would fit the publication, list the most important points and subpoints to prepare for your query letter. Put the points in logical order, based on questions readers would ask.

Review the sample stories you selected for similarity. Notice the style and voice. Is the writer part of the story or invisible? Examine the tone. If they are kings of snark, and you are sweet, it's not a good fit. Does the story follow a certain format that you can duplicate? See if they run long, detailed stories or lots of lists with provocative headlines. Does the magazine hold the reader's hand in the instruction, or does it assume a certain level of expertise? Does the writer sound breezy or authoritative? If it's a trend story, do you have a statistic to make the trend credible? Do a word count of one typical story, and plan how many points you can cover in the same amount of space. If your story raises questions, do enough research to answer them. If a similar story includes sidebars, come up with a few sidebar ideas.

Don't write the story yet. First figure out what kind of publication is likely to publish it. Then find the editor's name, and write the pitch.

•••

HOW TO BOIL WATER: A LESSON IN POSITIONING

MARTHA HOLMBERG, former publisher of *Fine Cooking,* understands that every food magazine has its own style, voice, and vision. Here's her take on how each pitch letter would slant a story on how to boil water:

"*Fine Cooking:* I've boiled water for years, and I've developed my own method that's fast and produces an even boil. I'll include information on pot selection, the best source of heat, the benefit of using a lid, some do-ahead tips, and I'll give recipes for salted water, acidulated water, and water infused with a bouquet garni. I could do a sidebar on making a bouquet garni.

"*Cook's Illustrated:* Good boiled water is crucial to good cooking, so we decided to experiment to find the best way to boil. I tried aluminum versus stainless, eight-quart versus twelve-quart, with a lid, without a lid, gas versus electric, starting with hot versus starting with cold, and our results will surprise you: cold water and no lid worked best.

"*Kinfolk:* Water connects us all, and ceramicist Kiera feels called to be part of the flow. In her custom water celebration service, she throws ceramic pots designed to contain pristine mountain water, boiled for purity. She supplies her global circle of artist friends, but it's doubtful that a regular reader could obtain any of this. Her company is planning an IPO."

"*Bon Appétit:* Tressa and Josh love brunch with friends. Poached eggs from their backyard hens frequently star on the menu, along with bacon from Winkie, the ethically raised pig they slaughtered (and made a documentary about) last fall. They've renovated their 1960s auto body shop to include a custom poaching pot, where they poach eggs to order as they sip barrel-aged breakfast Manhattans.""

Food & Wine: Enter the world of Trey, chef-owner of the white-hot restaurant of the moment. In his off hours, he craves nothing more than to hang with his friends at the renovated leather factory he shares with his designer girlfriend Giselle. Their casual evenings kick off with green tea martinis made from boiled Icelandic water and served in stemware designed by Giselle."

She's exaggerating to make her point that editors at each of these magazines have a firm idea of how their magazine differs. One of the main reasons they reject queries is because writers don't create enough of a slant to make the story appropriate. Another is because writers pitch a subject—boiling water—rather than a slant on boiling water. With Holmberg's clever examples, it's easy to see the difference.

Finding the Right Markets

Another way to decide who wants your story is to understand which kind of publication to target, what's realistic, and how to approach them.

National food magazines. Everyone wants to be published in one of the big food magazines. It's difficult to get a feature article accepted, though, unless you have written a cookbook, own a popular restaurant, have your own television show, are a well-known cooking-school teacher, have written for big magazines or newspapers, or have apprenticed under a celebrity chef. Some magazines, such as *Cook's Illustrated* and *Taste of Home*, take no freelance articles at all.

That's fine. You can be realistic. Let editors get to know and trust you by writing short pieces. Look at the listing of departments in the front of food magazines and come up with an idea for a 250- to 500-word newsy piece. *Saveur's* Agenda department, for example, might profile a producer, a food festival, and a bakery. Be innovative, inventive, and fresh, says Tina Ujlaki, executive food editor of *Food & Wine*.

While departments are usually collections of short work by different writers, columns are usually written by one person and provide clues on subjects the editors think are important enough to appear regularly. *Food & Wine* always has travel, restaurants, wine, and entertaining columns. *Bon Appétit* has regular writing on technique, healthy cooking, and restaurant recipes. *Eating Well*'s departments include two on nutrition. Typically these columns are rewards for trusted freelancers the editors have worked with for a long time, or written by industry professionals or celebrities.

Regional magazines. The biggest cover several states, such as *Southern Living* and *Sunset*, two magazines owned by Time Home Entertainment. Both *Southern Living* and *Sunset* take freelanced food and travel pieces and recipe-based articles. State magazines don't necessarily publish much food writing at all. *Texas Monthly* is an exception.

Trade publications in the food and beverage industry. *Nation's Restaurant News* and *Natural Foods Merchandiser* are a few of the food-industry trade magazines that cater to specific audiences such as restaurant management, retailers, and wholesalers. Many well-established freelancers work for these publications because they pay better than those oriented to consumers. If you are a chef or a caterer, or have worked in food service or production, industry publications could be an ideal outlet for you, as story ideas will come easily.

To learn more, try to qualify for a free one-year subscription to some food and beverage publications and study them for opportunities.

National travel magazines. Many travel features in these magazines include information about restaurants and dining as part of a destination. For example, *National Geographic Traveler* publishes articles such as "Confessions of a Cheese Smuggler." In a department in *Islands* magazine, you might see a piece on "Anguilla, a Wine and Food Lovers' Getaway."

Women's magazines. Some women's magazines have recipe sections. Examples include *Martha Stewart Living*, *Oprah*, *Family Circle*, *Yoga Journal*, *Health*, and *Woman's Day*. Some carry nutrition and diet-based advice articles as well. Chances are good that you need to be a published writer to get a pitch accepted at these national magazines. Competition will be fierce. You might also consider smaller specialty publications, such as *VegNews*, which are easier to get into.

Food sections of daily papers. I'd like to be optimistic, but I'm not. Newspapers take less and less freelance work. Most dailies are part of big chains like Knight Ridder or Cox News Service. The chains swap employee stories between newspapers, so food section editors have lots of stories from which to fill their pages without paying for freelanced stories.

The food section has a tight budget anyway, with most of it designated for buying food, recipe testing, food styling for in-house photography, culinary demonstrations, and professional development for staff members, says Heather McPherson, food editor of the *Orlando Sentinel*. She fills a four-page section each week by writing her own stories and subscribing to syndicates for other content. "We take very little freelance because budgets in newspapers across the country are shrinking," says McPherson. "You make the most with what money you have. I won't pay someone to do something I can do."

Aim for a local angle for newspapers. Here's a tip from *Washington Post* former food editor Jeanne McManus: "I like pieces that show the pulse of the city in which we publish the food section, pieces about people doing real things in the world of food."

Weekly papers. Usually these are alternative newspapers written with attitude for people in their twenties and thirties who go to clubs and restaurants. You'll always find restaurant reviews, but not all publications will have a budget to publish other food writing. Weeklies usually work a few days to one week ahead.

Virginia Wood is food editor of the *Austin Chronicle*. She says she fills two and a half pages per week with restaurant reviews, profiles, company stories, and cookbook reviews. Her assignments go to seven regular freelancers. Wood said two of these freelancers were working chefs she'd known around Austin who changed careers and were interested in food writing. Two writers who were also trained chefs approached her with good ideas or impressive clips. A restaurateur suggested a mutual friend as the wine writer. The final writer is the spouse of one of her *Chronicle* colleagues. "I didn't go looking for people with food service backgrounds, but five out of seven of us have spent years in the kitchen, which I think informs our writing in important ways," she concludes.

Other weekly papers are community-based and might be good prospects for first-time writers. Former *Saveur* contributing editor Peggy Knickerbocker started out at San Francisco's *Nob Hill Gazette*—"some silly thing about Thanksgiving," she recalls—and *North Beach Now*, with a story on the oldest cappuccino machine in the Italian neighborhood. From there she used her clips to approach the *San Francisco Examiner*, where she wrote a piece on cooking for people with AIDS.

City magazines. These tend to focus on restaurant reviews and capsule reviews to please their advertisers. Occasionally they profile specialty-food producers, such as an old-time candy bar manufacturer, or a piece on organic farms open to the public. They might have stories profiling local food people, or roundup pieces on where to get the best sandwich or coffee. Most produce an annual "Best Restaurants" cover story, which might have bits written by freelancers. The most sophisticated and most often copied city magazine is *New York*, so if you're really serious about getting into city magazines, you might subscribe.

General and association magazines and newsletters. National magazines such as those of insurance companies, the American Automobile Association, and the American Association of Retired People (AARP) are hard to crack, as are airline magazines. But all take food stories. Newsletters are a good option if you're starting out.

The Web. What are the differences between writing for the web and writing for print? Freelance writer and blogger Cheryl Sternman Rule says that web writing tends to be more personal and less fact-based. It also pays dramatically less.

"Because websites aren't constricted by ad-driven pages the way magazines are, editors are often more flexible about word count, subject matter, and even deadlines," explains Rule. "The turnaround time, from submission to seeing your piece online, becomes a matter of days or even hours, rather than the six-month lead time common in magazines."

To her delight, Rule has found editors have encouraged her to express her voice. "Magazines and newspapers enforce a uniform style, so quirkiness isn't always valued. As a magazine writer, part of my job is to represent the magazine, not myself. I've found almost the opposite to be true online.

"Of course, there's a flip side to all this creativity: Pay is substantially, shockingly less. Website editors are more likely to ask for supplemental material, such as photos and recipes, and they don't necessarily offer more money. And with competition especially fierce, writers have much less leverage to negotiate fees and rates online than they do in print."

Josh Ozersky, currently a freelance writer for *Esquire*, has a more optimistic take. "Get in the back door," he writes. "This one really is key. You can go to journalism school, write for ten years, and still not get into *New York*. Or *Time*. Or any number of other legitimate print outlets. But their websites have a bottomless appetite for content, and you can embed yourself within the sanctuary of a major brand by writing online there for almost nothing. This gives you an immense boost in legitimacy and can even lead to a promotion from new media to old, if someone should happen to be poisoned." (See a list of sites that pay for freelance work in the Appendix.)

Other freelancing opportunities. Contribute to anthologies, guidebooks, and reference guides. Look for opportunities in newsletters and on websites, based on what you know. When she was starting out, cooking school teacher and writer Thy Tran wrote the cooking chapter in *How to Fix (Just About) Everything*. For the book *Asia in the San Francisco Bay Area: A Cultural Travel Guide*, she wrote a chapter on San Jose's Vietnamese community.

Write Your Query Letter

Now that you have chosen your target market and publication, and refined your story idea, your job is to spin the subject to fit the publication or website. Write a short query letter explaining your idea and why you are the best person to write the story.

Target the editor who receives query letters. If the publication does not list a food editor on its masthead or on its website, call the editorial department. Whoever answers the phone can help you. Usually it's an editorial assistant or associate editor, and part of their job is to field questions from writers. Don't be shy. You want to know a couple of things: to whom should you pitch your story, and the editor's email address. Get the correct spelling of the editor's name and be formal in your email. Say "Dear Ms. Ujlaki," not "Dear Tina," if you've never met her.

You will also find editors on social media, such as LinkedIn, Twitter, and Facebook, and at conferences such as those put on by International Association of Culinary Professionals (IACP), and at big food shows and chef showcases. It might be good to read some of their Twitter feeds in case you see a subject that resonates with you, or to get a better understanding of their personalities.

Editors are flooded with query letters and reject almost all of them. Here's why queries fail:

- generic story idea, not targeted to the publication
- too long
- unfocused story idea
- badly written, with a boring lead
- just an introduction, no concept of how a story might unfold
- typos and misspellings, which suggest sloppiness, including spelling the editor's name wrong

"If someone says 'I'd like to work for you, contact me if you're interested,' I'll never contact them," said Holmberg. Like most editors, she didn't have time. She might put your letter and writing samples into a file, and mean to get back to them, but she probably won't.

So be concise, but also make the editor interested enough to respond. Stay away from saying how this story would be "perfect" or a "great fit." As editor Dan Jones at the *New York Times* said online, "A cover letter should be a brag-free zone. It should offer information, not opinion, about you and your work. I want to know, briefly, who you are (where you live, what you do). If you've published multiple books, mention one. If your writing has appeared in a lot of magazines, list three. When describing your story (not a requirement), better to tease in one line than summarize in four, and don't give anything away, especially how it ends! The basic rule for cover letters should be the same as for doctors: first, do no harm."

Often, query letters are three paragraphs long. Here are the elements:

The hook. Grab the editor's attention with the same kind of lead paragraph you'd write for the story. Your first few sentences must demonstrate that you can write and that you understand the audience's mission and readers. Here's one from food writer Janet Fletcher: "Everybody knows that broccoli is a great cancer fighter. But too many people overlook its cousins . . . that have comparable health benefits and underutilized potential in the kitchen. Kale of many kinds, kohlrabi, broccoli romanesco, and broccoli rabe are among [those] that deserve a wider audience."

If you reference a story or department, it shows you read the magazine or website and have thought about a story that is right for them. Editors will pay attention.

The pitch. Write your pitch right in the email. Explain the story idea in specifics, in just a few sentences. If you can't, it's a sign you haven't thought it through closely enough. Visualize the story, and explain how it will unfold. For a story with recipes, list the titles or make suggestions. State the length, whether it will fit in a particular section, and give a working title and a summary. State your plan of attack on how you intend to write the story and whom you need to interview. If you have thought of other elements such as sidebars and tip boxes, mention them. Editors are using little pieces these days, so your ability to cut the story up into boxes will help you.

Your credentials. State why you are qualified to write the story. The best reason would be that you have written stories like this before. If you have been published on an entirely different subject in an unrelated field, don't mention it, as editors will not see it as relevant. If you've never been published, bring up relevant work experience or personal experience or your blog. If you've already done some interviews or research, or have been granted access to a prestigious profile subject, these facts might compensate for lack of writing experience.

What if you don't have published work to point to? "That's okay— send me anything: a Yelp review you're proud of or a short piece you wrote but never published," wrote Falkowitz of *Serious Eats*. "Show me something to help me trust your intelligence and writing ability. Editors love taking risks on promising writers, but they need a show of good faith to do so."

If you have written for publication, find the most relevant stories, and link to a few of them.

The close. Thank the editor and say you will follow up in a few weeks. If you have a deadline, such as you're leaving the country within a month, say so. Do not say you'll wait for the editor to contact you. Chances are excellent that it will not happen.

Some final tips. Multiple story queries might increase your chance of getting published if you pitch two or three ideas of one paragraph each. For one national magazine, I pitched three stories. They had just accepted one idea from another writer, didn't like the second, but wanted the third. For another magazine, I pitched two articles and the editor wanted both. The challenge is to be concise.

These days, almost every editor takes email queries. Put a few key words or a likely headline in the subject line with the word "Query" preceding them. Don't send clips as attachments. Editors are suspicious of big files that download slowly or arrive in formats they can't open. If you have bylined pieces online—even on your own website—put links in the body of the email and make the editor's life easier.

Check the email several times for typos and spelling errors. Print it out and proofread it. If you send a badly written query with typos, or you have spelled the editor's name incorrectly, you'll turn the editor off and reduce your chance of being taken seriously.

●●

SAMPLE QUERY

Here's a letter freelance writer **TRACEY CEURVELS** wrote to *Relish,* a national magazine that appears in weekend editions of newspapers. While we were working together on getting her published, she researched back issues and saw a freelanced story about using different types of cheese to make French, English, and Italian lasagnas. So she figured the editor would like different renditions of pot roast. Ceurvels looked up one of the magazine's pot roast recipes and emulated the format.

Dear Jill Melton:

In the annals of New England culinary history, pot roast was known as a frugal dinner, since it calls for inexpensive cuts of meat like chuck, flank and bottom round cooked slowly in a covered pot. Perhaps for its practicality, it's also been a favorite pub offering. But now this old-fashioned Yankee dish is more appealing updated and infused with Asian, Indian, Italian and Mediterranean flavors.

While it's always been a standby at cantankerous Durgin Park in Boston's Faneuil Hall, where tourists enjoy eating up nostalgia, pot roast fell out of favor, replaced by more sophisticated meat dishes. Fortunately, at rustic Dalya's Restaurant in Bedford, Massachusetts, the practical dish has an elegant incarnation, thanks to chef Udiel Restrepo. His Mediterranean version of this poor man's roast beef is more tasteful than its historic twin with dribbles of heady, fragrant truffle oil and garlic mashed potatoes.

In this article of about 600 words, titled, "Not Your Grandmother's Pot Roast," I will include recipes for Mediterranean pot roast as well as an Asian version (Chinese 5-spice), Indian (with aromatic flavors such as cardamom and cumin), and Italian (parsley, sage and red wine) version.

My articles have appeared in the *Boston Globe,* the *New York Times,* the *New York Daily News, Hallmark, Condé Nast Traveler,* and *Chocolatier,* among other publications. [She also included links.]

I would love to write for *Relish* so I hope you will consider my idea.

Regards,

Tracey Ceurvels

The editor accepted the story, requesting Asian, Italian, and Mediterranean versions, but not the Indian version Ceurvels pitched originally.

••

Get a Response

You sent off the query. Now you wait. Typical responses range from two to eight weeks. Really. And often, you get no response at all.

When you've waited an appropriate amount of time, send a follow-up one-sentence email by forwarding the original query. Be polite and professional. Ask if the editor has received the query and had a chance to read it.

Sometimes editors respond with some version of "I need more time." If I don't hear back, I email again, with a shorter note. "Be persistent," said Tina Ujlaki, executive food editor of *Food & Wine,* at an IACP session. "It takes a lot to get through, and it might mean we just haven't got around to it."

If you still don't hear back, don't phone. Even if you get editors on the phone, they will not know who you are, won't know where they put the query, won't remember it, probably won't have time to look for it, and will have to get back to you.

Waiting for a response can get frustrating. "After spending about three weeks sending queries and clips with no success, I'd get so depressed

I took naps on the floor because if I slept in bed that meant I was really depressed," says writer Linda Furiya. But she persisted, and eventually an airline magazine hired her to do a roving feature on city dining. That article led to more assignments.

Some editors are so swamped that they don't bother sending any response at all. Be prepared for that outcome. Even established freelance writers complain that they get no response sometimes, so don't get too discouraged if it happens to you. The secret is to send out several different query ideas instead of one, so you're less attached to the outcome. If you hear nothing, pitch a new story, or move on to a new publication. Don't give up. Refocus.

What if editors want your story? They will discuss length and dead-line, and offer a fee. If you want the job and you're not experienced, take it and don't haggle over the money. It's considered impolite to do so before you have proven yourself. If the editor responds and fails to men-tion payment, it could mean it pays nothing, or it could mean they'll pay nothing if you don't ask. So ask. If you get an amount and you don't like it, I've heard more established freelancers suggest you pause. Sometimes just that is enough to get an increase. Or you could say, "It sounds a little low," to see if the editor will offer more. In fact, that could be your default response. You've got nothing to lose.

Sometimes, editors might like your writing but don't want the partic-ular story you've pitched. They might ask if you'd be interested in another story, perhaps one based on an idea they already generated.

Can You Make a Living as a Freelancer?

People contact me all the time to tell me they were asked to write for free. One of the most popular posts on my blog is about a woman who started a blog and then pitched recipe-based stories to two regional news-papers, only to have both tell her they would not pay her for her work. I asked readers what they would have done. The consensus was that because she was just starting out, it was acceptable if the writer needed the clip to move forward with her career.

But she should stop working for nothing as soon as she has a few clips. Or barter: one quarterly magazine gave me a free subscription in exchange for two articles a year. That's better than nothing.

I've learned I can work for almost free by being paid close to nothing. I've received $25 for cookbook reviews, $30 for restaurant reviews in a guidebook, and $150 for a three-thousand-word story. My experience is hardly unique, even for the big names. "I always dabbled in food writing as an aside but never planned to become a food writer. I never thought I could make a living as one, as the $50 and $75 I got for most of the food pieces I wrote proved," says GQ contributor Alan Richman of his early days in the business.

Why is food writing such a badly paid profession? A full-time freelancer put it this way: she asked if, when I was a magazine editor in other fields, I had a hundred people standing behind me willing to do my job for nothing. I said no. That's her situation, she explained. If she asks for more money, someone else will step in to fill her place for less, or nothing. Even freelance writers at the top of their game don't feel well compensated. When asked about the hardest part of freelancing, Estabrook said, "Money. Even when you're making top rates at magazines and doing books, it's a financial grind. Competition is such that publications aren't really forced to pay more than they do for articles." He added that even if he wrote an article every month when he was a regular contributor for *Gourmet,* he would make $50,000–$60,000 per year, with no medical care. "That's a grueling pace you probably couldn't keep up." Most food writers don't write full-time. They can't afford it. Says Wood of her regular writers at the Chronicle, "None makes their living as a freelancer, because it's almost impossible to do so." Again, keep your day job or work part-time at other jobs unless your spouse or partner can support you, you have a generous trust fund, or you can arrange to win the lottery. Or read Chapter 12 about other ways to make money.

When You Write Your Story

During a break in a writing class I taught, a student approached me and said she was a terrible writer. I asked her how many drafts she wrote. "One," she answered. Whenever I tell that story to fellow writers, they laugh. Your first draft isn't supposed to be good. Anne Lamott calls it a "shitty first draft" in her excellent book on writing, *Bird by Bird: Some Instructions on Writing and Life.*

The first draft is whatever you write to get started, after you have done your research and completed your interviews. Make it awful, incomplete, and out of order—whatever you want. Then go back over it several times, filling in pieces, shaping and polishing your work. Good writing doesn't flow out in a single piece, fully formed. It needs revision.

Start with a compelling opening paragraph, called a lead. Draw in readers by piquing their interest. Spend a long time getting it right. The best way to do so is to review the leads of previously published pieces in the publication or on the website. Obviously those leads worked for the editor, so try to copy them. Here are a few more strategies:

- Base it on common experiences everyone understands. Here's a lead from an article in *Bon Appétit:* "As desperately as I wanted to overhaul my seventies nightmare kitchen—it was ugly and claustrophobic, and the oven was held together with grease—I was scared. Was there a way to do the job without losing my money, my mind, and my marriage? Here's what I found out."
- Put readers in the center of the story immediately, a particularly good technique for travel stories. Here's the first sentence of a story on Bangkok in *Bon Appétit:* "It's hard to miss the distinctive flavors of Thailand in bustling Bangkok, whether you're slurping noodles at an outdoor market or quaffing cocktails in a skyscraper bar."
- Give a telling anecdote about one person to illustrate the point of your story. An *Eating Well* story on sugar addiction begins: "Long ago, Peg Duvall fell into a trap. As a teenager in the 1950s, Duvall studied diligently and led a life surrounded by high school friends. But she had a hard time relaxing at night."
- For a how-to piece, hook readers by reassuring them it's going to be worth it. Here's a lead in *Fine Cooking:* "Learning to love beets isn't nearly as hard as you might imagine, because a roasted beet isn't so much a beet as it is a sweet and tender roasted vegetable."
- Make a promise to the reader. In the first example, the sentence "Here's what I found out" tells readers you have something important and interesting to tell them.

Paint a visual image with words. Says Peggy Knickerbocker, "Capture your audience with something visual. I position the reader in the moment when I was captivated, and then go back and write the story. I have learned to write about something vivid, like kneading the dough, with little clouds rising into the air. *Saveur* taught me that."

Follow with a nut graph. Once you've drawn the reader in, explain what you're going to tell them. A nut graph ("graph" is short for "paragraph") bridges the lead and the rest of the story. It explains the point and tells readers what they will learn. Sometimes leads are so condensed that the nut graph is a sentence ending the first paragraph, as in the kitchen renovation story in the first example.

Near the top, after the lead, add a nut graph: tell readers why they should care, and what's in it for them. This is particularly true in newspapers, where you have to get to the point quickly. Readers want to know if this article will be worth their time.

Hold readers' hands. You know where the story's going, but your readers don't. Drop a trail of bread crumbs all the way through, to reassure readers you're telling them what you said you would, and foreshadow what will come next. Readers don't like to be surprised. Prepare them for a story that takes a turn or covers several points.

If you're writing a recipe-based story, chances are good that you'll write a lead and nut graph, then go right into the recipes. In this example from *Cook's Illustrated,* a nut graph frames the story: "Years ago, in the kitchen of a university apartment, my Taiwanese roommate taught me to create a simple noodle dish that involved no more than boiling the noodles. It was a cheap, quick, meatless meal on which a student tired of Salisbury steak could subsist. Could I create something that recalled that satisfying dish, yet was a bit more substantial—more suited to a weeknight dinner?"

Make sure the body of the story follows a logical path. All stories have a beginning, middle, and end. Before tackling the middle, draft an organizational plan of points you wish to make. Each paragraph's first sentence makes the decision for the rest of the piece. Thoughts should flow in logical order from one topic to the next. Once you have a structure, if you feel more comfortable starting in the middle, go for it.

Strong close. Does your story have one, or does it trail off? In the conclusion, tell readers what you've already told them as a way to wrap up. If you've relayed an anecdote or created a theme in your lead, circle around to it again in the conclusion.

HOW TO INTERVIEW

INTRODUCE YOURSELF. When you first contact your interviewee, politely explain the point of your story. Say where it will be published. If you haven't pitched the story yet, say you're calling to get permission to interview the person for a story. Once you have an interviewee's interest and consent, your query letter has more teeth. Request a convenient time to come by or telephone. Say how much time you'll need. If your interviewee doesn't want to do the interview until you have an assignment, see if you can ask a few short key questions that are essential to your pitch.

TRY NOT TO DO THE INTERVIEW BY EMAIL. Because people are busy, often they will answer with the smallest effort possible, and then it's hard to go back to them for more information. There's also no room for the best part, when the two of you spontaneously travel down a new path to new material. I do interviews by phone, using a headset, while typing on the computer. Some people tape interviews and then transcribe the notes.

CREATE A LIST OF QUESTIONS AND BE KNOWLEDGEABLE. Do your research and eliminate those that will annoy your subject, such as "What's the name of your award-winning cheese again?" Find out all you can by searching online, or talking to people who know the person.

ASK FOR CLARIFICATION OR DETAILS WHEN YOU DON'T UNDERSTAND. Clarifying questions are different from dumb or annoying questions. If your subject uses a word you don't understand, ask what it means. Feel free to ask "How do you know that?" or "How did it work?" when appropriate. Ask "Can you give me an example?" when something sounds theoretical. You're not the expert; you're the information gatherer, and you have to make sure you understand well enough to write about it later. You're representing the reader, so make sure that readers will understand what the interviewer says.

ASK OPEN-ENDED QUESTIONS. Yes or no answers don't tell readers anything. Your interview will be over before you know it, and you'll have no story. Ask questions such as "What led you to decide to? . . ." and "How do you feel about? . . ."

ASK A SURPRISE QUESTION. Sometimes even a silly question leads to an excellent quote.

FOCUS ON WHAT'S ESSENTIAL TO YOUR STORY. If you're interviewing Thomas Keller because a restaurant magazine wants to know how he runs several establishments at once, don't ask about his technique for making gnocchi.

REMEMBER THAT THE INTERVIEW IS NOT ABOUT YOU. It is not a conversation, but you can sound conversational. Express interest, even skepticism. Do not state your opinions, sympathize, or add meaning to questions. Don't tell stories about the time something similar happened to you. You're not there to entertain or make friends with your subject.

END ON TIME. Thank the interviewee for making time to talk with you. If you need more time, make another appointment. Send a thank-you note when you're done.

....

Edit Your Own Work

When you think you've drafted the story you want, your next step is to strengthen and shape it. Be ruthless. You might end up deleting half of it, moving paragraphs around, and rewriting the other half. None of this means you can't write. On the contrary, it means you are doing the work of real writers: revising. Here's how:

- Eliminate any throat clearing, where you have to warm up to get to the story. Make sure the first paragraph is truly the lead paragraph by setting the stage or getting to the point.
- Eliminate repetition by saying what you mean clearly. Don't keep writing the same idea in slightly different ways.
- Write in active versus passive voice. Active voice means someone takes action: "John cut the crusty bread." Passive voice means the action is more removed: "The crusty bread was cut by John." Passive voice flattens your writing.
- Create action by packing your story with verbs. Powerful verbs make your writing more vigorous and help readers move through the story.
- Adjectives are the curse of food writers. Find one specific word, and cut the rest.
- Tighten every sentence, eliminating all unnecessary words, particularly adverbs such as "very" and "really."
- Cut out tangents, or put them in sidebars.
- Remember to "show—don't tell." Instead of telling readers you didn't like sitting at the dinner table with your dad, show them what it was like. Put them there at the table with you.
- Revise by ear. Read your work out loud to feel its rhythm and flow. It sounds silly, but it's an invaluable way to eliminate clunky sentences and find parts that need clarification. When

you hesitate over a sentence's construction, work on revising it to read more clearly.

- If you have time, put your story away for a few days. When you come back to it, you'll be more objective about what to fix, and the fixes will be clearer.
- Edit for grammar, punctuation, and spelling. Proofread for typos. I can't emphasize this enough. There's nothing more irritating to editors than a careless mistake. It makes editors worry that you're not as accomplished as you seem. Have someone else read your work to look for errors.

"My process involves a lot of thinking before, during, and after," says freelancer Alan Richman. "It's not about polishing words but polishing the thinking, making things more focused."

What are the hardest things about writing articles? To quote Knickerbocker, "To be a good journalist, take the profession seriously, get the facts right, and present something new and fresh. Combine accuracy with creativity and passion."

• •
BOOKS TO HELP YOU BECOME A BETTER WRITER

- *On Writing Well: The Classic Guide to Writing Nonfiction,* by William Zinsser
- *The Elements of Style,* by William Strunk Jr. and E. B. White
- *Writing Down the Bones: Freeing the Writer Within,* by Natalie Goldberg
- *Bird by Bird: Some Instructions on Writing and Life,* by Anne Lamott

• •

Working with Your Editor

Once you submit your story to the editor, you may not hear back right away. Don't panic. Eventually your editor will read it and contact you about changes. Most stories need tweaking. Perhaps you left out critical details, or your lead is buried, or you need more information in certain areas, or the tone is wrong. Being edited is part of the process. Be polite, and accept the requests.

If you are having control issues about someone changing your work, get over it. Editors almost always ask for changes, no matter how long you've been writing. Yes, they can make edits you don't like. If you must object, pick your battle, and make a reasoned argument politely. Most editors, particularly at newspapers, don't even show you what they've done to your story before it is published. After a newspaper printed one of my restaurant reviews, I discovered that an editor interjected her own opinion, one contrary to my own. I called her and explained, politely, that my opinion was mine alone. She didn't do that again.

How to Keep Going

As I explained earlier, it's hard to make enough money as a freelance food writer to make a decent income. But there are ways to increase your chances of steady work, and to make more money. Here are some suggestions:

Network. Up until now, I've assumed you don't know the editor you're pitching to. But if you meet editors at conferences or industry events, follow them on social media, link to them on LinkedIn, or even meet them by chance, your job is to create an opening and to be memorable enough that editors remember you when you send them a story idea. If you meet them in person, get their business cards so you can follow up on email. To increase the odds, query the editor within a few days. Don't wait six months trying to get up the nerve. Get it over with. Six months from now, you might as well be a stranger.

Don't rest on your laurels. If the publication or website publishes your work, or an editor responds positively, pitch another story immediately, and try to establish a relationship with your editor. The more comfortable an editor feels with you, and the more you deliver professional stories on deadline, the more assignments you will receive. If editors like one story, they might like more, so keep pitching ideas.

Recycle. Freelance work can pay a little more if you recycle the same article to other publications. Most publications in the United States and Canada buy first North American serial rights, which means the publisher has the right to publish your work first. After that you're free to sell it again, preferably to noncompeting markets both here and abroad. For example, a piece you wrote for a food magazine on spa cuisine in Mexico might fit a travel magazine whose focus is more on travel and less on food. Perhaps there's another story if you can profile the chef, or do a roundup on other spas in Mexico. You may need to do a little rewriting and editing to make the angle more appropriate for the publication, which would be a plus, as it's best not to have identical articles published in several places. Read your contract carefully first to see whether it's possible to recycle your story.

By adding and subtracting according to the needs of other publications and websites, you can publish a similar story many times—and get paid each time. Just apply what you learned earlier about targeting and positioning. Do not disclose that the article was previously published, because you are going to revise it anyway. Magazines don't care unless you're recycling the same article that ran in a competing magazine. Then you're in trouble.

Pitch to trade publications. It's not glamorous, I know, but publications about manufacturing and retailing of groceries, beverages, produce, farming, and so forth usually pay much better than consumer publications. Keep in mind that they have a narrow focus, and you must know enough about the industry and have enough contacts to generate the right story ideas. Often you'll find well established writers' bylines there, because these publications often pay better than consumer magazines.

Take corporate writing jobs. For better pay, write for companies rather than publications, as long as there's no conflict of interest. Food writer Janet Fletcher got into commercial writing serendipitously. She was pitching to companies to become commercial sponsors for her new newsletter when one company offered her regular work. Her newsletter turned into a mini-magazine for a supermarket chain with seasonal stories, recipes, and product information. That job continued for about three years. Fletcher went on to write advertorials and special advertising sections that appeared in food magazines, and for ten years she wrote the newsletter of the American Institute for Wine and Food.

A significant share of Fletcher's income has come from commercial work. She writes website copy and develops recipes for corporations and commodity boards. The nonprofit boards, such as the Almond Board and the Beef Council, hire her to write text aimed at professional chefs. For the Culinary Institute of America, she writes web-based e-learning materials.

In this kind of writing, you're usually "pitching a product or a place or a service," says Fletcher, "but it's a soft sell with an editorial feel to it." Commercial writing has its downside. Most of your work doesn't appear with your byline, so it's harder to build your portfolio. But if you're a reliable writer with good ideas who knows how to keep clients, you can succeed. "Find a need and fill it," Fletcher advises. "Look for companies whose websites are not very good, or that don't have marketing materials and need them. Approach independent public relations firms."

Public relations firms, marketing agencies, ad agencies, manufacturers, retailers, and nonprofit boards and councils hire freelance writers for all kinds of commercial writing: press releases, brochures, website content, ghostwritten first person pieces, press-kit materials, label information, scripts for videos, pitch letters, research papers, and speeches. They might also give you work developing and testing recipes. If you're just getting started in this area, you may be willing to be paid less in order to build a portfolio of work and establish credibility.

The bigger question is how to find work like this. Blogger and freelance writer Amy Sherman of CookingwithAmy.com accepts most invitations to events, because she never knows whom she'll meet. At one meeting promoting travel in Alberta, Canada, she met a managing editor of a publishing house who offered her a bimonthly column on a website. After joining the San Francisco Professional Food Society, she met a marketing professional who hired her to fix chef recipes and help her client attract bloggers to promote products, and another for whom she wrote monthly newsletter.

"When you're self-employed, you're a small business person, and you have to know how to market yourself," she advises. "Most people have to do marketing. The sooner you get used to it and get good at it, the sooner you'll be successful." She considers her blog a place to highlight her writing skills and expertise, providing a showcase for corporate clients.

IS SYNDICATION WORTHWHILE?

Syndication is the ability to have your work published in multiple publications. Some say syndication is a great way to make money. If you are an established writer, you can query a syndication service about submitting articles or columns for distribution to major daily newspapers, community weeklies, newsletters, and websites across the United States and around the world. If the service accepts you, it takes 40 to 50 percent of sales. Sales are based on how many newspapers purchase your story or column and how much they pay.

These days, with reduced budgets and access to lots of free or inexpensive copy, newspapers are no longer a great market for syndication. In fact, one cookbook author told me he was only able to sell his column to one newspaper, which then demanded he also sell them all rights to print it. The syndicate will send payment if and when publications pick up your article or column. It takes a lot of publications to pick up your column to have it add up.

If you have a blog, you might find websites that aggregate blogs. Typically, however, they do not pay, promising you "exposure," in exchange for putting your copy on their website with a link.

For a list of syndicates, see dmoz.org/News/Media/Services/Syndicates.

• •

Writing freelance stories and blogs for pay is a competitive arena that requires good skills and creativity. Editors and clients like writers they trust who pitch well-defined ideas, understand what they want, turn in good work on time, and form a good relationship. If you can follow these rules and have a thick skin about rejection, you'll always be published. And despite recent hand wringing about the paucity of freelance work, dozens of magazines and websites still pay for good stories. I've assembled a lengthy list in the Appendix.

Then there's the role of passion, my theme from earlier chapters. Says Knickerbocker, "I don't think I've ever written something that has been an assignment that didn't come from me. [Otherwise] I haven't been able to write well about it. It's always something that has moved me very deeply, where I just have to get something off my chest and have to write the story. Someone's going to buy it. They're going to feel the vibrancy and the clarity.

"I kind of can't believe my life worked out the way it has, that I got to write and be paid for it."

• •

FOR MORE INFORMATION ON FREELANCING

BOOKS:
- *Starting Your Career as a Freelance Writer*, by Moira Anderson Allen
- *Writer's Market*, a directory published annually by Robert Lee Brewer

WEBSITES:
- Association of Food Journalists, afjonline.com
- The International Food, Wine, and Travel Writers Association, ifwtwa.org—open to food and wine writers, photographers who write, and established online journalists
- MediaBistro.com, a membership website with extensive tips for how to approach dozens of food magazines
- WritersDigest.com, which lists classes, conferences, and articles
- Writer's Market online, writersmarket.com, which provides listings and comprehensive information about where to freelance
- FundsforWriters.com/grants, which lists grants and contests

Writing Exercises

1. Make a list of ten how-to headlines of stories you can write with your eyes closed. Perhaps you're an expert on piecrusts, and your article would be about technique. Your headline will not be "All About Piecrusts." Instead, it will focus on your expert advice. "Make a Winning Piecrust Every Time" is a more specific, and more exciting, alternative. After you've written your list of ten headlines, pick one, and make a list of the steps involved. Now you have the middle of a story. Once you write the beginning and the end, the first draft will be complete.

2. Recycling stories based on the same subject and research is a terrific use of your time and a way to generate better income. Think up three stories based on one subject written for a general consumer publication, and then adapt them for an industry newsletter and a magazine aimed at mothers. Write a lead for each kind of story based on what the readership wants to know. A lead for a food safety story for a general consumer publication, for example, targets readers who prepare food without thinking too much about bacteria, and has a general lead about keeping the kitchen sanitary when cooking. A lead for a story for an industry publication quotes a government official discussing new labeling guidelines for meat. A lead for a publication aimed at mothers begins with the story of a child eating leftovers that have gone bad. For each lead idea, visualize your target audience, and slant the subject directly to them, addressing what might concern or interest them.

3. If you have not been published, come up with a story idea based on your own personal experience, and craft a query letter. A well-crafted query letter might be enough to sway an editor. Here's a sample story idea: "Since I returned to work after having a baby, I've had to plan ahead and buy cupboards full of canned and packaged food for my baby. My article will draw on my experiences of sampling prepared baby food such as crackers and cereal. It will recommend the top five products for busy mothers, based on taste, ingredients, and value."

6: DINING OUT

Writing about restaurants has to be one of the most glamorous jobs in the world. You'll dine for free at the best places in town, right?

Sometimes, if you're lucky. You may eat excellent, cutting-edge, and exotic food on occasion. But you'll also eat lots of mediocre and bad food, and pay for it yourself. And you might find it hard to keep from gaining weight. (As one reviewer told me, "Clothes always come in larger sizes.")

This chapter discusses two approaches to restaurant writing. There's the more recent blogging trend of covering restaurants, not reviewing them. In this case, the piece is about a restaurant or opening, not a critique. Bloggers might write about an opening they attended, accompanied by copious photography, or write a quick post about a new place they ate at once. They may or may not pay for the meal.

A restaurant review, on the other hand, appears in the larger national magazines and newspapers, including city magazines and alternative weeklies. They are criticisms of the restaurant, with analysis of the food, ambiance, service, and appeal. Their authors are thought to have superior palates and their judgment wields power. These restaurant critics may have full-time jobs with big expense accounts, but that's increasingly rare. Many are freelancers who are paid to visit a restaurant once or twice.

Professional reviewers try to be anonymous. Their meals are most often paid by their employer—website or print publication. Beginning reviewers or bloggers may pay for the meal themselves, or get a free meal from the restaurant.

Got it? The differences between these types of stories and writers may seem subtle, but they're indicative of a sea change in the United States in the last decade. Many good writing jobs were lost as newspapers and alternative weeklies slashed their dining budgets and placed less emphasis on reviews. They can't avoid the influence of Yelp, which offers consumer reviews written by anyone, thus reducing the power of professional restaurant reviewers. And they're also competing with food bloggers, who can beat them to a new restaurant opening.

This rising tide of food bloggers covers restaurants in new ways. I'll discuss the issues and trends first, and then move on to how professional restaurant reviewers work.

How Bloggers and Beginning Reviewers Work

The biggest difference between reviewers and food bloggers is that bloggers avoid an actual critique. This is for several reasons:

Many bloggers believe what their mammas told them—if you don't have anything nice to say, don't say anything at all. As a result, they "cover" restaurants, meaning "I went there, and this is what I had" kind of writing. Often their posts read like puff pieces, with gushing headlines. It's probably because they dine for free at soft openings, or receive comped meals. It's hard to not feel grateful, as if they owe the restaurant something, and they know they will not be invited to more free meals if the write-up is not positive. Yes, free meals let bloggers try new restaurants that may not be in their budgets, but then they might have trouble being objective. Another challenge might be to avoid writing what everyone else who was invited to the event is writing.

Lots of writers feel they are not qualified to critique the food. Bloggers are representing customers as eaters. Most customers have not been to chef school or worked in kitchens, and they don't know everything about every cuisine world over. Nevertheless, it takes time to have the confidence to judge a restaurant and its food. If you're going to have an opinion, you need to feel authoritative and accurate. Food bloggers are competing with established reviewers who have educated their palates for years, so it can be intimidating to put their views out there. If you feel that you need more gravitas, I have some ideas later in this chapter.

Some bloggers opine anyway, incurring the wrath of professional critics, who sneer at their lack of education. Said Josh Osersky in *Time* magazine, "The current crop of food writers, at least the online ones, are a cacophony of dazzled novices, opining confidently in an intellectual vacuum."

Bloggers want to be first, so they're looking for a quick news hit. Some bloggers just want their readers to know about a place, so it's more about breaking news and a few quick photos, so they can be the first. The post becomes an extension of word-of-mouth, delivered casually.

They don't have time or money to eat there more than once on their own dime. It's likely that bloggers eat only one meal before writing up the restaurant, rather than the two or three meals professional reviewers eat. That's because if they were invited to an event, it was only one meal, and if they're paying for it themselves, they don't necessarily go back.

Another trend that food bloggers have instigated is that they don't limit themselves to fine dining restaurants. When restaurant reviewing began, people didn't go out as much, and when they did so it was for a special occasion, such as a birthday or anniversary. Fine dining was the most obvious option, and part of the job of a reviewer was to help decide which place would be worth the expense. But now people eat out more often—at food trucks, dives, monasteries, underground diners, pop-up restaurants, and other more informal experiences that traditional reviewers usually won't touch. Perhaps that's why some publications have added reviews of more moderately priced and bargain restaurants.

Not all professional writing and reviews are of upscale eateries anyway, even though they are still the majority. Some reviewers stake out food from immigrant communities, including taco trucks and restaurants where the menu might not be in English. "I have my thing," *L.A. Weekly*'s Jonathan Gold said in a profile in the *New Yorker*. "Traditional—I hate the word 'ethnic'—restaurants that serve some actual hunger people have, rather than something they tell themselves they must have." He describes it as the "triple carom": the "Cajun seafood restaurant that caters to Chinese customers and is run by Vietnamese from Texas."

Writing about inexpensive restaurants is softer on the pocketbook anyway, since bloggers don't have an employer or client who is footing the bill. Since most food bloggers are hobbyists, it's also not possible to write off the cost.

Having your own blog means that you get to cover restaurants any way you want. You don't have to cover every kind of food. It's overwhelming to become an expert on everything, even for established reviewers. If you want to blog only about Korean food, you've got only one cuisine to master. Many food bloggers write about restaurants as part of the mix of what interests them anyway, along with recipes, photo essays, and how-to posts. And since blogs are potentially international, some bloggers feel that a focus on local places is too small.

While this chapter mentions citizen reviews for websites such as Yelp, it is not the focus, as my goal is to get you paid for your work. However, what you read here can make you a better reviewer if you start out in those mediums, particularly if you only want to review as a hobby.

And lastly, there's the advantage of your photography. Blogs and online sites can quickly post lots of photos of dishes. That doesn't happen with a traditional review in print. In most cases, the reviewer dines, leaves, and submits a story. A professional photographer arrives separately, later, to take the shots. The publication shows one photo of the food and maybe one of the restaurant, or the chef.

A FEW SUGGESTIONS FOR WRITING ABOUT RESTAURANTS ON BLOGS

- Don't expect a neighborhood joint to have the same attentive service as the French Laundry.
- Don't call attention to yourself and ask for special favors. You're representing your readers, who would get regular service if they walked in.
- Don't ask for a free meal. You don't want to get a reputation.
- If you do receive a free meal, and you say you like it in your post, do the decent thing and disclose that the meal was free (in the United States the "decent thing" is required by law).
- If you have an issue with the restaurant, don't blast it all over social media as a first step. It's not professional and can lead to stalking by chefs.
- If you don't understand something about a dish or ingredient, call the restaurant, and try to discuss it. It's better to educate yourself first rather than write with inadequate information.

How Professional Critics Work

No matter what kind of restaurant writing you're doing or want to do, you'd probably like to know how the pros review so you can up your game. This chapter shares questions that came up for me when I started reviewing, along with insights and tips from some of the best American reviewers. Many come from *New York Times* restaurant reviewers, who continue to dominate America in matters of opinion about food, chefs, and restaurants. You'll find more tips on the website of the Association of Food Journalists (AFJ) (afjonline.com), which lists a code of ethics and critic's guidelines. The AFJ, by the way, gives annual awards to the best critics in the country. Tom Sietsema of the *Washington Post* and Michael Bauer of the *San Francisco Chronicle*, both interviewed in this chapter, are multiple winners. Alan Richman, a contributing writer for GQ magazine, also interviewed, has won multiple awards as well, including more than a dozen from the James Beard Foundation.

As you read, you'll learn about the complex issues behind reviewing, particularly ethics, that make this field endlessly fascinating. You'll discover practical ways to get your first assignment and how to analyze a restaurant and its dishes. While there are fewer professional reviewers who have expense accounts, there are still plenty of publications and websites that want good writers on the subject of restaurants.

How Reviewing Is Done

Professional reviewing is difficult and time-consuming, even if all you do is write reviews. As a print reviewer, you may go out several evenings in a week. I went out three to four nights per week to write one review per week for *San Francisco Weekly*. Bauer, who writes two reviews per week, goes out almost every night. Sietsema heads out every day for lunch, sometimes breakfast, and sometimes two dinners if he's on deadline. He has kept detailed calendars for upward of sixty reservations per month. Gold, the first reviewer to ever win the Pulitzer Prize for restaurant reviewing, eats at three hundred to five hundred restaurants per year, and drives twenty thousand miles per year in search of good food. Some critics plan up to three months ahead and might visit one restaurant twice over several weeks.

Deciding Which Restaurant

First, as a reviewer, you have to choose where to go. At daily papers, the old "newsworthy" standard applies, explains Russ Parsons, food columnist at the *L. A. Times*. Questions he asks himself include: "Is there a reason people should know about this restaurant? Are people talking about it and want to know about it? Is it unknown and very good? Is it hyped and not so good? Does it in some way reflect something important about the community?"

While many new restaurants claim they're pushing the envelope, part of your job is to know whether what they are doing is truly new or just a new twist on something that was passé ten years ago.

To decide on restaurants, you have to be out and on the lookout, scoping out your town for new places that add variety to your reviews by price, location, or cuisine. Or you may have heard that a restaurant has changed chefs or made a major menu revision.

If you're starting out and you want to be published in print, you'll have to write on spec and then submit it. (That means editors are under no obligation to run the piece or pay you, if they don't like it.) Make sure you read your target publication thoroughly first, for several weeks. If there's only one review per week by one reviewer, they might not want another. Analyze what sorts of restaurants are critiqued. Don't pick a coffee shop frequented by seniors if the paper wants only hip, expensive places in certain parts of town. Don't write a 2,500-word review if reviews top out at 350 words. Your safest choice for a review will be a new restaurant. But don't sweat it too much—the point is to impress an editor, who might give you an assignment for a new article if they see promise in your writing.

If you're going to a fine dining establishment, find out about the restaurant and chef, perhaps where the chef worked in the past, and who designed the restaurant, if design is relevant. Try to get a menu.

Regardless of which eatery you choose, your next decision is when to go. Reviews of dinner are standard, unless the restaurant relies on its biggest crowd at lunch. Monday and Tuesday are the most frequent chef's nights off. Friday and Saturday nights put the most stress on the kitchen.

(Consider these for your own research, but they're not things to tell readers.) Go for lunch and dinner, but not just for lunch.

As for how many people to take, there's no right answer. Reviewing can be distracting. It's hard to taste, observe, and simultaneously participate in the conversation around the table. When you go alone, it's easier to soak up atmosphere, experience, and energy level. On the other hand, you may hate dining alone, and the downside is that you can't sample very much food. You could try taking one person who understands that you're working. Old friends or colleagues may let you concentrate and feel comfortable about not talking when you need to think. Most important is to choose people who will eat anything, and who will not take offense at rabbit, offal, or sampling ducks' tongues during dim sum. Make sure your guests understand that you might ask them to order particular dishes, not necessarily the menu items they'd like most, so that you can taste broadly and select dishes the restaurant is known for.

The best reviewers visit each restaurant at least two times, sometimes three if the budget allows. If you go just once, you won't know enough to make decisions. Service, food quality, and atmosphere vary. One night service might be exceptional, and another night your waiter may be taking a smoke break while you're waiting for the bill. Going multiple times helps you understand and more accurately gauge the spirit of the place. Another reason to go back is to sample more food. Sometimes you'll taste the risotto Milanese twice to see if it has improved or if it really is as spectacular as it was the first time. Or you decide you need more dishes to get a balance between grilled, baked, sautéed, and roasted dishes.

By now you're probably breaking out in a sweat, anticipating your next credit card statement. Cost can be a problem. Will you be reimbursed? The short answer is: it depends. If you send unsolicited reviews to a newspaper, you foot the bill. If you've been given an assignment, you'll probably be paid something. Later in this chapter you'll read more specifics about finances and payment.

Restaurant Checklist

Whether you're writing a print or online review, you'll look at a review from many angles when you get to the restaurant. Frank Bruni says in *Born Round* that when he spoke with his editors about taking the job, they discussed "the ways in which restaurants were about much more than food—they were theatres, social laboratories, microcosms of their neighborhoods and their moments—and the ways in which a broad spectrum of journalistic experiences might help a critic capture that."

Let's start with an extensive list of questions to ask yourself. All questions may not be relevant, and some are more important than others. Questions about food are always paramount.

At the beginning. How are you treated when you make a reservation over the phone and when you arrive at the door? Do you feel welcomed? Perhaps you can arrive a few minutes early and take in the scene. How full is the restaurant? Are diners enjoying themselves? Are diners getting similar-looking food and service at each table?

The service. Your waiter should be knowledgeable about the food and willing to find answers to questions you have or solutions to problems. Is your waiter attentive, overly chatty, or someone with an attitude? Do servers wait until you're finished before removing your plate, or do they let plates gather on the table? Does the waiter check in a few times? Are you told if your food is delayed? While you can complain to see how the waiter responds, your main job is to keep a low profile and not attract attention to yourself. How is the service at other tables? Do they get their food before you do, if seated at the same time or later?

The menu. Use it to examine the philosophy of the chef and restaurant. It's a good way to understand chefs' intentions, how courses flow, which flavors are important, whether seasonality is an issue, and the way they put flavors and colors together. Notice how categories are balanced. Is the menu pretentious, with too many foreign words not explained? Are the prices reasonable, given the surroundings and service? If it's an upscale restaurant, it might present a new menu every day, so you might not want to focus exclusively on particular dishes because they might disappear. If it's a corner family place, the menu may not have changed for years.

Evaluate the wine list and cocktails. Are the prices reasonable? Does the selection and presentation enhance the theme of the restaurant?

Does a waiter or sommelier help you select? Are they knowledgeable about the wines?

Ordering the food. Taste as much food as possible, particularly signature dishes. Often the menu will list which dishes are most popular, or the waiter will point them out if prompted. Bring guests, and taste their food. Choose a variety of dishes and courses, based on cooking techniques, ingredients, and styles.

Tasting the food. What is your gut reaction? Are flavors balanced and integrated? Is the dish exciting, fresh, or made with quality ingredients? Is it over-salted? Is it at the right temperature? Is the food visually appealing and properly cooked?

The ambiance. How does the setting and style compare to other restaurants of its kind? Are the tables large enough and not crammed together, and are the seats comfortable? Is it too noisy, or the music intrusive? What about the clientele? Does the restaurant appeal to a certain type, such as hipsters, couples, or business professionals? Would you take friends or family there to celebrate a birthday?

When you leave. How hard is it to get the check, and does someone acknowledge you when you leave? When you're out the door, what is your overall impression? Ask yourself whether you look forward to going back, why or why not, and whether you found dishes you can't wait to try again. What were the strongest and weakest aspects of the evening?

You're probably wondering how to remember it all. You can't, at first. Even the best critics had trouble initially. Bauer says he had the overwhelming feeling that he had to know everything, get it all down, recognize every ingredient in a dish, and react. "The first two years I was a basket case," he admits. "I didn't take notes—I had to remember. Talk about not having fun. I practically had an ulcer." Fortunately, his anxiety didn't last. Now he can have a good time and recall what's most important. "You don't have to remember every nuance of every dish," he advises. "Learn what you need to know. Let the other stuff go."

It's a good idea to take notes, but not at the table, because you won't want the restaurant staff to discover you. A notebook small enough to fit in your purse or pocket is a great place to assemble your impressions, preferably in a restroom stall or outside, after your meal. Or audio record your thoughts after leaving the restaurant, perhaps in the car. Bruni says he used his phone to send text messages to himself or stepped into the bathroom to call himself and give dictation into his voice mailbox.

If the menu is a daily printout, don't feel too guilty about stealing it. Later it will come in handy when you can't remember the name or ingredients of a particular dish, or when you want to evaluate the types of food presented. If you don't get a printed menu, most bigger restaurants post their menus on their websites.

Writing a Good Review

Good reviews are honest and fair, exercise good judgment, and are authoritative and accurate. Honesty is critical because it applies even if your friends love a place but you don't. If you're objective, you'll be less likely to get caught up in the romance, like claims that Fred's Breakfast Nook has been making the best pancakes for fifty years. Does the restaurant follow through on its promise? It's your job to find out.

Get to know your own prejudices and beliefs. Try to keep your "personal pollution" out of the decision, advises Dara Moskowitz Grumdahl, restaurant critic for *Mpls.St.Paul Magazine*. Bauer doesn't like sweet sauces, for example, and says so if he's reviewing that kind of dish.

Personal beliefs can become a problem if, say, you conclude the food didn't justify the high prices at a steak house. Could it be because you think steak shouldn't cost more than $25? If so, reveal your prejudice in the name of fairness. Ask yourself why you loved a dish. Is it because you love moussaka, or is it the way the chef prepared it, by doing something special?

Your goal is not to suggest how the chef might improve the food, because diners, not chefs, are your readers.

What About Negative Reviews?

Negative reviews are extremely rare. Publications don't like them, and so many writers believe that if they say anything that's not positive in a review, the review is negative. It just isn't so. That's an extreme point of view.

Think about the people who save up for a meal out, says Sietsema, who are counting on you to tell them the truth. You don't have to be cruel or take cheap shots. You just have to tell them the truth, from your point of view.

There's an unwritten rule in reviewing: critics are harder on expensive restaurants, because a costly place takes a bigger bite out of readers' wallets. High-profile restaurants can take the hit, compared to a small neighborhood place that will suffer. As former *Gourmet* magazine editor in chief Ruth Reichl once said, "When a restaurant charges twenty-five dollars for a bowl of turnip soup, pleasant is not enough."

What do you do when the food is uneven? Bauer once dealt with this issue by writing that a restaurant made "two dishes well and the rest not so well." Readers told him they went anyway, ordered the items he liked, and left happy. The restaurant met their needs. Sometimes everyone else at the restaurant is enjoying the signature salad with blueberries and pine nuts, but you don't like it. In that case, you say just that and explain why.

I like reviewers who use humor to make a negative comment more entertaining. Alan Richman loves a line he once read in a review of a Chinese restaurant: "The hot and sour soup only had to be one or the other." Here's Gold, writing about skewered coins of bull penis with a wincing simile, "It doesn't taste like much, this bull penis, pretty much just cartilage and char, but the spectacle is as emasculating as a Jonas Brothers CD."

In the end, restaurant reviewing is the most subjective form of criticism in the world today, asserts Richman. "There are no standards for how food tastes. Everything stems from the taste buds and taste memory of the reviewer." Most of the time, a restaurant is neither very good nor very bad. Your job is to see the shades of grey. Reviewers also wrestle with the issue of whether liking the food is the same as the food being good. It's your job to separate these two things and reconcile them, because you have to have an opinion.

Characteristics of a Great Reviewer

Great reviewers have passion, knowledge, authority, a great writing style, and stamina. They write intelligently, from a frame of reference established through years of loving food. They discern quality, ferret out pretentiousness, acknowledge flavors that don't go together, and can point to why a dish works. They give the reader a feel for the place, its rhythm and overall vibe. And they keep up their energy level and enthusiasm.

Passion is paramount. In Gael Greene's memoir *Insatiable: Tales from a Life of Delicious Excess*, she writes at the end, "I fully expect to go on eating and critiquing forever and that on my deathbed my last words will echo those of Brillat-Savarin's sister, who cried, 'Bring on dessert. I'm about to die.'" Alan Richman, after many years of reviewing, says he can't wait to see what a restaurant has in store for him. "I get a hop in my step," he enthuses.

He's also incredibly knowledgeable. You need a deep understanding of your subject to succeed. You already have experience dining in restaurants, you know and love food, and you probably love cooking. From there, you could increase your skill level by taking cooking classes. To understand the dishes at high-end restaurants, I twice took an eleven-week class in French cooking basics, repeating the course to understand the underlying principles and techniques of formally trained chefs.

Ruth Reichl suggests you train yourself. "There's not a school to go to," she said in an interview. "Work in restaurants for a while. Get a lot of experience. [A. J.] Liebling was oversimplifying when he said, 'The primary requisite for writing well about food is a good appetite.' That's not enough. You need to have a lot of experience. You need to bite off as much of the world as you can. Travel. It probably means not getting entangled with too many responsibilities."

Reviewers also thrive on research about food and trends. Do you devour cookbooks, food dictionaries, blogs, and specialty websites? Do you know the food scene in your town? Do you love to find unfamiliar raw ingredients in specialty groceries? Do you enjoy tasting the food of other regions or countries when you travel? Do you consult authorities when you have a question about tofu skins or a particular braising technique?

Critics understand and appreciate other people's cultures, even if they aren't experts in the cuisine. Education and research are particularly important when reviewing restaurants featuring cuisine you're unfamiliar with, where you learn how to approach it and what to look for in its elements. Some reviewers take along natives or experts in that specific cuisine, such as people who have cooked a particular food all their lives, or cookbook authors.

Cuisines of other countries are more accessible in the United States than ever before, and reviewers have to step up to the plate. "If you're going to review Japanese, Peruvian, Indian, Malaysian restaurants, you really need to have been to those countries and to have seriously studied what their food is supposed to do," said Reichl in an interview. "It's not enough to do it from a Western orientation anymore. You're dealing with a very knowledgeable public, and you can't be in the situation where the people you're writing for know more about the food that you're writing about than you do." She has called a consulate or embassy to see if an employee can accompany her to a restaurant to explain the food. At one publication, the art director was Korean and grew up eating Korean food, so Reichl took her to Korean restaurants.

No matter what challenges critics face, the best ones are excellent writers and storytellers. Jonathan Gold is a master of evocative detail. In a massive restaurant roundup for *Travel & Leisure*, he wrote of a Chicago steak house as "a battered old place under the El with blood-rare strip steaks the size of catcher's mitts, baked potatoes the size of footballs, and the best martinis in the world. Beefy, happy men tuck into huge platters of garbage salad—a time-honored Chicago thing not unlike a great antipasto run through a paper shredder—and croissant-size shrimp with cocktail sauce." Can't you just see it? He's given you evocative visual information on the place, the food, and the diners in two sentences.

Most reviews follow a similar format, and when you have to write within this format all the time, it can be challenging: they describe the setting, what's on the menu, the prices, the service, and the ambiance. Then they go into the appetizers, entrées, and dessert. The worst are the "bite-by-bite" reviews where people just go through the meal, describing everything they had, says Mary Margaret Pack, food writer for the *Austin Chronicle*. For variety, the *Post*'s Sietsema employs action, such as what people at the next table are saying and whether they're enjoying their food. Critics at alternative newspapers have the most freedom to mix it up by adding personal details.

As you can see, voice is an important part of reviewing. While it's not something you can fake, it's helpful to define it so your reviews are consistent. When I started out, I read the reviews of writers I admired to let their styles sink in. I tore out pieces I loved, particularly those with beautiful or witty writing, and collected them in a file. Luckily, Gold collected his in a book called *Counter Intelligence: Where to Eat in the Real Los Angeles*. A former music writer for *Rolling Stone*, he wrote reviews of neighborhood places for L.A. *Weekly* that are funny, irreverent, passionate, insightful, knowledgeable, and filled with witty references.

What about actually describing the food? The best reviewers use specific, evocative language. Three of the laziest adjectives I know are "nice," "wonderful," and "delicious." Most of us have resorted to them at times. They are so vague that readers don't know what you mean, other than something positive. It's harder to develop a taste lexicon, but a developed vocabulary is critical to being a successful food writer, particularly when you have to describe what's on your plate. "What surprised me the most is how hard it is," says Pack. "I read other reviews and see people struggling with the same kinds of things I do with the language." Which word makes her cringe most? "Unctuous."

• •

HOW WELL CAN YOU DESCRIBE FOOD?

This list certainly isn't exhaustive, but it gives an idea of specific language. Use these words sparingly. If you want more, read reviews, circle the words you like, and compile your own list.

TASTE AND SMELL:

acrid	cooling	peppery
bland	fruity	perfumed
buttery	herbal	piquant
bright	mellow	robust
briny	nutty	

TEXTURE:

brittle	foamy	slippery
chewy	gelatinous	velvety
crisp	silky	

APPEARANCE:

blanketed	melted	sprinkled
caramelized	mottled	stuffed
crumbled	murky	syrupy
crusty	plump	tired
drowned	sheared	trembling

lackluster	shiny	wet
leafy	smeared	wimpy
limp	spice-dusted	

SOUND.

| bubbling | fizzy | sizzling |
| crackling | popping | sputtering |

OTHERS:

alluring	denuded	liberal
comforting	dispirited	satisfying
complemented	impeccable	

••

Ruth Reichl, in an interview, reminds us that writing about food isn't just based on describing it. "One of the things I was lucky to learn early on is that you can't describe flavor, but you can put someone into a space where they can understand what you're talking about. If you really think hard and you try to imagine what the flavor is, if you hold it in your mouth and your mind for long enough, you can make other people experience that taste. You don't do it by saying, 'It's salty, it's sweet, it's citric.' You have to paint a picture."

Two loaded words I avoided using in restaurant reviews are "expensive" and "authentic." If a publication rates restaurants by price, such as inexpensive, moderate, and expensive, and gives a range in its rating system, then readers will know what "expensive" means. Otherwise it is undefined, leaving readers to wonder. The word "authentic" has pitfalls as well. My husband loves pad Thai, and ordered it often when we traveled in Thailand. Each restaurant served the noodles differently, even inside a thin egg omelet. Which is authentic? After all, the name means something like "fried Thai-style."

Once you've left the restaurant, if you didn't ask your waiter about certain dishes and you still have questions, it's acceptable to call the restaurant and identify yourself. If you're not sure about the hint of ginger in the tomato sauce, ask about the ingredients. Ask how the chef made the chicken taste so good. He might tell you he brined the meat for two days. (Ruth Reichl wouldn't agree with my suggestion, however. She says the last thing you want is a restaurateur saying, "She didn't know what she was eating; she had to call!")

When you're done with your piece, double-check all dates, name spellings, the address, telephone number, and hours. It's not a pain. It's part of your job, and better than getting a call from an irritated editor who just found out that you spelled the restaurant owner's name wrong. That happened to me.

The last characteristic of a good reviewer is stamina. You may have to sample the same dishes. "How many crème brûlées have I tasted in the last two years?" moans Grumdahl. "A thousand? But other people have only ordered them five times in their lives, and they're excited about them. What keeps me going is their right to have a good anniversary dinner." And you have to decide how much to eat. To quote Jane Stern, who with her husband, Michael, co-authored *Roadfood: The Coast to Coast Guide to 700 of the Best Barbeque Joints, Lobster Shacks, Ice Cream Parlors, Highway Diners, and Much More*, "We take a bite and if it sucks, we don't wait around for it to get better." I taste everything, but don't try to eat it all. That's why God made doggie bags.

How to Find That Great Undiscovered Restaurant

In addition to the coup of being the first to cover a new restaurant, good writers always look for the finds. Some reviewers look on Yelp and social media. Some ask cabdrivers and waitstaff where they eat. Some walk around town, see an interesting menu in a window, and check out the place. Once you're known for writing about restaurants, you'll get all kinds of recommendations, particularly if you focus on niche restaurants, such as vegan or Asian. But that doesn't mean they're worth writing about. You have to check them out.

Educating the Palate

This question gets to the crux of why so many food bloggers and writers think they cannot pass judgment (yet they do, by simply writing about a place). They don't think they're qualified.

Some reviewers think the ability to taste is an innate skill: people are born loving food and having a strong interest in it. Former *New York*

Times writer Mimi Sheraton says, "Taste is a matter of experience that varies widely with age, ethnic background, locale and era." And some think it can be taught. A good palate may have physical aspects and a different arrangement of taste buds that affect the experience of flavors. Cilantro, for example, affects people differently: they either love it or hate it.

Some reviewers say you don't have to be an expert to understand how something should taste. If you taste a sauce, for example, it's enough to get a sense of whether it tastes good, or whether flavors are discordant or lack proportion.

When I asked Gold about educating the palate, he was of two minds when it comes to many food writers, particularly bloggers. "Chances are pretty good that a food blogger isn't qualified to write criticism. (I hate the word 'critique')," he wrote me in an email.

"Real criticism tends to require a lot of work; the ability not just to describe food, but to contextualize it, and to make it sing. Restaurant criticism should be no less rigorous than any other kind of criticism—there is a lot of homework involved—and as food writers our standards should be no lower than those of our colleagues who review novels or the opera. Authority is dearly earned and easily lost.

"But in some important ways, your experience at a restaurant is as valid as anybody else's. You ate the avocado toast, you negotiated the glass of biodynamic Malbec, you were forgotten by your waiter when Keanu Reeves sat down at the next table. Nobody else had quite the experience you had that afternoon, and nobody will ever have it again. It's yours. I would suggest that you report the meal as a narrative rather than as a review, at least until you get the hang of the form, and that you refrain from implying expertise that you may not yet possess, but go ahead and write.

"The greatest tool in the toolbox is—as a critic of anything—your job is to basically, at least on a world historical scale, know more about the restaurants you're going to than even the people doing it," he told Eater.com. "You know why they're doing things. Even if not specifically, you know why on a historical scale they're doing things. You . . . taste dishes with the allusions to things, and you know what they're alluding to. You're coming across a dish, like a standard from new Nordic cooking or an elBulli thing, and your job is to know what that is. In the day of the Internet, it's even more important."

Bauer took the rare step of formally training his palate early in his career. He met his mentor, cooking instructor and author Madeleine Kamman, while working for a Dallas newspaper. He went to her cooking schools in New Hampshire and France, and then traveled around France with her for three weeks. "She really taught me how to taste sauces," recalls Bauer. "She would say, 'Can't you taste the carrot in that sauce?' We'd break it down. I had some really intense dining experiences."

If You Haven't Worked in a Restaurant
or Been to Culinary School

You may think you have to go to culinary school to understand the palate, but only a tiny percentage of food writers have experience in the culinary profession. This fact bothers some chefs, who ask how reviewers are able to judge food and restaurants without having been a chef or waiter.

But a reviewer's job is to advocate for the consumer, to represent the person who's spending the money. Most diners have not been chefs or waiters. They just want to know if they'll have a good dining experience and how much it will cost.

Restaurant experience can have its downside. As a reviewer, you can't feel sympathetic and take the restaurant's side when something goes wrong, and you might become obsessed with technique and focus too much on how the food should be made, rather than communicating your impressions of the final product and the restaurant. And if you know the chef, or have chef friends, it will be difficult to be critical.

"An eminent food journalist needs to be a master chef no more than a connoisseur of Bach needs be expected to perform the composer's preludes and fugues with immaculate precision," states James Villas, former editor of *Town and Country*.

Many reviewers don't cook, either. "Although I do not believe that one has to know how to cook to be a reliable restaurant critic, the knowledge certainly helps a critic to describe food convincingly and explain where it fails or succeeds," writes Sheraton in her memoir, *Eating My Words: An Appetite for Life*. "It is, however, no more necessary to cook well than for a drama, dance, or art critic to perform or paint."

Must Reviewers Be Anonymous to Be Effective?

The most powerful reviewers will still say yes to this question, even though bloggers rarely bother. Most feel that to truly represent readers, no one at the restaurant should know who you are. It's impossible to write an objective review if restaurants know you're coming or recognize you. They will not treat you the same way they treat other diners. You will get special attention, more food, and dishes that have been fussed over.

Some writers announce themselves so they can get the best table and service, and expect a free meal. Any of these behaviors signals you can be influenced or bought. Is that the reputation you want?

It's easy to be anonymous when you first start out. Your first year will be fine, because people don't know what you look like, and if you pay cash or use a credit card in someone else's name, you're safe. Eventually, however, if you persevere as a critic, you're likely to be recognized because waiters who spotted you once at one restaurant can change jobs and spot you at the new place. When this happens, you have to play it cool. Realistically, the restaurant can't do much except hover, send over too many waiters, or send over too much food.

Perhaps the most famous written account of being recognized appeared in Ruth Reichl's early critique of Le Cirque, a snobby New York restaurant, in the *New York Times*. The first part described her shabby treatment as an unidentified diner, and the second detailed what happened when the owner identified her: "Over the course of five months I ate five meals at the restaurant; it was not until the fourth that the owner, Sirio Maccioni, figured out who I was. When I was discovered, the change was startling. Everything improved: the seating, the service, the size of the portions. We had already reached dessert, but our little plate of petit fours was whisked away to be replaced by a larger, more ostentatious one."

Serious critics take steps to disguise themselves. They make reservations in another name, pay cash, or use credit cards with someone else's name. They call from outside the office because many restaurants now have caller ID. They wait until their guests sit down before arriving at the table, sometimes through a back door. They don't go to functions attended by restaurateurs and chefs, such as a restaurant grand opening, anniversary dinner, or wine tasting, where they could be recognized. Once you start reviewing, you will likely receive invitations to events like these. While they are tempting, decline them.

Many critics are surprised to learn how restaurants collaborated to identify them. Today, the Internet makes it that much more difficult to be anonymous.

Some people in the food community question whether disguises work. I've talked to restaurant owners and chefs who say they can recognize reviewers based on how much food they order and whether they taste the food of others at their table. In truth, many critics have been reviewing restaurants in the same city for several years, and perhaps they are recognized more than they would like.

In that vein, some reviewers have dropped their anonymity. Leslie Brenner, the dining critic of the *Dallas Morning News,* dropped hers in 2014, quoting from *New York* magazine critic Adam Platt, who dropped his the year before and allowed his face to appear on the magazine's cover. He said it was a "dated charade," but added he would not change his routine, such as booking under a pseudonym, because "the art of surprise has always been the critic's most useful tool."

If you're writing a blog, it's hard to be anonymous if you have the added complication of taking photos. I hope you won't set off a flash every few minutes in a darkened restaurant. Better restaurants don't allow flash photography, finding them a distraction to other diners. Go early enough to capture available light, sitting by the window.

Are Top Ten Stories and Roundups Reviews?

Yes. Articles such as "The Ten Best Places to Get a Cheesesteak in Philadelphia" qualify as reviews, because the author is critiquing and making decisions. These pieces are standards of many newspapers and magazines, and good ones to pitch.

How to Get Published

Now that you've absorbed the details of restaurant reviewing, you might be raring to go for a print publication. The first step is to be realistic. You're not going to break into a daily paper right away, where established reviewers fill the pages. Start small: either target neighborhood papers, or start a blog (see Chapter 4).

There's no disgrace in being published in small publications. Begin by collecting the local newspapers and magazines in your community. Find them at newsstands, cafés, clubs, coffeehouses, and libraries. Look online to find past reviews. Look through a few months of each publication to see what kind of articles they like. Make a pile of the ones that don't publish reviews and prioritize them, starting with the smallest. Maybe they'd start running reviews if they found someone good.

How do you get your foot in the door with an editor? You might call the paper, talk to an editor, and make a personal connection. The editor might give out tips about where to start. But that's unlikely. First, editors don't have time to chat with strangers, and few will encourage someone unknown to submit a review. Second, they don't know what kind of standards you apply to the food you review, and whether you've written false statements that make the publication liable for lawsuits. If they're going to give anyone a trial assignment, it's probably a person they know who has already demonstrated knowledge of food. It's not a great idea to cold-call an editor, unless you're lucky and you know someone on the inside who can ask them to take your call or talk with you in person for a few minutes.

The other way to go is to write one or two reviews for your target publication or website, emulating the style, tone, and word count, just to see how you like the experience. Write to the publication's audience. If you wish, submit your work with a cover letter explaining your passion and qualifications. If you have already been published and can attach clips, you're one step ahead.

You might do better with a related story, like a roundup. Check other media around town for ideas, or brainstorm with a friend (see Chapter 5 on freelancing). Use other kinds of pieces to prove that you know how to write and are knowledgeable about food.

If an editor eventually assigns you a review, it's time to ask practical questions. Find out if the paper will support you if the review is negative. Do they have an opinion about reviewing restaurants that also advertise in the publication?

Lastly, you might write your own guidebook to the city's restaurants. Many people have done so and done well. See more about writing guidebooks on page 218.

••

WHO PUBLISHES RESTAURANT REVIEWS?

Besides daily newspapers, here's a list of publications and sites that take reviews:

- weekly (alternative) and free newspapers
- regional magazines
- city magazines
- travel guidebooks
- city tourist information
- theater programs
- airline magazines
- Eater.com

Study these sources to see how reviews are written in terms of style, structure, length, and content. Look at the publication's masthead to see if the critic is on staff or a freelancer. Contact the appropriate editor to find out how he or she acquires reviews. Perhaps they are assigned, or perhaps the editor will take written queries or writing samples.

Write for the readers of that publication. Jonathan Gold, in an interview with Eater.com, said, "When I was at the *Weekly,* I figured that if I said something came with a sauce bordelaise, that I'd have to explain what it is. When I was at *Gourmet,* I didn't have to explain what a sauce bordelaise was, but if I made an allusion to Daft Punk, then I'd have to explain what that was. [Laughs] At the [*L.A.*] *Times,* maybe I slightly explain foreign word phrases more than I would. There are really good intelligent readers who read me every week, that won't necessarily know the difference between tonkatsu and tonkotsu. I think the worst thing you can do is write down to your readers."

Don't waste your skill on crowd-sourced free websites. Author Calvin Trillin jokes that the message is, "In a just world, I would be the restaurant critic of the *New York Times.* A bunch of phonies are actually doing this, but I am the one who knows."

••

About Payment

The eternal question of whether you can get paid for your work—this is an ongoing problem for freelance food writers. If an editor accepts your unsolicited piece, it's possible that the paper will not pay, or that they'll pay next to nothing, even if you get an assignment. If you write reviews for a guidebook for your city or an online restaurant guide, the pay might be a whopping $25 to $30 per restaurant. That's not much, but it's okay because you need published work to trade up to the bigger newspapers and magazines, which should at least pay for your reviews.

Nothing is standard when it comes to reimbursement for meals, despite a website guideline from the Association of Food Journalists that reviewers should not have to resort to "personal funds to help pay the bill." That's a subtle way of saying you probably won't be paid enough to cover all expenses plus your writing, even from the dailies.

If you get an assignment, ask lots of questions. Do they pay mileage, transportation fees, and parking? Are tips included in the meal reimbursement? How long will it take to get paid or reimbursed? This can be an issue if you get a credit card bill with fifteen restaurant meals on it, and you haven't received your check. Will the paper pay the late fee?

Grumdahl was initially paid $150 by an alternative weekly to write a two-thousand-word feature on one restaurant each week. She paid for the food out of that budget. That structure lasted two years, until the paper got more advertising and she became better known. You might be reimbursed for meals and visits to a restaurant and parking. Most publications don't pay for alcohol.

So if you love to dine out and tell people about your experience, this chapter has outlined ways for you to write about it, whether it's on your own blog, covering restaurant openings for a publication or website, or reviewing. People are dining out more than ever, and they need recommendations on where to go. The door is open to those who write well, educate themselves about all kinds of food, and develop a discerning palate.

Writing Exercises

1. Use adjectives sparingly. Write a 250-word review of the best restaurant meal you've eaten recently, using five descriptive words from the list on pages 146–147.
2. Overcome your leanings. Recall a dish you don't like that you ate anyway. Now write two paragraphs about your experience, as if you ate the dish at a restaurant and you know that many people love it. The goal is to acknowledge your own prejudices and overcome them for a publication's audience.
3. Do your research. Come up with a cuisine you've never had, and review a restaurant that serves it. Research the country's dishes and their origins and ingredients before visiting the restaurant, and then write the review.

7: THE COOKBOOK YOU'VE ALWAYS WANTED TO WRITE

There are many reasons to write a cookbook, or to keep writing them. You might love to entertain, create your own dishes, or be a paleo cook who's moving from her blog to a book. Successful cookbook writers begin with an enthusiasm for food that keeps them going and fuels their ability to come up with ideas for future books. The hard part is coming up with a book that excites both you and the outside world.

Notice I didn't say, "You want to get famous and make a lot of money." If that's your motivation, forget it. Writing a cookbook is too time-consuming to sustain such a notion for most. But if you're passionate, obsessed, and a good marketer, chances are that your cookbook will succeed.

It's easy to conjure up a first idea, but the first is not always the best. How to position or shape a book takes lots of pondering, research, and evaluating of pros and cons. You might change your opinion many times. Mulling it over is worthwhile. You can't write a worthwhile cookbook without a good idea, and you need to evaluate the competition to see if you have something new to say. This is true even if you want to self-publish.

This chapter will inspire you to shape your idea, think it through, and visualize the book you've always wanted to write, in terms of both subjects and eye appeal. It will tell you how to make a schedule, how to meet your deadline, and what kind of artwork to expect. Since I can't squeeze all the details on how to write a cookbook into one chapter, the following chapter tells you how to write recipes, the bulk of your book. For more on the literary aspects of cookbook writing, see page 165.

Once you have the idea for a publishable book, use it to pitch articles to newspaper and magazine editors to float your idea. If they publish the articles, it's a great sign that your cookbook idea has promise. It's also a way for you to establish expertise on your subject, which will impress an editor. How to get an article published is covered in Chapter 5.

Next you'll need to write a book proposal for an agent or editor, and with any luck, you'll get a contract. How to write a proposal, how to find an agent, and what to expect from a publisher are covered in Chapter 11. But you can't write a proposal without a good idea and an understanding of which cookbooks work and why, which is what this chapter is about.

Perhaps you want to self-publish an ebook, print book, or both. Even though most of the information in this chapter is geared toward traditional publishing, it will help you figure out your self-published book, too.

HOW THEY GOT STARTED

Everyone has to start somewhere, even successful cookbook authors. Here's how some of them began:

JULIE SAHNI. At a class on Chinese cooking, she told fellow students how she used a balti—an Indian wok—to cook at home. The students asked her to show them. She began teaching cooking classes and, from the recipes she developed, had the beginnings of her first cookbook, *Classic Indian Cooking*.

DEBORAH MADISON. A student of Zen Buddhism, she cooked at the San Francisco Zen Center and at Tassajara, a retreat in Big Sur, California. When the center opened Greens Restaurant, she became the chef there. The impetus for her first book, *The Greens Cookbook: Extraordinary Vegetarian Cuisine from the Celebrated Restaurant,* was to show customers who had requested recipes how to make the same quality dishes the restaurant served.

ANNE BYRN. A freelance food writer, she was a working mom who wanted to make great cupcakes for her kids but didn't have much time. She wrote a newspaper story about doctoring cake mixes and, based on the response, went on to publish *The Cake Mix Doctor.* The book has sold millions of copies.

DIANA KENNEDY. She arrived in Mexico in 1957 to join her future husband, a foreign correspondent for the *New York Times.* In 1969, at the suggestion of *Times* writer Craig Claiborne, she began teaching classes in Mexican cooking and in 1972 published her first cookbook.

MARTHA STEWART. She was a caterer in the Hamptons in Long Island, New York, before she became a lifestyle guru.

INA GARTEN. The author of the best-selling *The Barefoot Contessa Cookbook,* she also catered in the Hamptons, as did Julee Rosso and Sheila Lukins, authors of the Silver Palate series. (The three books in the Silver Palate series have sold several million copies.)

PAULA WOLFERT. She went to Morocco because her husband found employment there. Over the years, she became passionate about Mediterranean cooking, watching cooks in their homes and writing down their recipes. Today she's known as an authority on authentic Mediterranean food.

• •

What's a Good Cookbook Idea?

Agents and editors often give the same advice to someone who wants to write a cookbook: "You have to have something to say." That's true, but not very specific. They also say things like "Everyone reads, but not everybody writes. Everyone cooks, but not everyone can write a cookbook. It's harder than most people think." Agent Doe Coover told me that. Agents and editors are a tough group to impress, but hundreds of people have done it.

Let's get back to the good idea. Agent Lisa Ekus says she knows she's found one when she can't stop thinking about it. Typically, she reads incoming proposals once and puts them aside. "If I forget about it, it's not a book for me. If it lives with me and it excites me, I have to believe in the book, have a passion for the topic or writing, or think it's highly marketable."

Author Julie Sahni has more advice on what it takes to have a new idea: "A cookbook is more than a set of recipes. You have to have a message, a certain philosophy or technique or principle to pass on to the audience. It boils down to a simple concept: you know something more or something different than the reader. You have to inspire them."

What if you already have a cookbook idea? You've asked your friends and family if you should write your cookbook, and they've said yes. Friends and family are not as hard to please as agents and editors. The very first thing to do, when considering a cookbook, is to make sure you have a workable idea. The second is to scope out the competition. Here are my tests:

The book idea comes from your blog. Today, the easiest way to a book deal is to start your own blog and build a following of readers. Publishers are more dependent than ever on authors who not only know how to reach buyers of their book but also have tested their recipes on the public and may even be able to shoot their own photographs. They're signing food bloggers by the dozens. Read about blogging in Chapter 4.

You are passionate about the subject. As I've been saying, intense enthusiasm combined with knowledge is a powerful motivator. It's not enough to come up with a book idea, but if you communicate excitement, intensity, and knowledge in your writing, it can be contagious. Suzanne Rafer, executive editor at Workman Publishing Company, said in an interview that a potential author must ignite passion within her and successfully convey a creative spark and vision. Passion may be intangible, but editors and agents know it when they see it.

Martin Yan thrives on it. The author of several cookbooks, he travels extensively, teaching classes for consumers and chefs, taping television programs shown in fifty countries, and doing research for his cookbooks. "I love to capture some of the essence of individuals around the world and share my experience with people," he says. For one series and book, he targeted Chinatowns worldwide and interviewed chefs at the oldest and newest restaurants. He found families who had lived in each Chinatown for three to five generations and then asked the head of each household to walk with him and buy food for a meal. Yan went back to the family home, watched the cook in action, and shared the meal. "I see the entire picture of their life and heritage," he enthuses. "I am having a good time learning a lot of these things, which I may not experience again."

Laura Werlin was "seized by passion" when she decided to write her first book, *The New American Cheese*. She was a television assignment editor at a station in San Francisco when she decided to take classes on food writing. Eventually she narrowed down her food obsessions to artisan cheese from Northern California. When researching her topic, she discovered a national trend of artisan cheese production. "From that moment, I never looked back," says Werlin. She wrote a sixty-page proposal, got an agent and contract, quit her job, and wrote the entire book in three months.

"I had a very steep learning curve, having not written a book or recipe before. I probably did many things the hard way because I knew no other way. I never left my house other than to buy ingredients. I would write until ten p.m. On weekends, I sent my husband to a movie, and then I'd meet him at ten for a late dinner. I had never been an A-type personality until then." Both this book and her second, *The All American Cheese and Wine Book,* won national awards.

The subject is timely. This is tricky, because few successful cookbook authors actually study trends before writing their books. It's more likely they have good timing because they read widely and talk with other people who love food. When freelance food writer Anne Byrn made a batch of doctored cake-mix cupcakes for her kids and wrote a story about it for a newspaper, the paper added a sentence asking readers to send in their own cake-mix recipes and received five hundred responses in one week.

"The light bulb didn't go on instantly," Byrn admits. She wrote a follow-up story featuring six people who had sent in their favorite recipes. By then, Byrn had a hunch. Just to make sure it wasn't some kind of regional trend (Byrn lives in the South), she called six newspaper food editors across the country and asked whether readers requested cake-mix recipes regularly. All said yes, particularly for favorites such as the Better than Sex Cake. Byrn wrote her book and then wrote more. *The Cake Mix Doctor, Chocolate from the Cake Mix Doctor,* and *The Dinner Doctor* have sold several million copies.

This book was a departure for Byrn, a former newspaper editor who wrote restaurant reviews and traveled to Paris. "I have been such a food snob in my past," she admits. "But I live in a different world now, and I have three children. Big deal if I use a Duncan Hines mix." There have been consequences. Certain newspapers will not interview her. Nevertheless, says Byrn, "I wrote this book for mass Middle America, which I feel very much a part of. I'm not ashamed of that, and I do not live in Manhattan."

Alice Medrich capitalized on a trend as well, sharing her obsession with chocolate in five cookbooks, the majority of which won national awards. An obsessive recipe developer, she writes of her desire to share tools she created for herself, so that readers can "experiment and convert recipes with ease and understanding."

Some authors keep up with timely topics. "Developing salable ideas is not the same as just coming up with ideas," said author Nancy Baggett. "Salability involves meshing what I'm interested in and capable of writing about with what I, and hopefully cookbook editors, think the public might buy." She keeps up on new cookbooks; reads food blogs, food magazines, and newspaper sections; and follows trends and topics surfacing in the national media.

Agents and cookbook editors keep up with trends as well. The quick and easy trend, for example, is not going away. People still don't have a lot of time. Nor is the interest in dieting cookbooks, or those on special diets, going away.

Where you have to be careful, however, is when several ideas for the same book start floating around all at once. At least six cookbooks on mac and cheese came out in 2012, preceded by more than a dozen cookbooks on baking macaroons, and a half dozen books on Popsicles and other frozen treats. They can't all do well simultaneously.

The idea is in your area of expertise. Werlin and Byrn were not experts when they started their first book, but both became well versed on their subjects in a hurry. Medrich, by contrast, was already a chocolate expert and owner of a Berkeley chocolate store when an agent approached her to write a book. The best authors strive to develop in-depth knowledge of their subject. Even before they write books, they research extensively and write articles about their subject of expertise. They might also speak on the subject and hold cooking classes.

What, exactly, qualifies you as an expert? Let's say you have cooked Sicilian food for years. The recipes were handed down from your mother's side of the family. You might be an expert if, in addition to knowing family recipes, you devour all the information you can find about Sicilian cooking; speak Italian; travel to Sicily to watch people cook; write recipes on Sicilian food published in magazines, in newspaper articles, or on your own blog; or give talks about it.

Steven Raichlen, whose barbecue and grill books have sold millions of copies, said in a newsletter interview that branding himself as a barbecue and grilling expert has helped make a name for himself and build his identity in the food world. "What I've done now that I hadn't done before is focus all my energies on a particular specialty. Of course, the trick is finding a sufficiently broad and deep topic to explore to keep you interested for many years and that has the potential to reach lots of other enthusiasts."

Paula Wolfert has been relentlessly passionate about authentic Mediterranean food since her first cookbook on Moroccan food was published in 1972. It calls for a dessert with hashish seeds. She justified the recipe to her editor by arguing none of the other Moroccan cookbooks had it. Wolfert is one of a handful of successful authors who took an anthropological approach to further her expertise. She explored villages across the Mediterranean, met with women there, and asks them to introduce her to the best cooks. Sometimes she moved in with cooks so she can observe and take notes. "She has knocked on hundreds of back doors in obscure towns, searching for the cook who best executes a particular dish," wrote Peggy Knickerbocker in a profile of Wolfert in *Saveur*.

Wolfert even dealt with recipes in languages she doesn't know by developing a network of people who translate recipes from abroad. She also brought cookbooks in other languages to the United States and has people translate them for her.

If you don't have an area of expertise, claim one. Start a blog about your particular passion. It worked for several bloggers, including Clotilde Dusoulier of ChocolateandZucchini.com and Shauna James Ahern of GlutenFreeGirl.blogspot.com. Once they gained an impressive audience, agents and editors were interested. Ahern won a James Beard award for one of her cookbooks.

David Leite of LeitesCulinaria.com chose Portuguese cooking as his specialty, since it was his heritage. In *The New Portuguese Table*, he chronicled the Portuguese dishes disappearing from his family's dinner tables as older family members died. His book won a Julia Child First Book Award from the International Association of Culinary Professionals.

How long does it take to become an expert? That's up to you and how much time you spend thinking, blogging, researching, traveling, and testing recipes. W. W. Norton vice president and senior editor Maria Guarnaschelli, who edits cookbooks, takes the long-term approach. "Lynne Rossetto Kasper [*The Splendid Table*] and Rose Levy Beranbaum [*The Bread Bible*] were in their fifties when they wrote their books," she says. "Isn't an important work your life's work? In the end it will pay off."

Your idea is well focused. Lack of focus keeps many potential authors from moving forward. If you imagine a book that has to contain everything you've cooked that's good, you might put off doing it forever. Writing becomes an overwhelming topic. If you're in love with everything from apples to zabaglione, it's hard to decide what to leave out and what to leave in.

Examine your idea. Is it too general? Is it all about a topic? Think about how you would describe your cookbook to others. When you can form your description into a single sentence, you're much closer. Hone in on the most important subjects for readers, and make a list of points you wish to convey. Then whittle down the subject until it is specific and cohesive. Don't be afraid to discard. Throwing away can be liberating. Keep the ideas you've discarded in a file. You might want them someday for another book. (For example, a book on Mediterranean desserts might follow a book on Mediterranean main courses.)

You can be passionate about muffins, explains author Deborah Madison, but ask yourself why they're special to you, why muffins matter. "What is the story? Whom will it delight?" she asks. "Maybe it's stories about family, or maybe you add quick breads, and a book emerges." You could also narrow the idea and make it more specific, such as muffins that are paleo, sugar-free, or healthy.

Madison's enormous reference work, *Vegetarian Cooking for Everyone*, needed lots of forethought on structure and content. The book idea came into Madison's consciousness after teaching a weeklong class on vegetarian cooking at Esalen in Big Sur, California. While there, she realized it was a shame that there was no vegetarian *Joy of Cooking* in which vegetarians could find everything they needed in one place. She decided to write that book.

Even so, it was not "all about" vegetarian cooking. "It took a year just to come up with the table of contents," she recalls. She had to define the scope of the book and make decisions. Should it include breakfast foods, or breads, or recipes already widely available, such as hummus? She wondered what people would expect, whether to include sandwiches. "I had to become educated," she explains. "I was reading, thinking, and it changed as it went along." This new book was not personal like her prior cookbook, *The Savory Way*. "I wanted to make it a friendly guide for people I didn't know." It took six years to write, contains around one thousand recipes, and won a national award. Her new edition came out in 2014, with two hundred new recipes.

Single-subject books are tightly written books about one ingredient, piece of equipment, or type of dish. Author James McNair developed a reputation as king of the single-subject cookbook. In 1984, he launched his first book, *Cold Pasta*, and followed it with about thirty more books on subjects such as cheese, chicken, fish, pie, corn, and custards, all with gorgeous full-color photos.

Focus becomes an issue when you research your competition. If you want to write a book on Asian noodles and five books already exist, you'll have to change or narrow your focus to succeed. For more on evaluating competition, see page 252.

You love to tell stories. While publishers once thought of cookbooks as strictly how-to books, today they find it likely that cookbooks will be read rather than used for cooking. Time limitations and changing eating habits mean that the average number of recipes readers try in a cookbook could be as low as two. Think of your own cookbook collection. You may not have made any recipes in many, but it doesn't make them any less valuable.

Many people read cookbooks in bed as though they were novels. They provide escape from daily life and a source of guiltless pleasure. With longer stories and full-color photography, cookbooks can take you on a travel adventure, allow you to enter a foreign land, whet your appetite for exotic ingredients, tell the history of a country, and let you imagine a pleasurable dinner party you'll give someday.

That's what makes cookbooks different from just looking up an online recipe, and why they keep selling. Cookbooks put recipes in context, and present a whole to you, with ancillary information usually not included on a website.

The literary aspects of food writing can bring new excitement to a book. Joan Nathan authored *Foods of Israel Today*, an ambitious look at the diverse cultural and culinary lineage of Israel. She said that after senior editor Judith Jones of Knopf edited her book, she asked Nathan to take her and her stepdaughter to the Holy Land. "I introduced her to my Israel," says Nathan. "It was about a week before the Intifada. I had written about a village of vegetarians I'd heard about but had never been to, and Judith was very taken with the idea. We took a cab. Here we were, three women wandering around a Palestinian village." How's that for a testimony to skilled storytelling and writing? Your own editor is so fascinated by your work she wants to see the place.

You have a new approach. "If I hear there are too many books about Italy, yes, there are, but if you have something new to say about Italy, don't let it stop you," says editor Guarnaschelli. Americans are so in love with Italian cookbooks that they often command their own bookshelf in bookstores. Guarnaschelli worked with Lynne Rossetto Kasper on *The Splendid Table: Recipes from Emilia-Romagna, the Heartland of Northern Italian Food* in 1992. At that time, "no one thought anyone would be interested in the Emilia-Romagna area of Italy," she recalls. "They couldn't even pronounce it. Even I wasn't sure about using the name in the title." But they went with it. The book won awards and remains in print, and Kasper has a national radio show of the same name.

A Man, a Can, a Plan: 50 Great Guy Meals Even You Can Make takes an unusual twist on men's cooking. Printed on heavy paper and coated like a children's book so it won't stain, this book gives the not-so-subtle hint that men are like children when it comes to cooking. Recipes have photos of actual cans with plus signs between them. Are the recipes in the book unusual? No. But its unique differentiation, or positioning, succeeds. The book has been particularly successful among college students, author David Joachim told me, and has led to three more books based on a microwave, a grill, and a tailgate.

Your idea has potential as a series. Agents and publishers like to envision a long stream of revenue from you over the years, and for that matter, so might you. A series sounds like an easy idea, but today's publishers are the ones producing most collections, and they might hire a different writer to write each book.

Chuck and Blanche Johnson took a different approach and self-published their Savor Cookbook series under their own imprint, Wilderness Adventures Press. Their full-color books feature independent restaurants' stories, histories, and recipes, and have been sold in Costco stores.

A related point is that some bloggers have developed series on their blogs, and those series have lead to book ideas. Winnie Abramson, for example, started a regular section, "One Simple Change," on her blog, HealthyGreenKitchen.com. It's about making small changes for health and happiness, with many good points and observations. An editor at Chronicle Books found the series and suggested Abrahamson write a book based on it. Ashley Rodriguez blogs at NotWithoutSalt.com. She started a series called "Dating My Husband," in which she writes about her marriage and how she and her husband connect, and includes a recipe. Her book, *Date Night In: More than 120 Recipes to Nourish Your Relationship*, came out in 2014, just before Valentine's Day.

A large, well-defined audience will be interested in your book. Publishers want you to define exactly who will buy your book so they can sell to that audience. In the earlier example of a muffin book, you could slice your audience many ways. If the recipes have six ingredients or fewer and can be made in ten minutes, busy parents might snap up the book. If the muffins are gluten-free, you've targeted readers concerned about their health. If your idea is simply "All About Muffins," however, the audience is much harder to define. Who are these people who like muffins? Unless it's a major trend, it's impossible to know.

As mentioned earlier, if you have built up a large, well-defined audience for your blog, chances are good that an agent or publisher will be interested in a cookbook. If your blog is about gluten-free cooking, and you want to write a book about gardening, all bets are off. But if you're Ree Drummond, who has a huge, loyal blog readership (ThePioneer Woman.com/cooking), you can write *The Pioneer Woman Cooks*, and it will become a best seller.

Your idea is original. I'm talking about being a groundbreaker in the field. Back in 1969, a group of Berkeley, California, college students interested in Eastern religions and meditation gave up meat and created *Laurel's Kitchen*, a classic book on vegetarianism. Little information on meatless cooking and nutrition existed at that time. The group did its own nutrition research, and the book came out in 1976. "We weren't pushing tahini and weird mushrooms or seaweed, stuff that some of the other cookbooks that came along did a lot of," said coauthor Laurel Robertson in an interview. "Mostly we just made normal things without meat." Total combined sales for her first and subsequent four cookbooks are in the millions.

The Whole Beast: Nose to Tail Eating by British chef Fergus Henderson captivated chefs all over the country because it advocates consuming the entire animal. The book includes recipes for pig spleens, duck necks, and whole birds. Eating this way is de rigueur for many poor people, but Henderson, who serves offal in his renowned London restaurant, St. John, aimed his book at the carnivorous middle and upper classes.

More recently, *Jerusalem: The Cookbook*, took the United States by storm with its melting-pot collection of recipes and color-soaked photos of dishes and Jerusalem inhabitants. While many Middle Eastern cookbooks preceded it, the authors used ingredients in a new way, such as a tahini sauce drizzled over roasted butternut squash.

You have exclusive access to information. Let's say you've inherited a box of papers from a well-known person in the food world who has just died. When you search through the box, you discover his box of handwritten recipes, never before published. There's a good chance a publisher or agent will be all over it, and you. Another way involves doing so much research on a subject you become the expert by default, because no one else has amassed that volume of information, or cares to do so.

Your idea is not esoteric. Sure, your neighbor makes fabulous raw food dishes featuring seaweed, but the audience is too small to attract a publisher. Writing a book on a narrow subject is not the same thing, or entire books on grilled cheese sandwiches would not exist. Agents and editors often evaluate a book idea by whether the story would be better as a magazine article. "I have to believe there's a large market for the book," says agent Carole Bidnick, who sold Werlin's book on grilled cheese sandwiches. "I ask myself how many people would spend $25 to read this. If I can't come up with a minimum ten thousand people, I don't believe I can sell the book. If the sales aren't there, publishers are not going to buy the project." I just found five grilled cheese sandwich cookbooks online, so there must be many more readers.

The title rocks. Your ability to convey the meaning of a book in the title is critical. You don't want agents and editors scratching their heads. Straightforward is fine. Strive for brevity, wit, and specificity. Restrain yourself from being cute. Avoid inside jokes or phrases no one but you will understand. If none of your friends gets your title, that's a large clue. Clever puns are acceptable only if truly relevant to your book content. Here are some compelling attributes:

- Titles or subtitles in which the reader benefit is clearly stated, as in *The Meatless Diabetic Cookbook: Over 100 Recipes Combining Great Taste with Great Nutrition*. Other good benefit-oriented words are "fast," "easy," and "foolproof." I hope you can deliver on your promise, though. There's nothing worse than buying a cookbook and finding out that the recipes don't measure up to the title.
- The use of numbers that suggest a wealth of information, such as *1,000 Vegetarian Recipes from Around the World* or *100 Best Hamburger Recipes*.
- The use of "greatest" or "best," as in *America's Best RV Cookbook: The Complete Guide to RV Cooking*. It takes chutzpah, but it can be done well.
- Labeling a book as "new," as in *A New Way to Cook*. Again, the promise must be met.
- Humor, as in *Help! My Apartment Has a Kitchen Cookbook: 100+ Great Recipes with Foolproof Instructions*, which has sold more than 250,000 copies.
- Secrets, as in *Secrets of a New Orleans Chef: Recipes from Tom Cowman's Cookbook*.
- Words that suggest a book is comprehensive or definitive, such as *The Complete Meat Cookbook* or *The Wine Bible*.

If you're still stumped, look through your own cookbook collection for inspiration. Ask friends or family to brainstorm with you. No matter what title you choose, don't get too hung up on it, because the publisher has the final say, and chances are good it will change. If you have a established brand, however, the name of your blog is likely to appear.

It's an evergreen. This publishing term means your book will sell for a long time. That excites publishers. It might be a diet or self-help book, for example, neither of which goes out of style. Or it might be a work so distinguished—like *Mediterranean Cooking*—that it's been in print since 1976.

Classic Indian Cooking came out in 1980, and it's still selling. Author Sahni says she modeled her ideas after Julia Child, choosing ingredients readily available in supermarkets. And like Child's cookbooks, hers is still in style. "I give the example of crossing a stream with slippery stones," she explains. "You have to make sure your back foot is firm. You have to give the reader simple ways of cooking dishes with supermarket ingredients. Otherwise a lot of people will be put off."

· ·
WHEN YOU'D RATHER NOT BE ALONE: COLLABORATING, COAUTHORING, AND GHOSTWRITING

If you're not ready to write a book by yourself, or feel you don't have the credentials, collaborating can be a great way to become published more quickly. Here are three ways to work with a partner:

COLLABORATE. Book collaborations work best if a writer works with a more knowledgeable or well-known person, such as a chef or celebrity. The collaborator writes the proposal and the book and often tests the recipes.

As the writer, you take the chef's recipes, stories, and voice and translate them into a cookbook. You change the recipes into those appropriate for the home cook, testing to make sure they work: eliminate terms home cooks wouldn't understand such as "flame off," simplify elaborate or intimidating recipes, and cut down yields to servings of four to eight.

I've coauthored two pizza books with Chicago chef Craig Priebe. We have a great relationship, but even so, it takes sensitivity, as changing recipes can create a problem if chefs feel the integrity of the recipes will be sacrificed or lost. Many chefs cook without exact measurements, using technique and taste. They also use specialty ingredients not found in supermarkets. It's your job to measure and to educate the chef on the target audience, usually home cooks.

In our case, Craig drafted the recipes and sent them to me. I edited them and sent them back, making suggestions to cut down the complexity or replace an ingredient. Once he signed off on the recipe, I tested it and make further adjustments. For the headnotes, I interviewed him, or sometimes he sent me a rough draft. I wrote the book in his voice.

There are all kinds of ways to collaborate. In one collaboration I know of, the chef came to the writer's house to cook for her while she took notes and grabbed his hand to measure ingredients. Other collaborators go to a restaurant kitchen and watch the chef cook, and then create recipes for his or her review.

Once you approach a chef or restaurateur about a book, start by discussing the scope and content. It gives you a chance to get to know the chef, test the waters, and see if you two click. You also have to decide whether you are passionate enough about the book's content to devote months to writing it, and whether you can translate the chef's voice and style successfully. If you feel you've made a good match, the two of you will sign a collaboration agreement, spelling out the responsibilities, deadlines, and compensation.

The money you receive needs to be enough to cover your time and effort. Collaborators get paid in many ways. Craig paid me a flat fee, in an arrangement called a "work-for-hire," in which I received no royalties. He also reimbursed me for groceries, both mine and for the testers I hired to make some of my recipes. Work-for-hire fees vary wildly—anywhere from $10,000 to $150,000. Other arrangements include a flat fee and a percentage of royalties, or a percentage of the advance plus royalties, with no payment up front.

If you have made a big contribution to the book, your name may appear on the cover, preceded by "with." That detail should be covered in your contract.

Successful collaborators have agents and can win awards, regardless of whether they coauthor or ghostwrite. Mary Goodbody, Rick Rodgers, and Melissa Clark are examples of talented and hard workers who have had successful careers.

COAUTHOR. Coauthors do equal work for equal billing on the cover, where names are linked by "and." An example might be a recipe developer who hooks up with an expert in nutrition because she has less experience in that area. "You need two parties really willing to do their share," explains Nancy Baggett, who had a good experience cowriting books in a series. Each writer divides the work based on time, skill, or whatever criteria seem valid, and signs an agreement. "If you underestimate and undervalue the time you put in, you're kind of doomed," she cautions.

Yotam Ottolenghi and Sami Tamimi collaborated on *Jerusalem* and worked out their roles. Ottolenghi created, tested, and wrote the recipes, while Tamimi was the kitchen authority. "It was Ottolenghi who did the travelling, the interviewing, and nearly all the writing, but it was Tamimi who in many ways talked him through the experience," according to an article in the *New Yorker:* "We'd sit down and think about little things we'd done as children—things associated with a recipe," Tamimi says. "We'd tell stories. We'd compare the smells and tastes and sounds that were our memories of food." Ottolenghi and Tamimi were business partners, and had an established relationship, which helped.

GHOSTWRITER. Ghostwriters operate in much the same way as collaborators, but their job is to represent the chef and be invisible. The ghostwriter's name will not appear in the book, unless the author acknowledges them at the back. Usually the more money you receive as the writer, the less credit you get on the book. Fees are similar to those I discussed for collaborators.

While most ghostwriters are not allowed to divulge their clients, writer Barry Estabrook said he worked with Jacques Pépin on his memoir, *The Apprentice: My Life in the Kitchen*. Estabrook recorded Pépin in long, detailed interviews, "goading him" into talking about and remembering his past. He captured Pépin's voice beautifully and accurately for the chef's dedicated following of fans.

• •

What Kind of Cookbook?

If you're still not sure what kind of cookbook you'd like to write, look through your recipe collection. Do you have more recipes for Greek food? Do most of the recipes fall into a certain category, such as salad, or does your biggest stack focus on French technique? Or group the recipes by degree of difficulty, or by whether they would appeal to certain groups of people, such as busy working people or singles dining alone.

Perhaps you have a general cooking blog. It's possible that you can write a general cookbook, if publishers see you as a brand. The blogs SmittenKitchen.com, RecipeGirl.com, and SavorySweetLife.com fit into this category. But most cookbooks now have a theme and focus.

Here are some of the most popular types of cookbooks:

- Thematic books based on events such as seasons and holidays, but unless you're a big name, these are hard to sell.
- Single-subject books focusing on a specific ingredient, type of dish, or type of diet.
- Appliance books based on tools like slow cookers or pressure cookers.
- Audience-intended books focusing on groups of people, such as diabetics, college students, campers, or the budget-minded. The writing style and recipes would be appropriate to the audience. A cookbook for campers, for example, would have quick, easy, portable dishes with few ingredients, and steps that could be made ahead.
- Geographic books, distinguished by country or region. These might be travelogues, full of evocative dishes and photographs.
- Historical books, moving chronologically or covering a period.
- Hybrids. These books are crosses between two themes. Healthy Southern cooking is two times more focused than a book on American cooking.
- Menu-based cookbooks arranged by meals, such as picnics or holiday dinners.
- General reference books with an encyclopedic, alphabetical approach. These can also specialize in a single subject, such as vegetables.
- Amusing or quirky specialty cookbooks. Who can forget *White Trash Cooking*, which sold so well there's a twenty-fifth-anniversary edition?

The most traditional structure is soup-to-nuts: appetizers, soups, salads, main dishes, and desserts, but there's room to mix it up. From there you could subtract or add other chapters, such as breads, eggs, side dishes, vegetables, pasta, cheese courses, and fruit. To help determine the order of chapters you'd like to use, look at some other cookbooks you admire. Some cookbooks are organized by season, ingredient, technique, or country or region.

Once you delineate the appropriate categories or chapters, fill out the book by adding titles of every recipe in your brain. A serious cookbook requires at least a hundred recipes. Don't worry about finalizing the list at this point. You don't need finished recipes now, either. Putting the names into categories helps you whittle down recipes that should not be included. You might be famous for your coq au vin, but if you're writing a book on Latin food, it doesn't apply unless you can tweak your recipe to give it a Latin spin. Set aside the recipes that don't fit for your next cookbook. Be ruthless to ensure your book is properly focused.

If you have a blog, typically you can reuse about 25 percent of the recipes. The rest must be fresh.

Besides the lists of recipes, you might want to include some of the following:

- A shopping resource section to help readers find hard-to-locate ingredients on the web or in specialty stores in their city.
- A glossary or primer, if you are writing a cookbook that uses foods unfamiliar to your audience.
- A list or chapter on fundamental techniques, such as how to poach or brine, if you plan to use these methods in many recipes.
- A list or chapter on pantry supplies, if your book calls for ready-made ingredients such as canned stocks, roasted peppers, olives, or canned fish.
- A chapter on basics like stocks and sauces. If your book calls for lots of recipes using homemade stocks and sauces like pesto and hollandaise, you might collect these "sub-recipes" in the front or back and refer to them later within more elaborate recipes.

- A section on premade mixes, such as pancake, rubs, and herb combinations.
- A bibliography, if you wish to direct readers to books for additional learning.

Also consider how much narrative you want in your cookbook. If you like to write, you might choose essay-length chapter openers, narrative boxes, or sidebars. Consider whether stories are a central part of your book. They might not be appropriate for beat-the-clock cooking, but if you're writing a book like Grace Young's *Wisdom of the Chinese Kitchen*, which covers her family's recipes, Chinese culture, and the Chinatown where she grew up, you'll want essay-length writing. Young included biographical stories, information about Chinese food and healing, personal memories, and culinary traditions.

When your book idea has jelled thoroughly, and you've written a proposal, you're ready to find a publisher. Chapter 11 explains how to get your book published, whether you're looking for a traditional publisher or want to be self-published, and how the publishing experience will play out.

How Photography Fits into Your Idea

Now that you see your book taking shape, you've probably thought about how it will look. Hardly anyone envisions a text-only paperback. Why bother, when you can have a gorgeous all-color hardcover with photos that illustrate the beauty of each dish, landscapes of rolling hillsides, or gleaming shots of just-picked produce? Not so fast. Color photos are expensive. They require heavier paper stock and four ink colors instead of one. Even a text-based cookbook has extra steps for a color insert, where color photos are printed on higher quality and more expensive paper and inserted into the book. Heavier stock means a book that costs more to ship, and a bigger book costs more to shelve in a warehouse. The end result is a more expensive cookbook.

When editors review your book idea, they assess the risk and cost of publishing it. Adding color to your book increases risk because it increases cost. Some cookbooks lend themselves to photography, such as those on the cuisine of other countries or regions. Sometimes the beauty of a chef's presentation makes color photos appropriate. While color cookbooks are increasingly common, there's no guarantee that yours will qualify. Sometimes a book just doesn't warrant color. As Leslie Stoker, senior vice president and publisher at Harry N. Abrams, said in an interview, "A prune cookbook wouldn't have a broad enough book-buying audience to support its production cost. And a meatloaf cookbook just wouldn't have the visual appeal." Another choice is two-color printing. This works best when it's part of the design, such as illustrations, colored titles, or shaded boxes with type over them.

To become more familiar with these page design elements, thumb through your own cookbook collection, or go to a bookstore to discover details you may not have noticed before: the look of sidebars and tip boxes, the length of introductions and headnotes, and the use of pull quotes and other elements such as colored titles, boxes, and shading to enliven page design.

Publishers such as Chronicle Books, Ten Speed Press, Artisan, Clarkson Potter, and Stewart, Tabori & Chang routinely print four-color cookbooks. Most of the time the author pays for the photographs one way or another. Some writers get a small advance, and the publisher pays for the photographs. Some get a bigger advance but must hire the photographer. Some, like food bloggers or historians, provide the photos themselves. If you want a certain photographer or illustrator, state as much in your proposal. Otherwise the publisher will choose them for you.

A styled color photo costs anywhere from $500 to $1,200, depending on the prestige of the photographer. Established photographers can charge between $20,000 and $40,000 to do a cookbook shoot over several days. Usually the editor determines how many photos the publisher can afford and hires the photographer, but sometimes the author has a photographer in mind and can negotiate.

Photographers like to shoot their food photos in studios so that they don't have to schlep lights and equipment to a location shot. They also shoot in restaurants, home kitchens, and the outdoors. Most use natural light to bring out the beauty of the food. Some do the food styling, too, but may also use some combination of food stylist, prop stylist, and assistants who move the lights around and other tasks. All these people must be paid, and their cost figures into the book's advance.

The food stylist makes the food for the photos and plays up the natural beauty of a dish. "We make it the way it would look for real," explains photographer Maren Caruso. "Not over-the-top perfect so people are intimidated and will never prepare it." You've probably heard about hairspray on salad greens and shellac on peas. That's more for advertising, explains Caruso, where "the milk splash has to happen in a certain place."

A prop stylist provides all the plates, tablecloths, flowers, cutlery, and anything else needed in the shot. I attended a location shoot where the prop stylist drove up in a van and swung open its back doors to reveal a floor-to-ceiling cache: plates, platters, vases, flowers, tablecloths, napkins, cutlery, ribbon, and whatever else necessary for beautiful photos.

Do authors style their own food? It depends. Often the photo shoot takes place elsewhere, near a publisher's office, and the author's not part of it. Sometimes, if you have an artistic eye, and the photographer trusts you, it can work. Deborah Madison has cooked and styled the food for all her books. "I don't mind when someone else is helping me, but I want the right to say when something is a jumble versus arranged, or to point out when the dish doesn't look like anything I've cooked," she explains. Madison makes some dishes that might be hard to visualize, such as vegetable ragout. Of course, if you're also the photographer for the book, you're used to doing everything yourself.

So now you have an explanation of how to come up with an irresistible book idea, and what to consider when working it out into a cookbook. As you've learned from this chapter, you have lots of thinking ahead. Keep working out the concept and details. Brainstorm with friends. Focus your idea. Get your recipes in order. Next, it's time to start writing your cookbook, right? Yes, we'll get there. The next chapter explains how to write most of what's in a cookbook: recipes. Later on, in Chapter 11, you'll learn how to write a book proposal and get published.

Writing Exercises

1. Learn how to focus an idea by drilling down to specifics. If you want to write about the cuisine of a country you love, perhaps that's too broad. Instead, you could focus on a particular region.

How else might you customize your idea to interest a publisher, based on title concepts I've listed?

2. If you've already chosen the subject of your cookbook, define your expertise. Write a one-paragraph biography. Doing so helps you feel more confident about the project and might show you areas where you need more research. Perhaps you have a blog, have taken cooking classes on the subject, traveled extensively, cooked for a special diet, or grew up eating a particular cuisine. Have you written about the subject for a class, newsletter, blog, or newspaper? If you feel that you need more expertise, make a list of three steps you can take now to enhance your background.

3. When writers have trouble describing their book idea to me, I ask them to get the idea down to one sentence. Doing so requires you to focus on the most important points. Ask a friend to help. Keep explaining the idea until you can get it into a clear concept. Practice this sentence, often called the elevator pitch, when you tell people you're going to write a cookbook.

8: MASTERING THE ART OF RECIPE WRITING

My immigrant parents, Iraqi Jews born and raised in China, never used recipes. When they settled in Canada, they had to reinvent the foods they knew—no easy task when neither had ever cooked before. Because no restaurants served their food, to eat it, they had to make it. Eventually they re-created most of the main dishes, dairy products, pickles, sauces, and sweets they yearned for, tasting from memory and remembering how foods looked and smelled. An exception was the stuffed intestines my father smacked his lips over but my mother wouldn't allow in the house.

Both my parents are gone now, and ironically, they never taught me to cook. I have a few chicken scratchings on paper that hinted at a recipe, but when I tried to cook with them, I found instructions I didn't understand, shorthand for techniques I didn't know, or missing ingredients or steps that I didn't discover until it was too late. Nothing turned out right.

I kept trying. I cooked a few dishes repeatedly, refining the taste from memory, just as they did. Each time I cooked or baked, I wrote the recipe down, printed it out, and marked it up when I made the dish again. There was always something to improve: more or less of an ingredient, a little more simmering, figuring out how to make a pastry less tough or a step clearer. Today, I've got a handful of recipes I like, based on this process of experimentation and refinement.

And that's just one reason to create recipes. Perhaps your college-bound daughter wants to re-create her favorite dishes. Maybe your neighbor keeps asking for your fried chicken recipe. Perhaps you are a chef, caterer, or cooking-school teacher who wants to hand out recipes to students or customers. Or maybe you have a child who needs allergy-free meals, and you want to record the dishes you've made that work well. No matter what your desire or reason, you need to write trustworthy and workable recipes for food that tastes good.

A well-written recipe is poetry, like beautiful writing. Agents and editors can see a good one a mile away. Sometimes they test them. Agent Lisa Ekus, who represents both new and established cookbook writers, says if she's found an unknown writer whose recipes look interesting, she will ask the writer or chef to cook for her. "If I can see them in action and taste their food, I can sell the book more passionately. If the book is restaurant based, I try to eat in the restaurant." Agent Doe Coover says she tests recipes from proposals "all the time," because if an editor tries them and they don't work, "it's going to come back on my head."

A badly written recipe is a disappointment. When I first cooked from published recipes, I always blamed myself when the dish didn't turn out. I thought I had not followed a step properly or left something out. But it's possible the recipe was not written well, not adequately developed, or not tested thoroughly.

Today, when I read a recipe, I can judge whether it will work or how to adjust it if I think it won't. That's what happens after decades of cooking. But you don't want readers to second-guess your recipes. You want recipes that work the first time and those that are easily understood. Good recipe writers don't let go until they know their readers can reproduce the recipes faithfully and make dishes that look and taste as good as their own.

The best recipes not only are clearly written but include the personality of the writer. Consider the ending of Quick Cream of Chicken Soup, from my yellowed 1946 edition of *The Joy of Cooking*. After combining chicken bouillon and scalded cream, Irma Rombauer announces, "Add if you want to be luxurious: blanched almonds, ground (about 2 tablespoonfuls to 1 cup soup)." In just a few words, she reveals her playfulness, originality, and need to indulge.

If you are patient, exacting, and detail oriented, you can write a recipe. It's a form of systematic technical writing. In this chapter you'll learn how to write each part: the title, headnote, ingredients list, and method. You'll also learn how to develop, troubleshoot, compose, and test until you have a recipe anyone can follow and get the same results you did. Even if you've written recipes before—for yourself, a community cookbook, a neighbor, a friend, or even publication—you'll learn tips here that will increase your skill level. You'll also find answers to many common questions, particularly those related to testing, attribution, and copyright.

If you wish to write a cookbook, I can't emphasize enough how critical it is that you write recipes well. Recipes must be precise, accurate, logical, consistent, clear, complete, doable, and satisfying. The best create visual images in the minds of readers as they think about making or eating the dish. In the best cases, they are sensuous, immediate, and evocative.

That's what readers want most, regardless of whether they are blog readers, magazine editors, friends, or purchasers of your cookbook.

Developing a Recipe

You might think recipe writing is linear: you create a seafood pasta dish, write the recipe, and send it to a friend to see if they can re-create it accurately. It sounds simple enough. But that's not how it works. Here's an oversimplified example for the pasta dish: Let's say you taste the pasta dish and decide it could use improvement, maybe some parsley and lemon juice. You add "¼ cup parsley" and "1 tablespoon lemon juice" to the ingredients list and make the pasta again. Now it tastes better, but still needs more zing. You revise the ingredients list once more, adding more lemon juice and "2 tablespoons capers." You make the pasta again. Now you love it, and you're satisfied. That's recipe development.

Three is not the magic number of times to make a dish. What if you realized, upon tasting the third version of the pasta dish, you should have kept the lemon juice to one tablespoon instead of two? Should you make the pasta again, just to be certain? The best recipe writers would say yes. Some have been known to develop a recipe up to twenty times, particularly bakers, where recipe writing is a more exact science because of the chemistry involved. "Those of us who write good recipes tend to be obsessors," admits Alice Medrich. "You have to fight it and go with it at the same time."

Sometimes it's all about ingredients. When she's developing a recipe for, say, a layered cake, Medrich might change one of the cake layers to a different flavor, or change one of the fillings to custard, or take out nuts and substitute coconut. Other times she will start her development process with an ingredients and measurement grid. Let's say she wants a new chocolate cake recipe. She'll look through other bakers' recipes—those by writers she admires—and then fill in her grid with varying amounts of ingredients they specify. She'll put ingredients down one side and a list of measurements down the other. That way she knows which ingredients are basic and which are changeable. If all the recipes call for similar amounts of flour, Medrich knows the amount is standard, and she probably won't change it. She might test the recipe that calls for the most eggs to see how she likes the results. "It's like doing basic research before a history report," she explains. "It's about finickiness and curiosity, the teeny-weeny little details that make a difference."

....

THE BAREFOOT CONTESSA'S DOGGED RECIPE DEVELOPMENT

INA GARTEN, one of America's best-selling cookbook authors, develops and tests recipes repeatedly. Said her husband, Jeffrey, in an interview in *Parade* magazine, "Ina loves to have a good time, but she's also incredibly rigorous. She's like a scientist in the kitchen—very precise, very disciplined. She writes everything down, follows instructions to the decimal, and is always experimenting. She'll try something six different ways. Her experiments are very calculated."

Garten said she goes for no more than three flavors in a dish, each well balanced with the other. "It has to be clear what you're eating, she explained. "If it's a plum tart, you should know there are plums in there, and I do something with cassis that enhances the flavor of plums. I'm always thinking, 'How do I bring out the intrinsic flavors of a dish?'"

After she's happy with the recipe development, she watches an assistant make the dish, and then she tests each recipe on her friends.

....

Cookbook author Deborah Madison says she often gets inspiration from the garden and farmers' market when she's just "cooking freely in the kitchen." If she makes a dish she likes, she wants to repeat it. "I cook as intuitively as I can, and make notes like 'needs more tang or sharpness,' and then I start correcting the dish. I go back and forth until I find something I like." She limits herself to making a recipe three or four times.

Recipes may also evolve from dishes Madison ate in restaurants in which she noticed a flavor, unusual food presentation, or the texture of a silky soup. She makes notes on dishes she likes when she's away from the kitchen and refers to them when she's back. Some people have a good taste memory, she says, like her friend Clifford Wright, who specializes in Mediterranean cookbooks. "He can remember the taste of foods he's eaten abroad. Somehow, he nails the taste."

For a dish with several components, taste each part separately before assembling to see how they complement each other. Take into account appearance, taste, texture, and appropriate serving size. Remember that this is your recipe. If people you serve it to love it but you're not satisfied, keep refining or put it aside. If you publish a recipe on a blog and get a negative comment from a reader, replying with the defense of "my kids loved it" isn't very satisfying.

If you want to create recipes editors love, it's not just about making something that tastes good. "I'm a fan of clever," Bonnie Benwick, deputy food editor and recipe editor for the *Washington Post*, told me when I interviewed her for my blog. "A recipe has to be compelling, with a good technique. Or one that tells of a shorter, better, faster, more successful, foolproof way. Or there's some kind of revelation." Now I'd have to take another look at that seafood pasta dish example, to see if I could employ a shortcut, or add an ingredient that gives it a twist.

America's Test Kitchen is famous for having a staff of recipe developers who might make a recipe more than sixty times. "For a gingerbread cake, you'll test it at a range of different oven temperatures, with the rack at different levels," said Doc Willoughby, the company's executive director of magazines, when I interviewed him on my blog. "The amount of leavener might vary, and then there's the liquid you might use: water, milk, orange juice, and different kinds of beers. Someone will ask if lager is better, so you have to try different beers."

"For roast beef, if the goal is super evenly cooked, juicy meat, it's a different kind of testing. You get into a lot of science, like if you cook it to X degrees and let it sit, then put it back in the oven. Once you get started down that road, there might be forty tests to do to get those variables right," he explains. Of course you're not going to do all that in a home kitchen, but you can see why their recipes are bulletproof.

"If you're not satisfied with your dish, the process of looking at all the recipes you can find and asking how do they do it differently and what you could do differently will take care of it," he advises.

The best recipe developers know how to create international flavor combinations that are fresh and unusual. Sarah Kate Gillingham, founder of TheKitchn.com, said she attempts to re-create dishes she's liked, and thinks of ways to make it better, when I interviewed her for my blog.

She tries to remember what she thought at the time she first tasted the dish, such as "This would be better with orange peel, or with chicken thighs instead of lamb." Using her memory as a starting point, she heads into the kitchen to improve or change the dish, accessing a taste library of which flavors work together best. She tries to stay away from fads: "Not doing a ton of cardamom right now. It's been done."

When she's brainstorming a recipe, Gillingham turns to science books as a reference to see how people she respects think, such as those by Shirley Corriher or Harold McGee. At this stage, she's not tinkering with measurements yet. If she looks at similar recipes to dishes she's imagining, it's to decide what she would do differently to put a personal stamp on it. "I know the basic formula for most foods," said Gillingham. "A lot of that came from culinary school and the cooking afterwards."

Recipe Writing for a Cookbook

You want the right list of recipes to include in your book. How do you think about creating the recipes? "Choose dishes that best reflect your strength," advises Medrich. "You want the best results possible for [the] least time and work spent. Minimize drudgery. Streamline activities, increase convenience." Creating dishes with appearance in mind is particularly important for baking books, which often include color photos.

Many new writers aren't sure what level of instruction to give. I'm on the side that says not to make assumptions about what readers know. Most cooking magazines hold readers' hands and will expect you to do the same, if you're writing for them. Since you are not a new cook, you can't use yourself as an example.

Julia Child took beginning cooks seriously. When she lived in France and studied French cooking, she noticed that most of the cookbooks for serious students were chef's shorthand notes, with not much instruction for such techniques as how to fix a broken sauce or how to poach. Child wanted a "real teaching book" with clear reasoning and every step and technique thoroughly explained. In her first book, *Mastering the Art of French Cooking,* she described how a dish should look at each stage of preparation and told readers what could go wrong with the process, along with corrective measures. Her recipes are long, but they always work. And that is a big reason why readers appreciate her.

As an editor at Knopf in the 1950s, Judith Jones tried some of the recipes when she received Child's manuscript. She found the book revolutionary because it was "like having a teacher right there beside you in the kitchen, and everything really worked," she told the *New Yorker.* Today Jones is still an admirer. "She told us what to expect, how to achieve it, how to taste, how to correct our mistakes, and how to work out our own variations," she says.

Your first task is to accept that all readers are probably not exactly like you. They may not prepare ingredients before they start or have the same equipment. They might not understand the meaning of words like "blanch" or read your recipe all the way through first. They might not be as excited as you are about making several time-consuming dishes for a dinner party.

Madison acknowledges that real life intervenes in the kitchen. "Cooking is a dynamic and complex process, and I'm always trying to look at the whole picture," she explains. "Where in a recipe is there a gap where you can start something for the next day, set the table, or simply sit down and have a glass of wine with your partner? If you think of recipes only in terms of the final dish rather than a process, a meal, or an experience, then it's a rather limited way to see cooking." Bearing these thoughts in mind, in the next section I detail the process, best practices for each part of a recipe, how to write them, and how to test them.

The Recipe Writing Process

When you start writing recipes, you'll notice a certain amount of duplication in phrases and directions. Create a style sheet to ensure your recipe language is consistent. Use it to record unusual spellings and as a check on whether to use articles ("a," "an," "the") in the method. This practice helped me enormously when I wrote my cookbooks. I wanted to give instructions the same way for each pizza. They're still burned into my brain for the first book: "Brush the grilled side of the pizza crust with the Herbed Grill Oil. Dust with the Parmesan and sprinkle with the mozzarella."

Some recipe writing styles have become standard: figures always come first in an ingredients list, and tablespoon, teaspoon, pound, and cup are almost always spelled out. The assumption is to avoid confusion on the part of the reader. When you get a book contract, publishers may give you their own recipe style guide to follow. Magazines and newspapers have certain styles as well. If you're uncertain, read the publication's published recipes to see what style they prefer.

Overwhelmingly, recipe writing has a standard format: title, headnote, yield, ingredients list, and method. Édouard de Pomaine, an early-twentieth-century food writer, often wrote the method in the second person, telling you what you see and smell. Elizabeth David wrote in narrative style rather than listing the ingredients first. Instead she specified them within the method, and the method was all that appears. James Beard used this style as well in *Delights and Prejudices*. What follows, however, is the style that most publications and publishers use.

Recipe Titles

Recipe titles should be simple, descriptive, informative, and inviting. You don't want them to read like a menu item in a restaurant. And you don't want them to be vague, so readers can't envision the dish.

Like good writers, good recipe writers have their own styles. I like an accurate, specific title I can understand. Marion Cunningham took a straightforward approach in *Lost Recipes: Meals to Share with Friends and Family*. Titles are as simple as Southern Green Beans, Stuffed Cabbage Rolls, or Raised Waffles. She wouldn't consider such titles as Green Bean Surprise, Organic Cabbage Rolls Stuffed with Long-Grain Rice and Corn-Fed Ground Beef, or Judy's Famous Waffles: any dish called a "surprise" will be a mystery to your readers because they can't envision the dish, the second title belongs on a menu, and the third won't mean anything to readers, since they don't know Judy. If you must name Judy in your recipe title, at least explain her significance in the headnote.

It's easy to write a confusing title. You might think Stone Fruit Ice Cream is perfectly fine. But now you've asked readers to work. "Which fruits have stones in them?" they might wonder. "Does she mean plums? That doesn't sound good." And then they turn the page. If peaches make the best and most appealing ice cream, call it Peach Ice Cream, and list other stone fruit types as variations.

Readers want to be enticed. Even something as simple as James Villas's Creamed Leeks with Italian Sausage sounds good, because he added "creamed" and "Italian" as descriptors. "Easy" or "quick" are always inviting if they fit the style of the blog or book. Avoid adjectives like "the best" or "sublime." You probably think almost all of your recipes are the best or sublime. Let the title speak for itself.

For recipes from world cuisines, some authors go for the recipe title in its original language first, followed by an explanation in English, and some the other way around. The style of the book is a factor, as is the readers' sophistication level and the style sheet followed by the publisher. In *The Book of Jewish Food*, Claudia Roden names Chicken Soup with Rice in Arabic first: *Shorba bi Djaj*. Julia Child titles a recipe *Choux Brocoli Blancis*, followed by "(Blanched Broccoli—Plain Boiled Broccoli)." Grace Young, however, in *The Wisdom of the Chinese Kitchen*, calls my favorite dim sum dessert Sesame Balls, then *Zeen Doy* in smaller type, perhaps because people are unfamiliar with Mandarin and Cantonese. If you are writing a cookbook, compile a list of titles for each chapter. To ensure variety and liveliness, alternate their styles, complexities, ingredients, wording, and length.

The Headnote or Introduction

Here's your second chance to draw readers into the recipe. Headnotes set a mood, give the recipe a personality, or tell a story. You need headnotes for several reasons. One is because without them, the first thing readers will see after the title is "2 pounds pork butt, well trimmed." That's not terribly inviting.

These days, headnotes can read like novels. They tell stories or entertain. They're written in a conversational style. You might have a funny story about a kitchen disaster, or a particular memory or occasion you'd like to share. Blogger and cookbook author David Lebovitz used to write unusual headnotes such as, "I tried to flush this ice cream down the toilet." "Is that going to turn people off or is that funny?" he asks. "I write that way on my website, and people read it, so they must like it. That's the good thing about having a website: you get immediate feedback."

If you have no story, don't feel you have to fill a void or make one up. Instead, write about the connection of the recipe to history, dining rituals, and celebrations. Inventive sales pitches are fine, such as "This is one soup I make all winter long which has the double virtue of being scrumptious and effortless" (Laurie Colwin), or "My favorite chicken dish was the ring mold with wild-mushroom sauce served on a beautiful Sunday afternoon in late spring when the doors could be left open and the warm rays of the sun streaked across the dining table, saluting my mother for her efforts in presenting a beautiful meal gathered from field, forest, garden and barnyard" (Edna Lewis).

When you read a good headnote, you appreciate it. Your readers will want to do the same. Give them context for the larger issues. Janet Theophano, author of *Eat My Words: Reading Women's Lives Through the Cookbooks They Wrote*, explains in her book: "As cooks, we must first taste a dish in our imaginations, see it on the table, share it with guests—sometimes more fanciful than real—and then actually reproduce it from a text. A longing for the pleasures of the table reflects a concern for balance and harmony and an integration of the physical and spiritual nature of our existence. In this way, cookbooks are a meditation. Preparing a dish or a meal is not merely an effort to satisfy physical hunger but often a quest for the good life."

John T. Edge, author of *Southern Belly: A Food Lover's Companion*, has said there are five kinds of headnotes. Here are his examples:

- Cultural: In this neck of the woods, we eat hominy when . . .
- Historical: The Hot Brown sandwich was first concocted by Chef . . .
- Personal: I remember the night Aunt Minnie slipped on that banana peel . . .

- Instructional: Only soft winter wheat will do for this . . .
- Sensual: This cake rises so high that it looks like an Eisenhower-era bouffant.

Most of all, headnotes are often practical, particularly in magazines, where they tend to be shorter than in books. They tell readers what to expect. They state benefits such as saving time or using up leftovers.

Simplicity can be beautiful. Sometimes headnotes are no more than a set of brief, descriptive instructions. Here's an example from *Feasts for All Seasons*, by Roy Andries de Groot, a book on seasonal cooking that came out ahead of its time in 1966: "We like to serve asparagus as a separate course, before the main dish. The problem of cooking asparagus is simple. The tips are tender and should never be in contact with boiling water. The stems, on the other hand, must be boiled."

At a minimum, your job is to consider readers' needs, explain the recipe, and establish trust. If, for example:

- the recipe looks long and complicated, or is made in stages, reassure readers that it's worth their trouble, that they can make parts in advance, or that the dish comes together quickly.
- the recipe calls for advance preparation, let them know up front.
- the method uses a new technique critical to the recipe's success, say so here so readers can prepare for and focus on the task.
- the recipe includes an unfamiliar ingredient, explain where to procure it and why it's worthwhile. If the recipe calls for several unfamiliar ingredients, you're on thin ice, unless you're writing a book on a relatively unexplored cuisine and want to be accurate. A cookbook with lots of recipes calling for obscure ingredients makes agents and editors nervous. Reassure readers that if they can't find the exact ingredient, a substitute will work. For example, in her recipe for Zinfandel of Beef, Julia Child declares, "If you are out of zinfandel, use another good young red wine and call it simply Beef Stew in

Red Wine." I bet that Child, a responsible recipe developer, tested this variation.

- the dish can be made with variations, explain how adding or changing an ingredient works as an alternative.
- the dish is hard to imagine, describe it with specific words— not by saying delicious, wonderful, or great, but instead something like, "this sharp, refreshing sauce."
- the dish is traditionally served during certain holidays, or goes well with other recipes in the book, let readers know.
- you think it would taste best with certain wines or beers, you might make suggestions.
- the recipe needs a hint, help readers out. In *The Way to Cook*, Julia Child suggests soaking one cup of beans in ten cups of water to get rid of "the rooti-toots" they bring on.

I would be remiss if I did not include my pet peeves here. Please do not state in the headnote, "Add a green salad and a crusty loaf of country bread for a complete meal." You could say this about any Western or European entrée. And don't say that a dish is the best thing you've ever tasted. That's hype, and readers will discount it. Instead, show the reader how good it is with description. Describing what a dish tastes like, or its textures, is critical if you don't think they've ever tasted it before, or if you have created something new.

Attribution and Copyright

Attribution is usually discussed in the headnote. How do you address using a recipe with an unknown origin—such as a handwritten recipe from an aunt who got it from a friend? It might be an heirloom, from a restaurant, or from a cookbook or magazine. It's best to find the origin.

When in doubt, give credit, and you'll create fewer problems. Even if you have no idea, you can still say your best friend's mother gave it to you in the 1980s on a handwritten card. Or that it was adapted from, inspired by, or based on another recipe.

Bloggers run into this problem when they adapt recipes that are already published. Some think that they can take a cake recipe from one blog and an icing recipe from a cookbook and therefore they have created something new. Wrong! They have taken two previously published recipes written by others and merged them. It is unethical to reprint a recipe verbatim without requesting permission from the copyright owner (typically the author or publisher), even if it's for part of a recipe. It's better to adapt. But there is lots of griping about what constitutes "adapting."

Many people believe that if you make three changes to a recipe, it's yours. I am not a fan of that idea. Sometimes recipes are written in distinctive ways, so copying and pasting it while making minor changes to the amount of spices or salt isn't enough. The author can still tell it's her recipe. You have to go further, by changing the recipe in substantial ways. In addition to these changes, create a new title, write a new headnote, and rewrite the method. Even if you've completely reworded the recipe, to be safe, say where it came from.

As to the question of copyright, most publishers register cookbook copyrights in the author's name. The commonly held industry belief, however, is that only the headnote and method can be protected, not the ingredients list. You can't copyright "1 cup flour" and other ingredients in the list because they are too generic.

To the question, "How do I protect my recipes?" the US government answers: "a mere listing of ingredients is not protected under copyright law. However, where a recipe or formula is accompanied by substantial literary expression in the form of an explanation or directions, or when there is a collection of recipes as in a cookbook, there may be a basis for copyright protection." See this website for more information: copyright .gov/fls/fl122.html.

If you are self-publishing, you may request forms from the US Copyright Office at the Library of Congress (copyright.gov). If you want to reproduce a published recipe for a freelance article or for a website, you must contact the publisher and ask for permission.

Bloggers have a more insidious problem when people steal their recipes and photos by cutting and pasting them onto their own blogs or onto Facebook pages. Photographs are protected by US law, as are "collections" of recipes. But recipes are harder to keep just on your blog. Elise Bauer of SimplyRecipes.com recommends publishing a partial feed with a "continued" link, thereby creating an inbound link from recipe aggregators. She suggests setting up a Google Alert with your blog name as the search term. Google sends you an email whenever your blog is mentioned.

If someone does copy your recipe without your permission, leave a comment asking to remove it. If that fails, look up how to file a DMCA (Digital Millennium Copyright Act) complaint with the web host.

If you love a recipe from a blog and want to put it on your blog, write about it and name it, then link to the recipe. Do not cut and paste it in its entirety into your blog.

The Yield

At the end of the headnote, state the number of servings. Sometimes servings are based on precise measurements, such as "makes four half-cup servings," and sometimes you might have different sizes based on whether the item is an appetizer or main course. List cookies by the dozen. What constitutes a serving? That's a good question, and one that has caused me consternation when following recipes and editing them. All I can say is that you should try to be representative. Look up similar recipes if you are confused about yield.

••

RECIPE WRITING FOR CHEFS AND CATERERS

If you're a food professional who wants to write recipes for home cooks, you have challenges other cookbook writers do not. Most chefs and caterers create recipes to feed crowds. It's different to make a dish for four. Because you can make complex dishes, you might also make assumptions about reader knowledge and experience. My favorite example of a chef trying to write a recipe for home cooks is an opening sentence a friend read to me: "Roast a duck as you would for any occasion." If you don't understand why this is funny, you won't be successful writing for a home cook.

My friend had that recipe because she was rewriting a chef's recipes for home cooks. For best results, hire a recipe developer or experienced cookbook writer to rework the recipes you've written. Have someone who represents your reader, not a professional cook, test them. For more details, see "When You'd Rather Not Be Alone: Collaborating, Coauthoring, and Ghostwriting," on pages 170–171.

••

Ingredients List

Think of the ingredients list and the directions that follow as a formula. The most important rule of this formula is to list ingredients in the order they will be used in the directions or method. That way, if some ingredients require preparation, as in toasted nuts or thawed berries, readers see it right away. Or if they lose their place in the method, it's easy to scan the list to see which ingredient comes next.

The other rule about listing ingredients is that it's good to be specific. Instead of oil, specify olive oil if it matters, or extra virgin olive oil. State whether the butter is salted or unsalted. Specify onions and potatoes by size, such as "1 large onion, chopped." Sizes of cut vegetables range from largest to smallest: chopped, diced, or minced. And you'll want to put the largest quantity first, such as in a group of spices: 2 tablespoons oregano, 1 teaspoon salt, ½ teaspoon pepper.

Measurements can be tricky. Some recipe writers like to say "2 carrots, peeled and chopped." Since carrot sizes vary, you could also say "1 cup chopped carrots (about 2)." Readers like to know the exact amount for the recipe and the number of carrots, in case they have to shop.

Some writers prefer to state the weight, as in "½ pound carrots." Since most cooks don't have a scale at home, how would they know if the carrots they already have on hand are enough? If a food is sold by weight, however, give reader both measurements, such as "1 cup strawberries (about 8 ounces)." And for produce, you can assume that readers know it needs to be washed, so no reason to state it in the ingredients list.

When using canned foods, state the size, as in "1 (14-ounce) can whole tomatoes." If possible, use the whole can of broth to make life easier for readers. In the "making life easier" department, canned stock is acceptable in most cookbooks, and canned beans don't have to be soaked overnight. State your preference for dried beans, but also acknowledge that canned beans will work. If you only tell readers the amount required for dried beans soaked overnight, however, they won't know how many cans of cooked beans to buy instead.

In baking, know the difference between liquid and dry measure. Do not use a scale to measure ingredients, even if you think it's more accurate, unless you are a baker and your publisher has agreed. I know some chefs feel strongly about using weights for dry ingredients, but most American home cooks do not use scales to measure flour. Most do not use the metric system either, so keep measurements in cups, tablespoons, and teaspoons, unless you are writing for an international audience on your blog, or your publisher has requested metric measurements (for more on metric measurements, see the end of this section). Use large eggs, the standard size. If it matters whether water is ice cold, rather than cold, say so.

Consider whether a food should be measured before or after use. Distinguish between "1 cup almonds, chopped," or "1 cup chopped almonds." Similarly, "1 cup sifted flour" is different from "1 cup flour, sifted." Make sure you figure this out, as imprecise measurements drive recipe editors crazy.

Many people get stuck on how to refer to ingredients used twice in a recipe. Avoid double listing. Instead, write "½ cup plus 2 tablespoons olive oil." In the oil's first mention in the method, tell readers to add the "½ cup olive oil," not "the oil." Later tell them to add "the remaining 2 tablespoons olive oil." You could also say "½ cup olive oil plus oil for greasing the pan." Some writers use the term "divided" to follow a single amount, but I'm not sure it works. Often readers can't figure out what it means until they read the method.

One good way to deal with ingredients used twice is to separate them out into parts. If you separate the ingredients for pie with subheadings and groups, such as "piecrust" and "filling," you can call for the amount of flour in each recipe. These are called subrecipes. Write one method for the overall recipe, not a method for each subrecipe, unless the subrecipe can stand alone and will be referred to elsewhere in a cookbook, such as for piecrust.

Recipes with parts need subgroups with subheadings. Irene Kuo's Beef in Blackbean Sauce has a recipe for the "slippery coating," followed by a general recipe for the dish, and a third recipe for the sauce. I like this method because it's clear immediately to marinate the beef, stir fry it, and add sauce. Breaking up the recipe is particularly important if it's lengthy. If your recipe calls for a subrecipe on another page—such as stock or a sauce—cross-reference the dish. Too many subrecipes make readers turn to another page elsewhere in the book. Most don't like flipping from one page to another, or seeing that they have to prepare three parts first before assembling them all in the final fourth. Even on a blog, put the whole recipe in one place, not carved up in links.

While we're on the subject of subrecipes, I made what was, for me, a radical change when I cowrote my latest cookbook, *The United States of Pizza*. For this book, readers had to make the dough and often a sauce in advance. I listed the dough first in the ingredients list, since readers had to make it first, and then the sauce, since it had to rest an hour.

Traditionally, the common thinking is to call for the subrecipes based on when you employ them, which didn't make sense. There would be no dough and no pizza sauce ready to use if readers hadn't made them first. Bonnie Benwick of the *Washington Post* taught me this writing style.

When it comes to type of ingredient, call for the most commonly available whenever possible. This is particularly important for recipe writers who present food from other countries or particular regions of the United States. "We like to do things in authentic ways, but authentic ways are not necessarily the way to make things accessible," said Mark Bittman, *New York Times* columnist and author of *How to Cook Everything*. If you really want readers to use the hard-to-find ingredient because it's essential to the dish, or because the dish won't taste as good with a substitute, say so in the headnote. Give readers an incentive and enough information to search for it.

The same is true with brand names. Avoid them unless you think a dish will be diminished by not using a particular brand. Name it in the headnote, preferably, or in the ingredients list. If you list an optional ingredient, a substitution, or a variation, test each recipe that way to evaluate whether the change worked.

Typically, water is not used in the ingredients list, because it is not considered something that must be prepared in advance.

When it comes to salt, please don't take the easy way out. Specify the amount. You might think that you should leave it out and say "salt to taste" because people can put more or less according to what they like. That's true, but they can do that anyway. If you write "1 teaspoon salt," they can always adjust. But if you write nothing, they have no idea whether they're supposed to add ¼ teaspoon or 1 tablespoon. I think that's irresponsible. You know how the dish should taste, and you want their dish to turn out right. Take the plunge, and specify an amount.

If you're writing for an international audience, you will need to use both metric measurements (liters and grams) and imperial measurements (cups and pounds). Some cookbook publishers write this into their contractor style sheet, so you are on the hook for conversions. If you have a recipe blog that uses only imperial units you could increase your readership by adding metric measurements. While you can search for a list of conversions online, I like the one created at ChocolateandZucchini.com /conversions.

Method or Directions

The method is where you tell readers how to make the dish. At its most basic, it is systematic technical writing, written in a lively voice. At its best, method writing has personality. Editor Judith Jones advocates writing directions that sound like you're standing next to a friend in the kitchen, helping that person cook. "You want to give the impression you have done it many times and can cook with confidence," she explains.

When Jones reviews recipes, she looks at the quality of the writing and use of language. "It's not that the recipe per se is striking and new," she says. "It's what the writer does with it." One of her authors, Lydia Bastianich, wrote "a whole meditation on what you're doing while stirring risotto," she explains, "what you listen for, see, and smell. Writing like this comes from something within."

Put each group of actions in a separate paragraph. Sometime they are numbered, but most often not. Group tasks such as adding many ingredients to soup before simmering it. Sentences that start with a verb, such as "rinse," "chop," or "beat," make your writing active. If you're writing for a magazine or a publisher that has a recipe style sheet, you'll refer to it for guidance.

Often the first direction is to heat the oven, but this is not necessarily correct. Make sure readers do so at the right time. If you ask them to "marinate meat for 20 minutes," or "put cookie dough in the fridge for 1 hour," you'll want them to turn on the oven later.

Specify the size of commonly available pots and pans by small, medium, and large. Don't make readers guess what size they need and pick the wrong one. Baking, particularly, requires specific pan sizes.

Jones has strong opinions on recipe writing. She tries to undo formulaic writing. The word she likes least is "mixture." "You mix milk with a bit of salt—now it's called the milk mixture," she says incredulously. She suggests specific language instead, such as "batter," "dough," "custard," "sauce," "dry ingredients," and "liquid ingredients." Jones also likes Child's mastery of visceral action words. Another phrase she dislikes is "in a bowl, combine." "Recipe writing has become very sterile," she says. "People think you take the bowl out first. You don't always do it in a bowl, and why do you have to use six bowls?" I'm not a fan of the term "set aside." As Jones is likely to say, "What else are you going to do with it?

Throw it away?" Instead, give specific instructions only when necessary, such as "cover and refrigerate for at least 1 hour."

As you write your method, watch the length. There is such a thing as too much explanation. If the method becomes too long, simplify instructions, or put preparation into the ingredients list, such as "1 cup cooked rice" or "2 red peppers, roasted and cut into thin strips."

When you state a time on how long to cook, stir, or bake, use a timer to ensure the times are accurate. Give a second visual description for doneness, such as "bake until the custard is set, or until the top becomes golden brown." Or "sauté butter until it turns brown and smells nutty." Watch as you cook, and come up with accurate language about what's happening, such as "stir until sauce thickens (or hardens or reduces)."

Try not to use expensive or specialized tools readers might not have in their kitchens. Not everyone has a standing mixer or a food processor. Don't refer to appliances by brand names, such as the Cuisinart. If the recipe truly requires a particular tool or brand of appliance, note that in the headnote.

••

JULIA CHILD'S ACTION VERBS

If you write recipes regularly, you might be sick of using "add" and "place" in the method. (If not, you should be.) Here's help. Use powerful action verbs, the way Julia Child did. I spent a pleasurable hour reading through *Mastering the Art of French Cooking* to compile this list. Just look at this variety:

arrange	mince	settle
baste	mix	shave
beat	moisten	simmer
blend	mound	skim
brown	open	slice
build	pack	slide
bury	paint	slip
carve	pierce	slit
check	pour	smear
chop	prepare	soak
close	press	spoon
cool	prick	spread
correct	pull	sprinkle
cover	puree	stir
crumple	push	strain
cut	quarter	strew
decorate	raise	stuff
discard	reduce	surround
divide	refresh	taste
drape	reheat	thin

drop	replace	tie
dry	return	tilt
film	ring	tip
fold	roast	top
follow	roll	toss
force	salt	trim
form	sauté	turn
glaze	scatter	twist
insert	scoop	warm
lay	scrape	wilt
leave	scrub	wind
lift	season	wrap
make	separate	
melt	set	

ACTIONS WORTH EXPLAINING

Today, people cook less and less. You don't want to intimidate readers by using a term they don't understand. Doing so makes people feel stupid or frustrated, then mad at themselves because they don't know the word.

If your target reader is a novice cook, the following words are some you should either avoid or, if using, explain exactly:

blanch	cube	julienne
blend	deglaze	pan-broil
braise	dice	poach
combine	dredge	reduce
cook off	flame off	sweat
cream	fold	

Some terms require complex explanation and may bog down your method. Greg Patent, author of *Baking in America*, suggests that, because describing how to fold can take several sentences, you include a technique section where you can describe it once.

I'm holding out on "sauté," although many writers now explain that, too. And some people don't know what "separate the eggs" means. Move them further apart? I'm not kidding. A cookbook author told me someone asked him that.

The Role of Sidebars

Sidebars, also called notes or boxes, come into play when you want to give miscellaneous information in more detail. The information is never essential to the recipe and can be read if desired. Sidebars may have a shaded background, lines around the text to create a box, or colored text.

Subjects include:

- tips for preparation or technique (how to roast a pepper)
- serving suggestions or variations if you have a long list
- how to choose a particular ingredient (look for clams that are tightly closed)
- additional details about ingredients
- history or customs related to a dish.

Keeping Track and Evaluating

As you develop a recipe, keep track of the most current version by numbering and dating your various drafts and files. Keep all drafts. When you think you have a winner, review your recipe with a critical eye:

- Ask yourself whether your readers would make this dish. Does it meet their needs? Is it too complicated? Have you written a headnote that would draw them in?
- Make sure ingredients are listed specifically.
- Look for opportunities to explain a step more clearly.
- Look for missed steps, or steps in the wrong order.
- Check the ingredients list against the method.
- Check temperature times, yields, and pan sizes.
- Check that you have specified low, medium, or high heat and pan size when cooking on the stove.
- Check whether you handled all foods according to food safety techniques.
- Look for wordiness or illogical reasoning.
- Examine earlier drafts to ensure you purposely changed the amounts.
- Banish typos.

Testing, the Final Frontier

I know this book is about writing, but you are not done with recipes until you or someone else tests them and successfully reproduces the dishes. I'm a fan of having mere mortals—or whoever best represents your potential readers—test your recipes. Otherwise you run the risk of making assumptions about what readers know or of leaving errors they might find.

Joan Nathan says she likes to test everything in her book and still finds things she takes for granted. "I gave my daughter a recipe that asked for one pound of carrots. She gets everything from farmers' markets. She said she doesn't know what a pound is. So I decided it was about seven carrots." Nathan likes to keep in touch with readers. She finds that their result is not always the same as hers, even when they tell her they have made the recipe exactly. Readers also give her ideas. Someone who was allergic to coconut milk suggested using soy milk with coconut flavoring as a substitute, and Nathan says she would never have thought of that.

Nathan spends a day making six or seven recipes, hosts a dinner party for twelve, and then asks guests for their honest opinions. "My social life surrounds my cookbooks," she explains. Many other writers I've interviewed use this technique instead of recipe testers. Some feel recipe testers are not always trustworthy, as they might make unauthorized substitutions that will influence whether the dish succeeds, such as canned chilies instead of fresh ones, or kidney beans instead of pinto beans.

Some authors have testers come to their homes and cook. The authors watch the tester make a recipe. Like many authors, Nathan uses an assistant to help her test. She uses college interns three days per week, with one day set aside for cooking. Other writers might have assistants shop for them or prepare ingredients.

When testing your recipes, it's best not to give them to family members and friends. Chances are they will not be entirely honest in response, even if you give them a test sheet (see "Test Sheet Sample Questions" below) and tell them to be brutal. They may decide not to bring up something they don't like because they think their opinion isn't as valid as yours, or because they don't want to hurt your feelings. I also wouldn't give a recipe to a culinary school student or a professional recipe developer, unless they are your target readers. You want people you know slightly, who like to cook.

Many recipe writers don't pay testers. Others have found drawbacks to that system. Unpaid testers take forever and are less likely to provide thorough feedback, said cookbook author David Lebovitz in an interview. "When money is involved, people take it more seriously." He has paid home testers $50 to test three recipes. Others reimburse testers for ingredients. Regardless of how or whether you pay, acknowledge testers in your book.

If you have an online presence, you have testers built in. For Jaden Hair's first cookbook, she recruited testers on her blog Steamy-Kitchen.com and got more than two hundred testers. She asked them to test three recipes and provide honest feedback on specifics of the recipe and final dish, and to submit a photo of each dish. She found a volunteer to help manage the testers and testing feedback. She set up a private blog where they could respond, and as a reward, promised to name the testers in her book. David Leite of LeitesCuli naria.com turned to fourteen recipes testers, all of whom volunteer on his site, to test each dish in his cookbook *The New Portuguese Table*.

Food bloggers Garrett McCord and Stephanie Stiavetti recruited eighty volunteers for their cookbook *Melt*, so each recipe could be tested four times. I interviewed them for my blog. They couldn't pay anyone or reimburse ingredients. Instead, they promised to list the testers' names in the finished book. They had the testers sign a confidentiality waiver in case a tester wanted to share a recipe online.

"Of course, sometimes testers had problems," said McCord. "Sometimes testers misunderstood a step or made a substitution and didn't tell us. If more than one tester had a problem and the problems were all similar, then likely something was wrong with the recipe itself. Serious retesting on our side was needed to figure out what went wrong. Once we had an answer and rewrote the recipe, it would go out again to four more testers—sometimes the same ones, other times different ones depending on each situation.

"We asked lots of questions when a recipe didn't work out. Don't be bashful about doing so as you'll need specific answers. It could be anything from a simple misunderstanding or you might have left out an ingredient or step. Also, the tester could have made a reasonable cooking choice that you simply didn't foresee or consider, but that the recipe allowed."

They created a spreadsheet to track the testing, with contact lists, notes on who got which recipe, and who needed to get their feedback forms back.

Nancy Baggett, author of *The All-American Cookie Book*, saved her developing and testing notes so she could show documentation if anyone asked. "Just for curiosity's sake," she adds, "I totaled up the testing and found I had made 38,000 cookies."

ADDING NUTRITIONAL DATA

If you want nutritional data for your recipes, such as calories and fat per serving, you have a few options: buy software, use professional services, or enter the information into free online calculators. Some software and recipe writing programs (see page 277) offer nutritional analysis and are less expensive than professional versions, which cost around $800. Keep in mind that the resulting information has room for error based on what you feed it. A "serving size," for example, determines the result, but there are no standards on what determines a size.

Some recipe developers hire dieticians or nutritionists who have their own software programs. "There are so many nuances to correctly entering data for specific ingredients that I prefer to leave it to someone who does it regularly, knows the standards, and preferably is a dietician," says Rosemary Mark, a professional recipe developer. "Someone who owns software should also be continuously updating with new ingredients and nutrition data."

If Mark needs approximate data, she uses online software (such as nutritiondata .com or recipes.sparkpeople.com/recipe-calculator.asp), but says they often don't have data for more unique ingredients. There's also the old-fashioned way of calculating each ingredient and then adding them up using ndb.nal.usda.gov but that's "very tedious," she adds.

By the end of this system of developing, writing, and testing, you should have a batch of well-written, accurate, consistent recipes. Look at all the benefits: If you've always wanted to create a lasting chronicle of your cooking, you will have succeeded. Great recipes mean editors will take you seriously. Readers who need explicit instructions will be grateful. And those who fantasized about making a dish like yours will get it right the first time.

TEST SHEET SAMPLE QUESTIONS

Whenever possible, ask questions that avoid a simple yes or no answer. Here are examples:
- Did you use the ingredients in the order listed?
- What kind of questions did you have about the directions?
- Did the ingredient quantities seem to work, or would you have added or subtracted anything? Were any ingredients difficult to find? What was your substitution, if any, and how do you think it may have affected the dish?
- How would you evaluate the time it took to prepare the dish?
- Was there anything confusing about the recipe steps?
- How did you choose which utensils, cookware, or equipment to use?
- Would you prefer that be specified?

- How were your results? What did you like or dislike about the flavors, textures, and tastes of the dish?
- What was visually appealing about the dish?
- How would you evaluate portion sizes, preparation times, and level of difficulty, on a scale of one to ten for each? Please elaborate on your answer. Say if anything was too hard or too time-consuming.
- How does this dish taste to you, on a scale of one to ten?
- How likely would you be to make this dish again? Why or why not?
- How did this recipe compare with similar ones you have tried before?
- Overall comments?

REFERENCE BOOKS

- *The New Food Lover's Companion,* by Sharon Tyler Herbst and Ron Herbst. Definitions of culinary terms, origins of foods, and explanations of techniques.
- *The Recipe Writer's Handbook,* by Barbara Gibbs Ostmann and Jane L. Baker. Much more detail than I could ever include here.
- *Recipes into Type: A Handbook for Cookbook Writers and Editors,* by Joan Whitman and Dolores Simon. A good complementary book to the above title, as they have different content and organization.
- *The Oxford Companion to Food,* by Alan Davidson. Useful for clarifications on ingredients and for writing headnotes.
- *On Food and Cooking: The Science and Lore of the Kitchen,* by Harold McGee. Scientific explanation, culinary lore, and food history in a fascinating compendium.
- *CookWise: The Secrets of Cooking Revealed,* by Shirley O. Corriher. Explanations of how certain outcomes of cooking occur and help with how to make changes.
- Your own cookbook collection. When words fail me on how to explain a technique, write a headnote, or describe an ingredient, I often turn to trusted authors to see how they do it. Aside from the ones mentioned in this chapter, other outstanding recipe writers are Richard Olney, Craig Claiborne, Rose Levy Beranbaum, Madeleine Kamman, and Flo Braker.
- For historic recipes, consider the work of Auguste Escoffier, Antonin Carême, and Édouard de Pomaine.

Writing Exercises

1. Write a recipe for your favorite sandwich. Include a headnote at least three sentences long. Now check your ability to be specific. Did you ask for a certain type of bread or for slices of a

certain thickness? Did you specify the type of mustard (not the brand name)? If you called for an exotic mayonnaise like aioli, did you include the recipe? Did you specify special equipment, such as a panini maker? If so, describe how readers can make the sandwich without it.

2. Find origins. In your files, find a half dozen handwritten recipes given to you by others, with no credit listed. Contact each person to find out where the recipe originated. If they can't remember, consider how you would alter each recipe to make it your own, or what you would write in the headnote to explain the situation.

3. Determine the sophistication level of your readers. If you plan to write a cookbook, look in your cupboards and refrigerator, and notice foods and spices you think your target reader probably will not have. Decide which will be essential to your cookbook, and which you could leave out or use substitutions.

9: CRAFTING MEMOIR AND NONFICTION

In the last decade or so, hundreds of books on every possible subject related to food have flooded the shelves. Fueled by the success of Ruth Reichl's memoir *Tender at the Bone: Growing Up at the Table*, they picked up steam. Chef memoirs became the rage. Food history books, once thought obscure and esoteric, entered the mainstream with books like *Cod: A Biography of the Fish That Changed the World* and *Salt: A World History*. Single-subject books on topics such as chocolate, oranges, and vanilla abound. Guidebooks on food and travel, biographies, and exposés such as the seminal *Fast Food Nation: The Dark Side of the American Meal* have crossed over into other categories of the bookstore. Reference books demystifying foods, their origins, and uses are plentiful.

So if you prefer not to write a cookbook, or if you've already written one and want to try another form, consider food-centric books. To succeed at narrative or reference food writing, you have to be a great detective and researcher rather than an expert. After all, what is the appropriate background of someone who wants to write a book on, say, the history of barbecue?

Take Andrew Smith, author or editor of several books including the *Oxford Encyclopedia of Food and Drink in America*, who had no expertise in food when he started writing for publication. In fact, his field is international relations. Smith entered the food-writing world after using a candy bar to explain complicated international topics to fourth graders.

He pointed to a map of the world to show where chocolate comes from, where it's manufactured, and where the money from candy bar sales goes. He realized that talking about food is a great way to get people interested in "all the things they wouldn't normally care about," such as history, culture, and science.

This chapter talks mostly about memoir, which is also useful to anyone who wants to write personal essay. From there you'll find lots of other forms that will help you with your own ideas of what to write, whether on history, cultural anthropology and philosophy, reference, guidebooks, biographies, food and health, adventures, and politics. Some of these are based on reporting in addition to personal essay. The door's wide open for food-based books.

Food-Based Memoir

Why are we attracted to reading this genre? We use our love of food to access family, culture, and emotions. First-person books based on food memory and autobiography are usually joyous, even when the memories evoked are bittersweet. Some are filled with intimate memories of life, love, and food, particularly the memoir-like *The Gastronomical Me* by M. F. K. Fisher.

One of Fisher's disciples, Ruth Reichl, the former editor of *Gourmet*, came out with her first memoir in 1986. She single-handedly fired up a new generation of food memoirists with the best-selling *Tender at the Bone*, a sensuous coming-of-age tale of a career spent following her appetite.

"It had been a forgotten genre," recalls Reichl. "M. F. K. Fisher had done it; then nobody had done it again until fifty years later. I didn't understand it was going to be a game-changing book. It touched a nerve. I feel like my whole career, my timing is based on that I was interested in food when almost no one in America was. Then suddenly everyone was interested, and I was the person already there." Her sequel, *Comfort Me with Apples: More Adventures at the Table*, gave further credibility to food-based memoir as a category.

Soon food memoir became a genre. One year after Reichl's first memoir debuted, Frances Mayes caused a sensation with *Under the Tuscan*

Sun: At Home in Italy, a memoir about fixing up a rural Italian villa, living with her husband, and cooking. It also included recipes. In 2000, Anthony Bourdain's classic, Kitchen Confidential: Adventures in the Culinary Underbelly, became a New York Times best seller. The first blog-to-book memoir arrived soon after: Molly Wizenberg's A Homemade Life: Stories and Recipes from My Kitchen Table, a coming-of-age memoir based on her blog, Orangette. The food memoir floodgates opened after that, with memoirs by chefs (such as Blood, Bones, & Butter: The Inadvertent Education of a Reluctant Chef, by Gabrielle Hamilton), travelers, cookbook authors, farmers (notably Farm City: The Education of an Urban Farmer, by Novella Carpenter), fiction writers, and newspaper reporters and critics. Some food-based memoir has even been made into movies, such as Julie Powell's Julie & Julia: 365 Days, 524 Recipes, 1 Tiny Apartment Kitchen and Nigel Slater's Toast: The Story of a Boy's Hunger. The former was said to have inspired thousands of women to become food bloggers.

These memoirs aren't just about food, and that is why they succeed. Adept storytellers write about people, relationships, and emotions, where conflict between characters is as important as stellar meals. The most successful food-based memoirs combine extraordinary stories with beautiful writing. "It seems to me that any good memoir is about relationships and telling events, so it doesn't matter if it's about food or not," says Amanda Hesser, author of the memoir Cooking for Mr. Latte: A Food Lover's Courtship, with Recipes. "Food can provide an organizing principle to the book or can serve as a sensual element or symbolism, but if the core narrative isn't there, it's not going to be a very interesting memoir."

"What makes good food writing is an exploration of the way that food shapes our lives, the way we interact with food, the way that food is a part of our relationships and the shape of our lives," agrees Wizenberg. "Not everyone thinks about food the way you and I do, but food gives their lives a certain shape, and they all have emotions and strong opinions about it."

Food-based memoir has its own characteristics. It may sound obvious, but the stories must center on food. "This is both limiting and liberating," explains Shoba Narayan, author of Monsoon Diary: A Memoir with Recipes. "Limiting because you don't include aspects of your life story that are not food related. Liberating because this gives it a tight structure and therefore one less thing the writer has to obsess about."

While many excellent books can guide you through the general topic of memoir writing (see "Great Books on Memoir Writing," page 214), they do not cover the specifics of this particular genre. Here are the most important characteristics:

Food memories. Reconstruct meals and dialogue from around the table, cooking events, and how you learned about food and food traditions. Describe the sights, tastes, sounds, and smells of the kitchen and who was there. Tell people about what they couldn't possibly have tasted or known by themselves.

Focus on the senses. Most of your scenes will take place in locations where food and eating are at the forefront, whether it's in the kitchen, dining room, garden, restaurant, market, cooking school, cafeteria, picnic area, or the woods. Put the reader there with you, experiencing all the sensations.

Sophisticated storyteller Isabelle Allende's *Aphrodite: A Memoir of the Senses*, her lusty celebration of sex and food, takes a different approach by combining more than a hundred recipes with poems, stories, photos, and drawings, and discussions on the sensual art of food, attracting your mate, and the effect of smell on libido.

Recipes. Just about every food memoir I've read includes recipes, except for those by restaurant critics.

The number of recipes to include seems to be up to you, or your editor may have suggestions. Some books contain just one or two at the end of each chapter. Some have dozens. Reichl has said that in her first book the story drove the recipes, while in her second the recipes drove the story.

Decide whether recipes are fundamental to your book's story, whether they deepen it and add texture and context. In Hesser's book about her relationship with a man who later became her husband, she detailed the meal her future mother-in-law made, the first meal Hesser made for Mr. Latte, and the first meal he made for her. These events are critical to the book's story line.

Memoir has characteristics particular to its genre as well. The first is that it covers a certain period of time, perhaps a single aspect of your life. It's not your life story, or you would call it an autobiography. Memoir tells of an emotional, physical, or psychological journey you experienced over a certain time, such as going to culinary school, or moving to Japan to learn a tea ceremony. The best memoirs read like novels. This style is called literary nonfiction, or narrative nonfiction, in which the quality of writing is as important as the story. Here are the elements of memoir:

Insights are critical. The story is not just about what you did, but how what you did changed or affected you. Without these insights, the book will be a recounting, with little liveliness and depth.

When thinking about your topic, consider how your experiences relate to readers and their lives. Sometimes things that fascinate you will not translate well to your readers. If you deal with broadly relatable themes of accomplishment, such as graduating from culinary school, taking a fantasy trip abroad, or leaving home and forging your own life and cooking style, you are more likely to succeed. Make readers feel as though they are experiencing your story, help them learn, or give them inspiration to duplicate your experience for themselves. Show them how the world works. To do so, you'll have to get out of the way. Otherwise readers will be passive, reading about you and what you did, and not experiencing your story directly. Be part of the scene without dominating it.

Here's an example from A. J. Liebling, who pays for his feasts in Paris with money wired from his parents. He writes in *Between Meals: An Appetite for Paris*, "At the Credit, I would be received with scornful solemnity, like a suitor for the hand of a miser's daughter. I was made to sit on a bare wooden bench with the other wretches come to claim money from the bank, all feeling more like culprits by the minute. A French bank, by the somber intensity of its addiction to money, establishes an emotional claim on funds in transit. The client feels in the moral position of a wayward mother who has left her babe on a doorstep and later comes back to claim it from the foster parents, who now consider it their own."

Can't you imagine Liebling at the bank, seething? You share his disgust and discomfort, right down to how it feels to sit on a hard surface. You agree that the bank is unreasonable to treat him this way, because things like this have happened to you. And you're having fun reading his diatribe because it's witty. On the other hand, he could have written, "I really hate going to the bank. I don't like the way they treat me. I feel as if I've done something wrong. They have no right to keep me from my money." Now, it's all about him, not about the scene. You don't know where he is, you feel no compassion or outrage, and there's no humor to provide levity. You watch him have a tantrum, from a distance. That's boring.

The story evokes emotion from the reader. You want readers to feel joy, sadness, and a host of other feelings.

Additionally, your story must seem real to readers, and you must have enough distance to make realistic assessments of how you felt at the time. If readers are not convinced, it doesn't really matter what happened or how it unfolded. Many people use memoirs as a form of therapy. It's fine to do so, but your story may not be publishable if you are the only one who understands the course of events, or if there is no action or dialogue. You must be capable of objectivity about that period in your life. If not, turn it into fiction.

Strong characters come alive on the page. Even more minor characters need vitality. Describe the person's appearance in specific detail to create a picture for the reader. One writer who excels at character study is Ludwig Bemelmans. His hilarious memoir *Hotel Bemelmans*, a behind-the-scenes tell-all about a New York hotel in the 1920s, was recently reissued.

In memoir as in fiction writing, your character and tone are essential to the book. You'll probably have to make yourself into a character as well, even one that isn't exactly true to life. I like memoirs that show a writer's excitement about that fascinating part of his or her life and the wonder of it. Another way to show character is to use humor and self-deprecation in your writing.

If certain people are critical characters in your story, interview them now. You think they'll always be around and there's time, but you can't be certain. I conducted oral histories with my aunt and mother before they died. Now I have a transcript of their memories. I can listen to the tapes to add texture and credibility to my characters. On the tape, I hear how my auntie paused to take long drags on her cigarette, for example, and the raspy quality of her voice. But my dad died young, and I had thought there was lots of time.

If you feel apprehensive about exposing certain thoughts or incidents, there are ways to create boundaries between yourself and readers. Just as you want to be careful not to overdo the emotional aspects of your past, you must be prepared to live with whatever you disclose about yourself. Reichl said she "didn't talk about the really bad stuff in the first book. I didn't want to hurt people's memories." At the same time, your duty is to tell the essential emotional truth, and not get lost in what you think you should be feeling. You don't have to reveal everything about yourself. Choose what's essential to the story, and reveal these secrets throughout the book.

To play it safe, some writers employ false names for individuals they want to protect, those who might be hurt or upset by the way they are portrayed. Because I was trained as a reporter, I'm not fond of this technique, where emphasis is on telling the literal truth. Since no two people remember an event or individual exactly the same way, however, writers can take license, as long as the point is to bring out the inherent truthfulness of the story. Some authors also merge characters or alter the setting or timing. That sounds like fiction to me, but you have to decide what you can live with. If you're afraid you can't accurately reconstruct a conversation, put a disclaimer in the front of the book saying you did your best to get the essence of what people said.

Typically, you shouldn't let the people mentioned in your book read your manuscript before it's published, because they will find things they don't like. Find ways to reassure them without getting specific about their role in the book. If you're afraid you'll hurt or embarrass a loved one, make that person less identifiable in the book. If you write something potentially damaging, a publisher might ask for a written consent form from that person.

Reichl got permission from Colman Andrews, cofounder of *Saveur*, to write about their affair. She didn't send him the manuscript. Andrews told me the story: "She took me to lunch at Fleur de Sel in Manhattan and told me she had written about me and our relationship in the book, then asked my permission to use my real name and the actual circumstances. If I was uncomfortable with that, she said, she would be willing to give me a pseudonym and change some identifying details. She added that she didn't think I'd mind anything she had written.

"On the principle that one probably shouldn't do anything in life that one wouldn't be willing to read about later, I told her to go ahead and use the 'real' me. And as I told her later, it turned out I did mind some of what she had written, not because it made me seem like a cad (which I probably was), but because it made me sound so humorless about food and wine, which I'd like to think I wasn't. But ultimately, I can't complain. She did a good job of capturing the spirit of the times (and of our relationship), even if she played a bit fast and loose—as she readily admits—with the facts."

The dialogue of your characters rings true. In writing *Kitchen Confidential*, author Anthony Bourdain said in an interview that he "did not want real working cooks and restaurant people to read the thing and say, 'What the hell is this? I don't know any chefs who talk like this! This is not my life!'"

You tell the truth. "If you're not honest, it's boring," says Hesser. "It's the texture of relationships that's interesting, and if you smooth it all out, it's going to be insipid."

You are careful of the nostalgia trap. If you're writing about the past, nostalgia can be dull. No one wants to read about a perfect past of discovering food during childhood, where a loving mother and grandmother were ingenious cooks who made complicated meals by hand. Avoid sentimentality as your main theme. Be willing to write about something mundane or imperfect.

Memoir writing includes extensive research so that you can choose which details to include. If your memoir captures your family's past, look for documents other than recipes that give clues about that time, such as marriage and death certificates, letters, maps, family trees, photos, music, movies, and magazines from that era to give you a sense of the times. If you plan to write about an adventure while you are living it, such as cooking on a houseboat in France, collect and save the things around you to unlock memories later. Take photos. Write in a daily journal. Save menus, tickets, and relevant newspaper stories.

You use plot devices from fiction, such as conflict, suspense, and tension, by creating desire. "All storytelling from the beginning of recorded time is based on somebody wanting something, facing obstacles, not getting it, trying to get it, trying to overcome obstacles, and finally getting or not getting what he wanted," writes Sol Stein in *Stein on Writing*.

"Why are we so attracted to stories?" asks Paul J. Zak, a brain researcher, in a piece about the attraction of storytelling. "My lab has spent the last several years seeking to understand why stories can move us to tears, change our attitudes, opinions and behaviors, and even inspire us—and how stories change our brains, often for the better."

The challenge is to create a universal story structure, he said. An engaging story has a dramatic arc. "It starts with something new and surprising, and increases tension with difficulties that the characters must overcome, often because of some failure or crisis in their past, and then leads to a climax where the characters must look deep inside themselves to overcome the looming crisis, and once this transformation occurs, the story resolves itself."

Your book has a narrative arc. This is the critical point in a novel, where tension is at its highest, and you have used suspense to build up to this moment. "The biggest thing was finding my way to a story with a narrative arc," says Wizenberg. "It required diving in. I didn't know what the arc was going to be until it was there."

The ending reflects the story. Your conclusion shows how your life and impressions have changed, and the consequences of that change upon you.

Know how the story ends. A big part of defining your memoir is to determine where it stops. You have to be over the experience to put it into perspective. When you write your story, you will lead up to the end, foreshadowing it throughout the book, and you must know what to conclude. Your book must have a definable beginning, middle, and end. In *Animal, Vegetable, Miracle*, by Barbara Kingsolver, the subtitle says it all: *A Year of Food Life*.

You might start by figuring out the reason you want to write a memoir in the first place. Does it fill a powerful need? Do you have an unusual story or a life-changing experience? Was it the first time you did something? Did you overcome adversity in a way that will inspire others? Do you want to record an event from the past, your accomplishments, family history, meals you ate, or recipes?

The structure of a memoir can be a series of anecdotes, vignettes, or essays strung together into a larger, overarching narrative. It can be chronological or written as diary entries. A memoir is not about every event, or even the most important ones during that time, unless they are relevant to the central story of your book.

Organizing a long manuscript requires vigilance. You will continuously distill and discard, and it may take you some time to get to the exact theme to pursue. You may write a list of points you wish to make, or a skeleton or outline, and change it several times. That means you're making progress because you're thinking it through.

If you're worried your life might be too boring, you're not alone. Hesser said as much in an interview. Even though she was a full-time *New York Times* writer, she said she was afraid she wouldn't be able to find or gather stories. "I didn't want it to be just self-involved blather about my life," she admitted. Even though it's hard, keep your inner critic at bay. Hesser knew she had a good story. She probably felt vulnerable by publishing such personal aspects of her life. You must believe you have a good story, too, particularly if you have told it and people respond positively.

For more on writing memoir, read some of the books I list below, or take classes to jump-start your writing.

• •

GREAT BOOKS ON MEMOIR WRITING

- *Inventing the Truth: The Art and Craft of Memoir,* edited by William Zinsser. Famous authors on how they wrote their memoirs.
- *Writing About Your Life: A Journey into the Past,* by William Zinsser. Part memoir and part writing advice from an author with a fascinating career.
- *Old Friend from Far Away: How to Write a Memoir,* by Natalie Goldberg (audio book). A practical yet impassioned call to write from a well-known writing teacher, with exercises.
- *Unreliable Truth: On Memoir and Memory,* by Maureen Murdock. How identity shapes memory and why people remember the same thing differently, with writing exercises.
- *Writing Life Stories,* by Bill Roorbach. Terrific exercises at the end of each chapter to get your imagination roaring.

• •

Food History

Do you wonder about the history of foods, cooking, food preparation, and food etiquette? Consider writing about food from the past and providing new insights. Many forms of food-based books include history. For memoir, you'll want to find your own culinary history and family information about who cooked where and what they made. For a book about travels in Mexico, you might want to investigate the origin of tortillas, if that's part of the adventure. Researching origins and significance of foods in history makes the material come alive.

Food history needn't be dry or boring. Jessica B. Harris, an educator and culinary historian, incorporates food history in her celebrated cookbooks, discussing regional food differences and subjects such as the edible history of Africa, all with scholarship and sophisticated storytelling. Betty Fussell's *Story of Corn* will entertain you while explaining how corn transformed the way the entire world eats.

If you are passionate about a subject that requires delving into history, your book can bring fresh perspectives to old stories, says food historian Sandy Oliver. So many questions need answers. She's curious about many things, such as "What did the pilgrims eat for the first Thanksgiving? Was the Italian Catherine de' Medici responsible for French haute cuisine? Is it true that people spiced meat highly in past times to hide the bad taste of spoilage?"

While many food history books languish in obscurity, some make their way into the mainstream, as demonstrated by Mark Kurlansky's *Cod* and David Kamp's *The United States of Arugula: The Sun-Dried, Cold-Pressed, Dark-Roasted, Extra-Virgin Story of the American Food Revolution*. Most historians wouldn't think of food as an appropriate category, says author Andrew Smith. The field was wide open when he entered it twenty years ago. He believes it still is. "Anybody can pick a topic," he says. "The secret is to talk to people about things they know but have never thought about before, and are shocked and surprised when you start giving them context."

What all good food history books have in common is the hundreds of hours of careful research authors put into them. Accuracy is paramount. "If you're working from your own memory [as in a memoir], no big deal, but in a historical context, you have to be right," says Oliver, author of the award-winning book *Saltwater Foodways*. To research historical cooking, you must go past theorizing and re-create the food as accurately as possible, she says. If you're interested in fireplace cooking, for example, "go find a fireplace and cook something in it. Or take a vacation. Or visit house museums. Living history museums sponsor all kinds of weekends," Oliver advises.

To get started, she suggests you "go to the library and read everything you can lay your hands on for a week or more. Or do library research on the Internet." For research, you can't just use the Internet, as tempting as that is, because incorrect information is cut and pasted repeatedly and eventually treated as gospel. You have to check dates and information, or you will not be taken seriously as a writer. Get to know other food historians who can advise you on how to write food history well. Oliver lists culinary history groups across the country on foodhistorynews.com. Many big cities have groups you can look up called "culinary historians."

For general information on writing food history, go to food-culture. org, and join the Association of the Study of Food and Society, which lists links to programs and conferences. An excellent, detailed resource is Rachel Laudan's blog post "Getting Started in Food History" (rachellaudan .com/getting-started-in-food-history), which lists resources for research.

How long does it take to write a history book? Oliver estimates that writing a one-subject book can be covered in a year or two. "Grab something out of your life experience that interests you terribly," she advises. That's good advice for any kind of book.

Cultural Anthropology and Philosophy

These books study the social, symbolic, political, and economic roles of food and cultures. Often written by academics, they may require peer review and are often published by university presses. Some emerge from masters' theses or doctoral dissertations.

These books have a hard time getting into the mainstream, partly because they are written in a scholarly tone for a specialized audience and are often expensive to purchase. Many cite previous works and are heavily footnoted, perhaps intimidating the casual reader. They are also not as accessible as books in the cookbook section of bookstores. Instead, search for them in the history, philosophy, or anthropology sections. For example, my paperback edition of *No Foreign Food: The American Diet in Time and Place,* by geography professor Richard Pillsbury, suggests on its back cover that it be placed in "American/Cultural Studies."

Some books in this category cross over. *Much Depends on Dinner: The Extraordinary History and Mythology, Allure and Obsessions, Perils and*

Taboo of an Ordinary Meal, by Margaret Visser, tells the story behind ordinary items found on the American dinner table, such as butter, salt, and roast chicken. *USA Today* reviewed *We Are What We Eat: Ethnic Food and the Making of Americans*, by Donna R. Gabaccia, and said, "Today's multiethnic American diet offers intriguing insight into the character of the nation. . . . Gabaccia explores the journey of these ethnic foods from pushcarts to the national marketplace and how . . . ethnic cuisines have retained their essential and often ritualized role in American life."

Another respected book is the anthology *Food and Culture: A Reader*, edited by anthropology professors Carole Counihan and Penny Van Esterik. It examines the social, symbolic, and political-economic roles of what—and how—we eat. While M. F. K. Fisher and Frances Moore Lappé (*Diet for a Small Planet*) penned two of the essays, academics, historians, cultural anthropologists, and researchers wrote the rest. Topics in this kind of food writing can be challenging to the general reader.

Reference

These books are structured as a series of listings, like dictionaries, where you look up something to do with food. Sharon Tyler Herbst spent years refining and updating various versions of *The Food Lover's Companion*. Her book has sold more than one million copies. Another book I love and use regularly in my kitchen is David Joachim's *Food Substitutions Bible*, which tells me exactly what and how much to use when I don't have the required recipe ingredient on hand.

Smaller reference works on the subject of your passion might be a bit less ambitious and more doable. If general topics seem too enormous, tackle a narrower subject that serves as more of a guide. Some of these books do quite well. Ben Schott's quirky *Schott's Food & Drink Miscellany* contains an addictive blend of oddities, such as how to cook a swan, how Hemingway liked his martinis, and why asparagus makes your urine smell. *Newsweek* called it "as hilarious as it is addictive," and *Vanity Fair* reviewed it as "utterly indispensable."

Even the big reference books don't take forever. Author and editor Andrew Smith told me his *Oxford Encyclopedia of Food and Drink in America* was published three years after he got the contract. He hired dozens of freelance writers who wrote entries and indexes. Like other big reference books on food, the *Encyclopedia* is an invaluable research tool. If you don't want to buy these huge books, go to a library large enough to keep them. The best known are:

- *The Cambridge World History of Food*, edited by Kenneth F. Kiple and Kriemhild Coneè Ornelas—looks at the relationship between what we eat today and what humans ate millions of years ago.
- *The Encyclopedia of Food and Culture* (part of Scribner Library of Daily Life), edited by Solomon H. Katz and William Woys Weaver—covers food in relation to society.
- *The Oxford Companion to Food*, edited by Alan Davidson—comprises an enormous, authoritative work on food, seasonings, and cooking
- *The Oxford Encyclopedia of Food and Drink in America*, edited by Andrew F. Smith—covers every aspect from a historical and cultural context

Literary lists are another form of food reference. If you enjoy searching publications for pithy quotes, you could collect your findings in a compendium of witty one-liners and quotes about food. Some books trace the history of words and explain their usage. Lists of historical cookbooks or food-based poems, bibliographies by people who collect cookbooks, and books with meal suggestions for reading groups are just a few of the book ideas that might inspire you.

If you like essays, apply to have yours reprinted in an anthology. Holly Hughes created an instant annual work when she compiled the first *Best Food Writing* in 2000. She guaranteed her success with a foreword by Alice Waters, and the series is still going strong.

Guidebooks, Both Local and Abroad

If you like to travel—even locally—and you've devoted yourself to finding insider information—like where to find vegetarian restaurants on the road, you could write a guidebook. Packed with useful, practical information, these books are written by those who pick an area and become experts on it, guiding the reader with careful research. These days, they compete with the Internet for in-depth, up-to-date information, which makes them more challenging to publish.

Laura Taxel spent two years writing *Cleveland Ethnic Eats*, a profitable guidebook. If you're considering writing one of your own, here is her advice:

- Look for an unmet need, a lack of organized, easy-to-use, easy-to-access information on a topic people want to discover.
- Define a specific geographic area to cover.
- The yellow pages already exists, so don't think all you have to do is gather names, addresses, and phone numbers. A guidebook's value is in the personalized, value-added information a knowledgeable author provides.
- Invest time and legwork in gathering a significant sample of your listings, and put together a meaningful representation of the book's content before you take your idea to a publisher.
- A guidebook requires a big investment of time and out-of-pocket expense up front. You'll have to pay for your own transportation costs, food bills, and telephone calls.
- View your guidebook as an ongoing project. Regular updates require a steady infusion of new and corrected information.

If you've written a book that sells, you'll have to keep it up to date. Taxel revises hers annually. "You won't make big bucks fast, but it can become a steady source of revenue and make you a recognized expert in a particular market, which leads to many other writing and speaking opportunities," says Taxel. "That's what *Cleveland Ethnic Eats* has done for me."

Take the same kind of guidelines and go abroad to your most beloved tourist destination. You may want to pitch a book idea to a travel-based publisher. What you decide to write depends on your area of interest, your ability to find information meaningful to other visitors, and whether you have the means to travel and pay your own bills.

Biographies

Fascinated by a certain figure in the food world? Write a biography. Laura Shapiro, an accomplished author of two historical books, *Perfection*

Salad: Women and Cooking at the Turn of the Century and *Something from the Oven: Reinventing Dinner in 1950s America,* turned to a biography of Julia Child after Child's death. She calls the book "an extended essay about Child and her impact on the culture, who she was and what she meant. I could only do it after her death. It's more of an appreciative analysis," she explains.

How do you come up with the right person to profile? It can be anyone who strikes a chord. "You have to want to lose yourself in that person. That person has to be big and interesting enough, or small and interesting enough, with depth you can throw yourself into," says Shapiro.

Two other examples of biographies publishers found worthwhile are *Stand Facing the Stove: The Story of the Women Who Gave America the Joy of Cooking* and *Cooking for Kings: The Life of Antonin Carême, the First Celebrity Chef.*

Shapiro says the biographies she used as guides are *Epicurean Delight: The Life and Times of James Beard,* by Evan Jones, and *James Beard: A Biography,* by Robert Clark.

Food and Health

These are two always-trendy topics that are even more successful when they go hand in hand. As special diets become more mainstream, books on everything from wheat-free, dairy-free, and paleo diets to general "let food be thy medicine" treatises are crowding the shelves. Most are advice-based cookbooks, written by doctors, nutritionists, and dietitians, with a few chapters of advice in the front. This is another area where bloggers and self-educated experts are building credibility, such as Vani Hari's book *The Food Babe Way: Break Free from the Hidden Toxins in Your Food and Lose Weight, Look Years Younger, and Get Healthy in Just 21 Days.*

Your decision about what to write will be fueled by your enthusiasm, interest, experience, and ability to find and explain technical information. If you feel you need expertise, team up with a credentialed expert and cowrite the book. Ask experts for access to their information and credit them in the book. Or interview experts and quote them to give more credibility to your project.

Kitchen Science

One of the best-known books on kitchen science is *On Food and Cooking: The Science and Lore of the Kitchen*, by Harold McGee, a reference book that explains everything from lactose intolerance to the composition of a corn kernel. He wrote it as a companion guide to cookbooks in which readers could discover more in-depth information about cooking, particularly the chemistry, history, and uses of foods.

McGee taught English and writing at Yale University, and he trained as a physicist and astronomer. Recently he updated and expanded the second edition into a more general food reference book. His biggest problem was knowing where to stop. "Writing half a page about coffee isn't going to cut it anymore," he admits. He thought ten pages would be better, but "each subject is fascinating and could be a book." When I asked him how he could verify the accuracy of hundreds of entries, he said, "You do the best you can; then the world decides whether you did a good job. It has to do with personal standards. If you skim the subject, you are most likely to make mistakes. I try to burrow down a few stages, and then I feel confident about the material." This is excellent advice for researching any kind of book, but then again, it took him ten years to write the second edition.

Biochemist Shirley Corriher wrote *CookWise: The Secrets of Cooking Revealed* and *BakeWise: The Hows and Whys of Successful Baking* about the way food works in a recipe, to enable cooks to get the results they want. Her books explains such things as why cookies made with butter turn out flat and crisp, while cookies made with some shortening are soft and puffy.

If you want to write about how to become a better cook by understanding science, this category might be for you, if you have something new to say.

Adventures, Food Journalism, and Politics

Many of the categories in this chapter overlap, particularly here, where adventure-based, journalistic books are likely to include memoir, food politics, and food history.

If you're interested in chronicling a hands-on experience, such as attending cooking school or working in a restaurant, you've come upon a topic publishers like. Bill Buford, a staff writer for the *New Yorker*, wrote *Heat: An Amateur Cook's Adventures as a Kitchen Slave, Pasta Maker, and Apprentice to a Dante-Quoting Butcher on a Hilltop in Tuscany*. That's the longest subtitle I've ever read. In *The Making of a Chef: Mastering Heat at the Culinary Institute*, Michael Ruhlman explains how the most prominent cooking school in the country trains chefs, and included his own thoughts as he went through the process. Both books are also memoirs, capturing a slice of time in the authors' lives.

Speaking of culinary adventures, *A Cook's Tour*, about chef Anthony Bourdain's world tour, chews up and spits out the usual food and travel journalism in which a writer might typically discuss more rarified meals. Bourdain took what was then a new approach. Here's his first sentence, in the form of a letter to his wife: "I'm about as far away from you as I've ever been—a hotel (the hotel, actually) in Pailin, a miserable one-horse dunghole in northwest Cambodia, home to those not-so-adorable scamps, the Khmer Rouge." If you have a reporting background and don't mind causing trouble, you might investigate a part of the food industry. *The Jungle*, a novel by Upton Sinclair, set the standard in 1905, when Lewis exposed the inhumane conditions of Chicago's stockyards. Most investigative reporting is nonfiction, however. Eric Schlosser's *Fast Food Nation* enjoyed a deservingly long ride on the best-seller lists because of his prescient timing, excellent journalism, and passionate writing. *Food Politics: How the Food Industry Influences Nutrition and Health*, by Marion Nestle, takes an insider's perspective. It's an eye-opening read as well.

UC Berkeley professor of journalism and science writer Michael Pollan eclipsed them all, however, with *The Omnivore's Dilemma*, which examines America's "national eating disorder" by tracing four meals, and subsequent books *In Defense of Food* and *Food Rules*, each with several weeks on best-seller lists.

"More people feel that food is the solution. That is, they see food as the way to change the world around them," explained Brian Halweil in *Edible Manhattan*. "As a result, food writers carry the weight of the world on their shoulders. People don't learn how to eat from doctors and nutritionists anymore, they learn from Michael Pollan and Barbara Kingsolver.

"In this sense, food writers today have more in common with Upton Sinclair than with Maureen Dowd, or with restaurant reviewers, for that matter. That is, food writers are required to keep the bigger context in mind; are required to shine a light not just on a restaurant's service or noise level, but on how the foods got to the plate. Weaving in issues of sustainability and ethics must be done tactfully and artfully, but it must be done."

If you're not into issues of sustainability, company profiles are popular ways to write about food and who controls the food industry. A background as a reporter would be particularly useful here, as these are not vanity books, in which the company approves the content before it can be published and often controls it. But that's not out of the question either, if you want a work-for-hire position—meaning you are retained to write a company's history. A related book, *Candyfreak: A Journey Through the Chocolate Underbelly of America*, takes more of a travel memoir approach from the perspective of the candy-obsessed author, Steve Almond.

Nonfiction food writing continues to expand in exciting and novel ways, now that the genre has opened up past memoir. I hope reading this chapter made you as excited as I am by the prospects. The variety shows how mainstream the subject of food has become and how it can be translated into many styles. If several book ideas popped into your head as you read, capture that list. Book ideas have to come from somewhere, and one of my goals in writing this book is to help you generate yours.

Writing Exercises

1. Generate food-based memories for your memoir. Map out the street where you lived as a child, and write about the food you tasted from other homes. Draw the street where you grew up on a sheet of paper. Add a drawing or X marking the spot of each building. Add the names of families you knew or kids you played with. Now draw upon your memory of eating foods for the first time. Write about three or four times when playmates or their parents presented you with a food you had never eaten before. Create the scene. Remember your apprehension or excitement. Recall the taste on your tongue. Once you have

documented a few strong images, weave them together in a story. Write about how you felt eating those new foods, how they changed you, and whether you eat any of them today.

2. Flex your research skills with an essay on food history. Name your favorite spice. Now write five hundred words about it. Discover the country of origin and how the spice is harvested, processed, and sold. Find out whether it was used in a famous historical dish or prized by certain people. See whether traders took it on trade routes to another country, and how that country used the spice. Say how it's used today and how you cook or bake with it. If you like, conclude by developing a recipe using the spice.

3. Write a short essay on a current events topic that really gets you going, such as factory farming, fast food, or eating locally. Does your point of view add something new to the conversation? Who are the major figures worth interviewing or reading about? If you find you love this subject, start with a few freelanced articles about it to determine interest.

10: A RECIPE FOR GOOD FICTION

So far this book has been about nonfiction, the biggest category of food writing by far. But writing fiction, it turns out, is not that different. In both cases, your job is to tell a story, develop compelling characters, convey passion, put the reader in the scene, and let the food play the leading role. Both fiction and nonfiction include suspense and tension to drive the narrative. Both use food to establish the place, time, culture, and mood. If you've read the other chapters, you've been prepared for fiction.

In fiction writing, you get to make up characters, plot, and dialogue. Your story can take place anywhere in the world, during any period (or even on a distant planet in the future). You get to merge people you know into a single person and take revenge on people you don't like—as long as they won't know it. If some events haven't turned out well in your life, they can turn out well in your fiction. If you've always hated your mother's cooking, a character can have a mother who's a celebrated chef.

In fiction, food is a device that helps you develop characters based on how they cook, which foods they like, and how they eat. It also creates a mood or sets a scene, and establishes the time. "Food is everything," says Phyllis Richman, author of *The Butter Did It: A Gastronomic Tale of Love and Murder*, *Murder on the Gravy Train*, and *Who's Afraid of Virginia Ham?* "It's part of the relationship between Chas [Richman's main character] and her lover, Chas and her daughter, and it's the murder weapon. While they're having an argument, the daughter cooks, and Chas sets the table. Food is what occupies them. It facilitates working out problems among characters, explains characters to one another, and identifies people."

In that vein, a skilled writer might shape a character's personality based on how the character handles food and how and when he eats. In *The Garden of Eden*, Ernest Hemingway writes: "He went out to the empty kitchen and found a tin of Maquereau Vin Blanc Capitaine Cook and opened it and took it, perilous with edge-level juice, with a cold bottle of the Tuborg beer out to the bar. He opened the beer, took the bottle top between his right thumb and the first joint of his right forefinger and bent it in until it was flattened together, put it in his pocket since he saw no container to toss it into, raised the bottle that was still cold to his hand and now beaded wet in his fingers and, smelling the aroma from the opened tin of spiced and marinated mackerel, he took a long drink of the cold beer."

Wow. I've read that paragraph at least two dozen times, and it still slays me with its muscular sensuousness. Look at the specific language, how he slowed down the moment. Now what do you know about this character? He's strong, masculine, sexual, and deliberate. He takes great pleasure in food. He doesn't litter.

In some fiction, food itself becomes a character. In *Five Quarters of the Orange*, by Joanne Harris, an orange becomes the villain by taking on evil powers. The smell of oranges brings on a woman's crippling headaches. She will not permit them in her house. Her daughter steals an orange and uses it to control her by placing it on her mother's pillow, triggering migraines. Other negative roles food can play include dismay, disgust, detachment, disillusion, destruction, danger, or even death—the all-important D-words.

The assent to eat—sitting down to dinner, taking a cup of tea— can become the catalyst for action. In *Anna Karenina* by Leo Tolstoy, Levin, the main character, drinks an awful lot of tea, often at the start of a paragraph as a way to begin a scene. He might order tea sent to his study, signaling the beginning of work. Or he might sit with others and have tea, as in: "Levin was sitting beside his hostess at the tea-table and had to keep up a conversation with her and her sister, who was sitting opposite him."

By default, much of the dialogue in novels with food themes takes place over food at parties, cafés, and particularly at dinner tables. Edith Wharton's *The Age of Innocence* uses food to advance the plot, eventually: "After a velvety oyster soup came shad and cucumbers, then a young broiled turkey with corn fritters, followed by a canvas-back with currant jelly and a celery mayonnaise. Mr. Letterblair, who lunched on a sandwich and tea, dined deliberately and deeply, and insisted on his guests doing the same. Finally, when the closing rites had been accomplished, the cloth was removed, cigars were lit, and Mr. Letterblair, leaning back in his chair and pushing the port westward, said, spreading his back agreeably to the coal fire behind him, 'The whole family is against a divorce. And I think rightly.'"

Sometimes the plot relies on the elaborate meals the main character makes and the dialogue that results. In *Serving Crazy with Curry* by Amulya Malladi, a woman gets fired from her job and suffers a miscarriage. Feeling shame for abandoning her traditional Indian family, she attempts suicide. Her mother saves her life. The woman moves in with her parents but refuses to speak, taking up cooking instead and prompting her family to engage in conversations over meals that draw them closer.

There are all types of culinary fiction, from murder mysteries to children's books to novels based on food to joint themes of food and sex. While many classic writers are never thought of as food writers, they write beautifully on the topic, as illustrated above by Hemingway, Tolstoy, and Wharton. Even children's books with food themes present a satisfying challenge. This chapter explores all types of food writing in book-length fiction. Its goal is not to teach you how to write fiction, but to generate story ideas by giving you examples of successful titles and plot lines, and to help you shape your individual voice, style, and view of the world.

Food in Classic Literature

It's said that good writers are great readers. Now that you've read examples that show how fiction writers insert descriptions of food or meals to move a story along or to depict emotion, once you start looking at classic literature, you'll find useful examples everywhere. Here are some of my favorite books:

- *The Age of Innocence*, by Edith Wharton, tells the story of a man engaged to a society girl who longs for a life of passion with someone else, set against a New York backdrop of grand dinners and parties.
- *Down and Out in Paris and London*, by George Orwell, includes his experiences in the unpleasant hotel and restaurant world in which he worked in the 1930s.
- *Feast of Words: For Lovers of Food and Fiction*, edited by Anna Shapiro, gives you a taste of many writers and their love of food. She pairs inventive menus and recipes with passages of fiction by authors such as Charles Dickens, Doris Lessing, and Thomas Hardy. Her book is instructive because it is organized by themes found in classic novels, such as "Starved Love," "Penitential Meals," and "Eating the Social Index."
- *The Great Gatsby*, by F. Scott Fitzgerald, details summer parties out on the famous lawn: "On buffet tables, garnished with glistening hors-d'oeuvre, spiced baked hams crowded against salads of harlequin designs and pastry pigs and turkeys bewitched to a dark gold."
- *The History of Tom Jones, a Foundling*, by Henry Fielding, employs a witty eighteenth-century narrator who says literature is like a meal, in which the paying customer expects to be entertained and satisfied.
- *Moby Dick*, by Herman Melville, describes foods of his times as a way to show authenticity and detail. Here's a picture of seafood chowder: "It was made of small juicy clams, scarcely bigger than hazelnuts, mixed with pounded ship biscuits, and salted pork cut up into little flakes; the whole enriched with butter, and plentifully seasoned with pepper and salt."
- *Swann's Way* by Marcel Proust includes a wistful passage about a madeleine and introduces the famous passage about the relationship between food and memory: "But when from a long-distant past nothing subsists, after the people are dead, after the things are broken and scattered, taste and smell alone, more fragile but more enduring, more unsubstantial, more persistent, more faithful, remain poised a long time, like

souls, remembering; waiting, hoping, amid the ruins of all the rest; and bear unflinchingly, in the tiny and almost impalpable drop of their essence, the vast structure of recollection."

WRITING SHORT STORIES

If writing a novel sounds a little overwhelming, there are always short stories. Generally, short stories are about a transformative event for one main character. They have fewer characters than novels, no subplots, and less backstory. You have to streamline because you have less space. A classic short story that involves a baker is Raymond Carver's "A Small, Good Thing."

Most literary magazines publish short stories of between three thousand and five thousand words. Stories of less than one thousand words are considered flash fiction, and there is even a magazine called *Flash Fiction Online* devoted to that style. If you write a piece longer than twenty thousand words, it can be called a novella.

Culinary Crime Capers

Great dining has often been a part of mystery novels. In the 1960s, Nero Wolfe, Rex Stout's sleuth, had a rule that no one could interrupt a meal, including those prepared by his personal chef, Fritz. Meals were an integral part of the plot in Agatha Christie books, from arsenic in the food to the way the murderer stalked his victim at a dinner party to exposing the murderer at tea. More modern examples of culinary crime are Nan Lyons's *Someone Is Killing the Great Chefs of Europe*, and television personality Anthony Bourdain's thrillers set in the restaurant industry and seasoned with culinary detail: *Gone Bamboo* and *Bone in the Throat*.

Some writers create food-based murder mysteries based on ordinary characters. They have moved the genre away from stories about hardboiled detectives who never eat, to cozies, books that focus more on character and relationships. Joyce and Jim Levine, who have written more than forty books together, describe the genre: "Cozies are light mysteries depicting real-life people solving mysteries in unusual ways. The genre is steadily broadening as their popularity increases. Traditionally, the cozy was a British novel featuring sweet elderly women and other harmless protagonists. Probably the best known is Agatha Christie's Miss Marple series.

"Today's cozies occur in every place and time with men and women as sleuths. They have an amateur detective, although there is often a police officer in a supporting role. The amateur sleuth gathers clues by listening to gossip and by paying attention to surroundings. The cozy sleuth attracts murder. Murders happen everywhere around him or her. The sleuth has access to a large number of people, usually through a career.

"The cozy is heavy on dialogue, light on gritty depictions of death and the murder itself. They are full of suspense and dark corners of intrigue. But cozy murder mysteries are tamer than their thriller counterparts. Descriptions of the crime scene are toned down. Sex is never graphic. The stories are thoughtful rather than thriller. The books generally have strong, quirky characters and are set in interesting places. Cozy sleuths come from many different occupations and from any time or place."

That means the main character could be a food journalist, baker, caterer, innkeeper, chocolate maker, or coffeehouse owner, as they are in the books I've discovered. Here, the plot ideas are often campy and the titles full of puns and double entendres. Recipes are always part of the form, although the amount varies.

Phyllis Richman, the top restaurant reviewer of the *Washington Post* until her retirement, wrote her three cozies while working full-time. "I had been doing my job for so long I needed some freshening," she explains. "I had been thinking for decades about doing mysteries. I also thought if I wanted to get published, it would be easier to do so from the *Post* than from retirement." She stayed home one day a week to write, and after fifty-two weeks, her first book was ready.

Richman used her insider knowledge of the restaurant business as a theme for three books, as cozies are usually written as a series. In *Murder on the Gravy Train*, Chas Wheatley, restaurant critic for the fictional *Washington Examiner*, flies to Paris with her chef lover for a benefit gala. When her lover dies of an apparent heart attack from soaring cholesterol, Wheatley knows better. She continues writing her reviews and recipes while investigating his death. In *The Butter Did It*, Wheatley finds something rotten with the food at one of Washington's most popular new restaurants. The head chef is missing. Wheatley tracks down the dead chef, eating her way from one restaurant to the next and giving readers an inside look at the restaurant business. In *Who's Afraid of Virginia Ham?* a new reporter, angling for Wheatley's job as food editor, dies by eating lethal Virginia ham at a work function.

At first Richman had to get used to new tools of plot, character development, point of view, and dialogue. But there's nothing that different about fiction, she decided. "It's just another form of restaurant reviews and travel writing."

Probably the most famous of the food-themed cozy writers is Diane Mott Davidson. Some of her mysteries have appeared on the *New York Times* and *USA Today* best-seller lists. When starting out, Davidson wrote two regular mysteries before selling her third, *Catering to Nobody,* to St. Martin's Press at age forty-one. An avid cook and fan of Julia Child, she convinced the publisher to include four recipes.

Davidson's writing group suggested she focus her murder mystery on Goldy Korman, a caterer, who was then a minor character. "For Goldy, cooking heals," said Davidson in an interview. "If she can cook, she can get a feeling of control over the world. Cooking is more than just comfort food, it's about nurturing oneself while nurturing others." Davidson's recipes come from food ideas suggested by friends, colleagues, restaurant dishes, or sometimes right out of her head, featuring ingredients she thinks would taste good together.

While Davidson started out as a mystery writer, Joanne Fluke wrote psychological thrillers before moving to culinary capers. Now all of her murders have to do with baked goods. In some of her books, the pastries provide a clue. In *Lemon Meringue Pie Murder*, the protagonist, Hannah Swensen, discovers one of her pies at a crime scene and finds out how it got there. Baked goodies win friends and get people to talk, says Fluke, particularly at Swensen's own bakery and coffee shop in fictional Lake Eden, Minnesota. There she hears local gossip and private conversations as she refills coffee cups. Food is also a facilitator, says Fluke, where Swensen uses her cookies and desserts to soothe pain and calm nervous people, thus disarming them and prompting them to talk.

Fluke catered in college to make extra money, but the author traces her passion for baking back to childhood. Her grandmother was an assistant pastry cook for a wealthy family. "Gammie used to bake every winter morning to warm up the kitchen, and all it took was a whiff of vanilla, chocolate, or cinnamon to get me out of bed in plenty of time for school," recalls Fluke. "When I was old enough to reach the table, Gammie and

Mom taught me how to bake. It was something we all did together, and I'm sure that's why the kitchen is still my favorite room in the house."

Fluke wrote her first culinary mystery, *Chocolate Chip Cookie Murder*, in 2001. Swensen returns home upon the death of her father and opens the Cookie Jar bakery. She becomes an amateur sleuth when she finds a dead delivery truck driver still holding a chocolate chip crunch cookie in his hand.

••

A CULINARY MYSTERY WRITER TELLS YOU HOW

I asked mystery writer Joanne Fluke to pass on some simple ways to get ideas and writing going for your upcoming food-themed book. Her three-notebook idea, which follows, is particularly good. I've learned from experience that notes I've taken at the scene or soon thereafter are much more detailed than if I wait and write them later. Her advice about honing your skills is something you've read before in this book, but it can't be said enough. Here are her suggestions:

BUY THREE NOTEBOOKS. Use one to jot down all your favorite dishes, especially if you're going out to dinner and trying something new. Write down the name and your impressions. You may think you'll remember the great meal you had at that little French bistro, but you won't. Use the second notebook to take notes while you read everything you can get your hands on in the genre you've chosen. Write down what the authors do that you like. Use the third notebook to note what the authors do that you don't like.

START WRITING. Try the techniques from the second notebook to see if they work for you. Avoid the things in the third notebook like the plague.

HONE YOUR SKILLS. Take a writing class or join a critique group if you think it'll help you. Get a copy of *Writer's Market* and study it for practical advice and information.

TAKE NOTES. When thinking about your story, jot down little notes about the characters. When the story and characters are clear in your mind, outline it so that you won't forget.

BEGIN WRITING YOUR BOOK. If that first paragraph eludes you, try writing the last chapter first. Then, when you write the first chapter, you'll know where you're going.

WRITE EVERY DAY. Work hard. Be optimistic, but don't give up your day job.

••

Two other writers who write culinary capers are Mary Daheim and Joanna Carl. Daheim crossed over from a career as a historical romance writer. Her Bed and Breakfast series includes *Just Desserts*, in which an innkeeper solves the mystery of a murdered visitor. Other titles I love are *Nutty as a Fruitcake* and *Legs Benedict*. In *The Chocolate Frog Frame-Up*, part of the Chocolate Chocoholic mystery series by Carl, small-town chocolatiers debut their chocolate frog at a Fourth of July party. The first customer to buy it dies, and a chocolate clue leads to solving the murder.

Certainly you can read these books for fun. While you do so, notice how authors advance the plot, throw in plot twists, and create suspense and tension. Without suspense, there's not much of a mystery at the end, when you reveal the culprit. You need narrative drive, or the promise that something's going to happen. These authors know how to build events and suspicions to a crescendo. If you're interested in learning how to write mysteries, see "Useful Reference Books for Fiction Writers" on page 234.

I love how these writers don't take themselves so seriously. I can't resist telling you about a few more ways writers create funny titles and plots:

- In *On What Grounds*, by Cleo Coyle, the manager of a historic coffeehouse arrives to find her assistant manager dead.
- In Coyle's *Through the Grinder*, business is booming, but customers seem to be dying after drinking her house coffee blend.
- In *Too Many Crooks Spoil the Broth*, by Tamar Myers, a mean-spirited innkeeper solves the murder of a dead guest. *Eat, Drink and Be Wary: A Pennsylvania Dutch Mystery with Recipes*, and *Parsley, Sage, Rosemary and Crime* are two more titles I love.
- *Death by the Glass: A Sunny McCoskey Napa Valley Mystery*, by Nadia Gordon, investigates the seamy side of the restaurant and wine world. Wine professionals, cooks, and gourmet friends help a chef-owner of a Napa Valley restaurant solve a crime.
- In *A Catered Murder*, by Isis Crawford, a caterer and travel writer, a best-selling author of vampire fiction drops dead at an affair the main character caters.

When your characters are caterers, bakers, innkeepers, restaurant critics, chefs, and candy makers, you can live vicariously by imagining their lives. Take a moment to picture one of these characters, the hero of your book, coming upon a dead body. In your mind you've already constructed the scene, imagined your hero physically, and identified the body. These details could be the start of your own mystery novel. Write down the scene while it's still fresh.

··

USEFUL REFERENCE BOOKS FOR FICTION WRITERS

This chapter offers just a taste of fiction writing. For more, try these books:

- *Description,* by Monica Wood. Includes advice on how to use description to awaken readers' senses. Part of the Elements of Fiction series.
- *The Art of Fiction: Notes on Craft for Young Writers,* by John Gardner. The classic guide by a renowned novelist and professor. Good advice for writers of any age on plot sentence structure, diction, and point of view.
- *How to Write a Damn Good Novel: A Step-by-Step No Nonsense Guide to Dramatic Storytelling,* by James Frey. Detailed descriptions of common pitfalls and how to avoid them.
- *Stein on Writing: A Master Editor of Some of the Most Successful Writers of Our Century Shares His Craft Techniques and Strategies,* by Sol Stein. Well-written, useful advice on how to fix flawed writing, improve good writing, and create excellent writing.
- *Write Away: One Novelist's Approach to Fiction and the Writing Life,* by Elizabeth George. A personal approach to mastering the tools and techniques necessary to writing the novel.

If you're interested in mysteries, you'll find around a dozen books on how to write them, many written by successful mystery writers, including:

- *How to Write Killer Fiction: The Funhouse of Mystery & the Roller Coaster of Suspense,* by Carolyn Wheat. Lots of useful tips and insights explain the difference between mystery and suspense and how to plant clues.
- *How to Write a Mystery,* by Larry Beinhart. Here is advice on narrative drive, the promise that something will happen. It's not systematic, but offers useful recommendations on how to approach plot, character development, and other writing techniques.

··

Main Characters in the Food Business

Like culinary capers, lots of novels have main characters in the food business as well. Culinary romances are another category of fictional food writing. In *Cooking for Love*, by Sharon Boorstin, a Beverly Hills cookbook author dreams about food and the man who got away. She finds him on Google twenty-five years later, leading to a culinary adventure halfway around the world with her girlfriend. *In Three Good*

Things, by Wendy Francis, a divorced woman opens a bake shop devoted to kringles, a Danish pastry. Her ex comes back and threatens her relationship with another man, but the book is also about her sister and their relationship. *Good Grief*, by Lolly Winston, has a different baking theme. A woman quits her job and discovers her talent as a baker. Winston's book is also a laugh-out-loud funny and poignant story about surviving the loss of a spouse.

Some novels in the culinary romance category focus on the dual pleasures of food and sex, filling the senses to near overflowing. Why do food and sex go together so well? "Food is our most public sensual pleasure," explains Phyllis Richman. "It's second only to sex in terms of sensuality, and since you can't really do sex in public, reading about it fulfills a basic need."

Perhaps the best-known book in this category is *Like Water for Chocolate: A Novel in Monthly Installments with Recipes, Romances, and Home Remedies*, by Laura Esquivel. The daughter of a rancher falls in love and uses magical realism to pour her emotions into her cooking. Each chapter opens with a recipe. *La Cucina: A Novel of Rapture*, by Lily Prior, tells the story of a girl growing up on a Sicilian farm who spends most of her time in the kitchen. She meets an Englishman in Palermo, and together they explore their culinary and sexual passions.

Here are more sample characters and plots based on food, to give you ideas for your own story, or just to enjoy as a reader:

Food writer. The best-selling *Heartburn*, by Nora Ephron, tells the story of a food writer whose husband cheats on her. Ephron makes a convincing case of how her heroine got into food writing, starting out as a journalist (how Ephron got started in real life), then writing a food column for a newspaper. Recipes are included.

Restaurant owner, chef, waiter, or reviewer. If you've ever worked in a restaurant, owned one, or you have been a reviewer, you must have lots of material for a good yarn. If you haven't and would love to imagine this lifestyle, consider these plotlines:

- *Crawfish Dreams: A Novel*, by Nancy Rawles. A Creole who moved her family from Louisiana to South Central Los

Angeles opens Camille's Creole Kitchen and recruits her family to help her get the restaurant on its feet.

- *Crescent*, by Diana Abu-Jaber. A chef in a Lebanese restaurant has her passions aroused only by the preparation of food, until a handsome Arabic literature professor starts dropping by for a little home cooking. Falling in love brings Sirene's heart to a boil, stirring up questions about her identity as an Arab American. The author worked as a cook throughout college and for a few years after.

- *Eating Crow*, by Jay Rayner. A London restaurant critic attempts to redeem himself after a chef commits suicide because of a bad review.

- *The Food of Love*, by Anthony Capella. Based on Edmond Rostand's *Cyrano de Bergerac*, but set in Rome, an Italian Casanova falls in love with an American art student and tells her he's a chef. He can't cook, but his less attractive friend can, so he uses his friend's skills for a culinary seduction.

- *High Bonnet: A Novel of Epicurean Adventures*, by Idwal Jones. Written in 1945, this book reveals a restaurant world in Paris entirely devoted to food. Anthony Bourdain called it "porn for cooks."

- *How I Gave My Heart to the Restaurant Business: A Novel*, by Karen Hubert Allison. A woman and her boyfriend open a successful restaurant in Manhattan and give up their outside lives.

- *Liquor: A Novel*, by Poppy Z. Brite. A New Orleans alcohol-themed restaurant's bumbling owners close the place down. The author's husband was a chef at Commander's Palace.

- *Love and Meatballs*. A daughter works in a family restaurant and becomes torn between two men. Author Susan Volland is a classically trained chef who had written freelance articles and recipes for magazines and cookbooks.

Chocolate shop or sweetshop owner. In *Chocolat*, by Joanne Harris, a woman opens a chocolate shop in a rustic French village and angers the church by appealing to pleasure-starved parishioners. Taste the chocolates in your mouth as you read.

Cheesemaker. In *The Mammoth Cheese*, by Sheri Holman, an artisan cheese maker and his daughter go on a historic journey to re-create a huge Cheshire cheese once given to Jefferson, presenting it to the current president.

Television producer. My *Year of Meats*, by Ruth L. Ozeki, features a Japanese American documentary filmmaker invited to work on a Japanese television show meant to encourage beef consumption. She becomes increasingly aware of the beef industry's practice of using synthetic estrogens on cattle and plans to sabotage the program.

What About Recipes?

Some culinary fiction authors swear by including recipes in their works. Others put them in grudgingly, and some don't do it at all.

"If I didn't include recipes, my house would get egged, people would call to yell at me on the phone, and I'd receive a slew of angry emails and letters," says Fluke. Twice now, she's written in passing about a cookie and a cake without including their recipes. She mentioned Lisa's White Chocolate Supreme Cookies in *Chocolate Chip Cookie Murder*. "I got so many letters and email messages I had to create a recipe and put it in *Blueberry Muffin Murder*," says Fluke. "I also got in trouble when I wrote about Rose's Famous Coconut Cake in *Lemon Meringue Pie Murder*. I didn't have a recipe for that either, but hundreds of people asked for it in emails so I had to come up with one and put it in *Sugar Cookie Murder*."

Richman's restaurant-based mysteries include a recipe at the back of each book. In the narrative, she makes a point of writing about dishes in enough detail that they're workable; some chef-readers have tried them out and told her about their efforts. Ephron uses a similar technique in *Heartburn*, but with more specific measurements and instruction, so they read more like recipes. Twenty recipes appear in the book, inserted conversationally as part of the story. It's an effective way to keep the narration going, but the style makes these recipes harder to read than those in a more traditional structure.

As you can see, there's no one right way to add recipes. I prefer them at the end of each chapter, in traditional recipe format, with an index by title in the back so readers can look them up alphabetically. Diana Mott Davidson wrote her first twelve cozies with recipes that followed a description of a dish. After that, recipes appeared at the end.

An example of a popular novel with recipes is *Friendship Cake*, by Lynne Hinton, about five seemingly different women who bond over cake, with seventeen recipes. Maya Angelou was an enthusiastic endorser.

Children's Books

If you've always wanted to write young adult or children's books, why not combine your passions and write about food? Food in children's literature can serve several purposes, no matter what your intention. Primarily, of course, it tells a good story, just like adult fiction. Stone Soup (there are various versions by multiple authors) tells an old French tale of three hungry soldiers who convince inhabitants of a village to make them a soup that starts with boiled rocks. In *Blueberries for Sal*, by Robert Mc-Closkey, two sets of mother and child, one a momma bear and cub, go on a hunt for blueberries and end up intermixed. In Maurice Sendak's *In the Night Kitchen*, a boy stumbles into a night kitchen, where bakers prepare cakes for the morning.

Food is not only a source of entertainment for kids but also an educational and experiential tool. Here are some other ways writers employ it in children's fiction:

It can make eating look enticing. *Eating the Alphabet*, by Lois Ehlert, shows fruits and vegetables so enticing that even finicky kids will want to eat them. *The Seven Silly Eaters*, by Mary Ann Hoberman, comprises rhymes about how a mother accommodates picky children who will only eat certain foods such as applesauce or eggs.

Aids you can't use in adult novels can help younger readers indulge their senses. The Wiggles' *Yummy, Yummy Fruit Salad* has fourteen scratch-and-sniff stickers in flavors like apple, banana, watermelon, and grape.

It can introduce new foods. Some authors build songlike lyrics around food. Amy Wilson Sanger's World Snacks series explains sushi, dim sum, Mexican food, Jewish "nosh," and soul food. Here's a line from *A Little Bit of Soul Food:* "When I wake up I smell biscuits / and gravy for our grits. / I say thanks for smoky ham / cut into little itty bits."

It helps children understand other cultures. In *Henner's Lydia,* by Marguerite De Angeli, readers see how a Pennsylvania Dutch community makes cider in the backyard and what kinds of food the community members eat, such as apple butter and half-moon pies. Artist and poet Grace Lin's *Dim Sum for Everyone* describes the pleasures of a Chinese dining tradition. Joanne Rocklin's *Strudel Stories* weaves a tender tale about seven generations of family members who bake apple strudel, from Odessa to Brooklyn to the Pacific.

Food can be a learning tool. In *Chicken Soup with Rice: A Book of Months,* by Maurice Sendak, children learn activities they can do during different months and seasons while sipping this soup. In January they eat it while slipping and sliding on the ice, while in July they find a turtle selling it at the bottom of the ocean.

Whether you plan to write a mystery about a cook, a novel with a food-based theme, or a children's book, all the fiction writers I've interviewed share similar advice. They suggest joining a critique group with regular meetings and producing work to share with the other members. They recommend reading books on how to write novels, and reading novels to understand how authors use food to craft scenes, plot, and character. They suggest you take classes. And most of all, if you want to be a writer: write. Do it every day.

Writing Exercises

1. People in your book or short story must seem believable to your readers. Build up characteristics by writing a sketch. Go to a restaurant with a pad of paper, and take notes about your waiter. Describe the person visually, then get inside his head and imagine his life in the workplace and at home. Does he

work fourteen-hour days, ending with drinks at bars at three in the morning? Does he spend tips on heavy-metal music? Describe his home, how he cooks, what he likes to eat, and whether he is a food snob.

2. Write a dramatic dialogue between you and the waiter, based on the food. This is a next step in developing the waiter's character, where you imagine a conversation based on your personality and what you know about him. Write several lines of dialogue suggesting the beginning of a relationship that may continue later in your story. You can choose to create conflict and tension (you hated the food; he was snippy), but not all drama is negative. In the previous example, perhaps he stalks you later for revenge. If it's positive, maybe he's a flirt, and you build suspense that the two of you will meet elsewhere.

3. Choose a food, and then write a story that is set in a particular historical period. If you chose beans, for example, you could write about cowboys hunched over a fire, camped out at night while driving a herd of cattle. Next, write a dialogue between two people who are consuming your chosen food. Incorporate action related to the food in the scene, such as how one cowboy slurps the beans from a tin cup, or how another tears bread and leaves crumbs in his mustache. Try writing three paragraphs.

11: HOW TO GET YOUR BOOK PUBLISHED

Back in Chapter 7 you learned how to think about your book idea, and in Chapter 8 we covered recipe writing and development. Now it's time for the next step. You probably think that means writing your book and publishing it. Not yet.

To be professionally published, you do not write the book next (the exceptions are fiction and memoir; more on this below). Even if you want to self-publish, there are things to put in place beforehand.

Why? This is the way the nonfiction book publishing industry works, so to succeed, you need to follow the rules. On top of that, the rejection rate for book proposals from both agents and publishers is around 98 percent. Yes, just 2 percent of book proposals are accepted and made into books. So if you're going to put the time into writing a book, let's get you into the 2 percent that succeeds.

Another thing is that agents and publishers are drowning in book proposals, and they often don't read past the first page. They are looking for a quick reason to turn down yours and move on to the rest. Your job is to not give them one.

Where many proposal writers fall down is being impatient. I understand this, since it's much more fun to write the book than a sales pitch and strategic document about the book. But that's how you get rejected, when you don't address the warning signs and holes. Let's say you want to write a cookbook on Italian desserts, for example. What are your credentials as a writer on this topic? Do you teach cooking classes on the subject, write a blog on it, or lead tours in Italian neighborhoods or in Italy? Editors want people who know their subject matter and have already been recognized, to lower their risk. They want some assurance that you can write an excellent recipe. So creating credentials—if you don't have them now—will make you more likely to succeed.

To be traditionally published, you need to show, in a book proposal, that your idea is brilliant, you are the right person to write it, and there is an audience waiting for your book. (The exception is fiction, where you submit a full manuscript for your novel, instead of a proposal.) If you have thousands of social media followers, cooking class students, or visitors to your restaurant, no problem. If not, it may take time to create a big enough audience for the dessert book.

This chapter describes a book proposal in detail. It will help you write one for maximum success and impact. Once you're ready to send it out, you'll learn whether to submit it to a publisher or agent, how to find an agent, and what to expect when a publisher wants your book. If you'd like to self-publish, you'll also learn more about how it works.

How to Write a Killer Book Proposal

A book proposal is a business plan for your book, written before you write the book, with a sample chapter or sometimes two. For nonfiction, on first contact, agents and editors will want to know who you are, how you came up with your idea, whether it's original, how you will promote your book, whom you know in the media, whether you have a built-in audience, and if you've ever been published. If you send your finished manuscript with a cover letter that says, "Please publish this," you're not answering any of these questions. You're not selling yourself. Selling is a big part of the game, as is having something new and fresh to say. Many big publishing companies don't even accept unsolicited manuscripts at all, let alone read them. Instead, they want a proposal. While these bigger houses only want to see proposals through agents, many people are published without one. More on that later.

As a book proposal coach, I've helped people write the proposals that excite agents and editors, resulting in advances from between $5,000 to $125,000 from all kinds of publishers, from small to large. The best advice I can give you is to be patient. I've found that many people rush to get their book proposals out the door before they are ready. When I suggest they write a few articles, teach a class, or speak on the subject to build up their credibility, many resist. "I just want to get the book proposal finished," they say.

Yes, but unless it's solid, a finished book proposal won't do you any good.

Honing your book's idea, your reputation, and your audience, before you write your book, will dramatically increase your chances of success. And here's a great side effect: once you establish your focus and credentials, your self-confidence goes way up, and you'll write a stronger and more convincing book proposal.

Backing Up Before Going Forward

Agents and publishers look for all kinds of red flags when reading proposals, such as a boring title, uninspired writing, lack of focus, and lack of platform. Two things to work on when writing a proposal are your book's focus and your author platform. Your book's focus refers to your ability to carve the subject matter into a digestible, sharply defined topic or angle that will be realistic to write. It's too late, for example, to write a general cookbook on preserving pickles, unless you have an enormous audience. Besides, it's overwhelming to attempt such a broad topic. At least two authors have new books on Asian pickles. This subset taps into a current trend, and it's much more manageable as an idea.

Your platform refers to your ability to establish a base of interested readers who are likely to buy your book. A blogger with thousands of readers per day; a newspaper or magazine columnist; a cooking teacher who does fifty classes per year; a television show host; a well-known restaurateur, chef, or caterer; or a consultant who speaks all over the country are examples of people with platforms. Potential purchasers of their books know them, and they can get in front of their readers with regularity.

If you do not have a big platform on the subject of your book, beef up your credibility now, before you send out your proposal. One of the best ways is to get published on the subject of your book. Stories with your byline show that someone else thought your writing was good enough to publish and make you more desirable. If you don't believe me, consider this quote from Rux Martin, head of her own imprint at Houghton Mifflin Harcourt, who has edited cookbooks by *Gourmet* magazine and Jacques Pépin. "It would be virtually impossible for someone to have a proposal that would excite me and be worthy of consideration who had never written for publication."

Sure, there are exceptions. It may be enough if you have never been published elsewhere but you blog on the subject and your page views are in the hundreds of thousands. But many editors and agents want to see your byline elsewhere as proof that people outside your blog will want to read your book.

Getting published on the subject of your book is a way to test the idea and confirm its value. Doing so shows publishers that readers are interested in the subject. (If you have not begun writing for publication or blogging, read Chapters 4 and 5.)

Do you need prior publication or a book proposal if you are writing a novel or memoir, or plan to self-publish your book? No, but it doesn't hurt. As a novelist, you will be more attractive if you get short stories published first, but this may not be essential. To approach agents and publishers with fiction, you don't need a proposal. You write the whole book first and send agents or editors a cover letter with a few sample chapters. If you're writing memoir, write the proposal after you complete your manuscript, and include a sample chapter or two. If you plan to self-publish and sell your book, you don't need a proposal, although it will help you to flesh out the table of contents, the competition, and the promotion plan. You don't need a proposal if your book is only for yourself or family members, or you are compiling a community book or recipes to raise money within a defined audience. If so, you might want to skip ahead to the self-publishing section on page 270.

The Landscape

Around the world, millions of food and wine titles are published each year. While publishers keep churning out cookbooks, the market is getting tougher, says agent Jane Dystel, head of Dystel and Goderich Literary Management. There are too many cookbooks, and some publishers have cut back or cut out publishing them, she says. But on the other hand, "There are always going to be new cooks and new consumers who want to do fresh things." And perhaps the rise of noncookbook food books shows there are lots of opportunities outside the cookbook world.

The competition will be intense. Many publishers get hundreds of proposals a year and publish only a few dozen books. And of those they publish, they may have come up with the idea for the book themselves, and they found a writer to create a book they want.

Even though it's a tough market, you can succeed. You have to know what agents and editors want, which can be elusive. "It really boils down from personal taste," explains agent Doe Coover, who represents such authors as Jacques Pépin, Rick Bayless, and Deborah Madison. "Some decisions stem from what I think is salable. I have to feel passionate about it. I have to know I'm not going to be daunted if the first two publishers turn it down, or the first six. I have to know I'm in it for the long haul." Coover has represented first-time authors as well as the stars, but obviously she's picky. If you follow the advice in this chapter, you'll have a much better shot at getting an agent at her level or a good editor and publisher.

Writing the Book Proposal

A book proposal includes your bio, a table of contents for the book, sample recipes if you're writing a cookbook, and samples of your writing. It explains the target market, the potential competition and how your book differs from it, and how you will promote the book. Regardless of whether you want an agent or plan to submit directly to a publisher, you need a proposal. It's normal to spend at least six months writing it.

You might have heard that you can send a one-page query letter instead of a proposal. That's true, and it's a lot less work. But if agents or editors like it, they will say, "Yes, this sounds interesting. Please send the book proposal." Now what? You haven't written it. Six months or a year from now, when you finish the proposal, your cover letter will say, "Remember when I sent you that query and you liked the idea?" Write the query letter after writing the proposal, so the proposal will be ready to go if you get a green light.

A book proposal might be as long as 12,000 words. It might take you anywhere from six months to two years to write. That's fine. It's best to take your time and get it right, unless you want to be the first out of the gate with some red-hot trend. Remember that you're writing it to agents and editors, not readers—these are not the same audience. Only the sample chapter is written directly to your end readers. A book proposal must answer these questions: Why you, why now, and who cares? Here are the main elements:

Title page. Create a cover page with the book's title and subtitle, and all of your contact information, which includes your name, email, mailing address, and website. If you have a gorgeous photo of the food for your cookbook, include it.

••

HOW TO WRITE AN IRRESISTIBLE BOOK TITLE

- Be short, witty, and specific to your book's content. Don't come up with a general title that leaves readers wondering, such as *Meals Anyone Would Love* or *My Favorite Recipes*.
- Research the names of competing or similar books, and draw from them. Someone spent a great deal of time on them, so why not benefit? Researching will also show you how books like yours are named, and what's appropriate.
- Short, direct words are instantly successful in titles. You've only got a moment or two to communicate, so get the qualities of your book across quickly. Cookbooks, particularly, have titles using words like "Greatest," "Best," "Quick," "Easy," "Complete," and "Secrets of."
- Some titles draw you in. They are evocative and sensuous, or meant to evoke curiosity, such as *Bitter*, or *Blood, Bones, & Butter*, *The Breath of a Wok*, or *Songs of Sapa*.

For more on this subject, particularly when naming cookbooks, see pages 168–169.

••

Table of contents for the proposal. If your proposal is long, it needs a table of contents listing sections by page number.

Summary or concept. Agents and editors are busy. An acquiring editor is the one who is most likely to buy your book. These editors might spend about a third of their time acquiring manuscripts, and maybe 10 to 15 percent editing. The rest of the time they are dealing with business issues, contracts, meetings, design, and marketing. They could be responsible for several dozen books in a year.

A summary gives these readers an immediate understanding of the book, as soon as they begin reading the proposal. Craft two or three dynamite paragraphs that sum up the book, the market, and you. Here's the proposal summary for a book by a former client, *My Nepenthe: Bohemian Tales of Food, Family, and Big Sur*, by Nani Steele:

"*My Nepenthe* weaves together stories and tales of the famous California restaurant. It celebrates the magic and history of a place through its food and the family that started it. In 2009 Nepenthe will commemorate sixty years of bringing writers, artists, dancers, travelers, actors, and cooks together around the table, including author Henry Miller, who used it as his favorite watering hole. Today about 200,000 people visit Nepenthe per year.

"A lyrical feast written by the owner's granddaughter, who grew up at the restaurant, *My Nepenthe* covers the food, the unconventional family, the colorful people, and the art and architecture that were the genesis of this legendary restaurant. The book includes 60 favorite recipes culled from the restaurant, the café, and the family's archives. I am a freelance food writer, food stylist, and recipe developer. I opened Café Kevah, named after my maternal great grandmother, at Nepenthe when I was 26 years old and later became a pastry chef. I now live in Oakland, CA with my two children."

You probably do not know enough to write the consummate summary right now. Write a draft summary, and leave it as a placeholder. Go back when you've finished the proposal, and punch it up. By then you'll have a stronger and more focused notion of what it should say.

Overview. This is the proposal's introduction. It tells the agent or editor what kind of book you plan to write and why. The overview is like a mini-proposal that sums up all the points you will make. Even though it comes first, write it at the end, because it's hard to sum up the proposal and the book idea at first. Writing the proposal forces you to think through the book's structure and content. Often you're still fleshing out and refining the book as you write.

The overview

- must engage the agent or editor immediately, in the first few sentences. They may stop by the bottom of the page if you have not dazzled them or made them curious or excited.

- establishes your idea as solid and salable.
- describes the book's main points, scope and breadth, material to be covered, your writing style, and the book's special features.
- tells how readers will benefit from reading your book.
- makes a case for why the market needs a book on this subject now.
- explains how your book is different or unique.
- explains why you are qualified to write this book.
- tells the reader the size of the manuscript or how many recipes it contains, and how long it will take you to complete it.

To begin your overview, pull readers in. It should read like a novel or news story, pulling readers along, involving and exciting them, creating sensual images in their heads. An anecdote might work at the beginning—even statistics, if they grab attention.

Once you hook your readers, summarize the elements listed above in a few compelling paragraphs. Help them visualize your book by outlining the material you will cover, the main points, the philosophy behind the book, its unique conception, and its organization. Explain what you will include, such as the number and types of recipes, special sections, or sidebars. Be as specific as possible without resorting to a list of chapters (that comes later). If appropriate, use anecdotes or name a few dishes and describe them, using all the senses. Think of this section as the book jacket copy. If you're not sure how to word it, read a dozen or so jackets of books you have at home.

The overview is the main place for you to discuss your book in detail, about how you came up with the idea, why you're passionate about it, and how it will be new and different. Take your time.

If you're writing a cookbook, explain how this book will be better than a database of free recipes readers can find online easily, and explain your recipe writing style. Tell agents and editors your strengths when it comes to writing this type of material. Are you a terrific recipe developer, with a gaggle of people who test for you? "Can you write about food traditions and cooking practices in a serious way? Or can you write about regional and cultural background in an enlightening and fun way?" asks

Sydny Miner, now a publishing consultant and former vice president of Crown Publishing Group.

Talk about yourself and why "you are the ideal person for the job because of passion, experience and expertise. Tell us how you still will be involved with the subject two years from now, when the book appears. Publicity interviews will be as much about you as they are about the book," advises Miner.

Describe your voice. Will it be friendly, knowledgeable, or witty? Will you attempt to break down complex concepts? If you've described your book as humorous, do you know how to use humor? It's not enough to say, "The book will be funny." Demonstrate humor within the proposal. Tell how the book benefits your readers, what's in it for them. Close the overview with a strong statement that reinforces your most important point.

Do not insist that the book must look a certain way. The publisher determines the design. If you think photos or illustrations are critical to your book's success, explain why. A guidebook on identifying oysters, for example, would be harder to use without visual images. If you plan to provide your own artwork, such as illustrations, historical photographs, or old letters, say so here. For more on the visual aspects, see pages 174–175 in Chapter 7.

Target audience and market. Agents and publishers want to know if a definable market exists for your book. This is part of what constitutes your platform. The target audience identifies who will buy the book and why.

Even though you'd like it to be so, your book is not for everyone. Saying so implies you have not thought through who will buy it. Look for definable populations. Quantify the groups by finding statistics or other identifying information. Identify your readers in as many ways as possible, such as income level, gender, or frequency of visits to fine restaurants.

It's okay to identify more than one kind of reader, as long as you build a solid case for each. When Andrew F. Smith began compiling the audience for his book *The Tomato in America: Early History, Culture, and Cookery*, he found tomato-lover societies, huge tomato festivals with twenty-five thousand attendees, and tomato-growing contests attended by tomato lovers. When he wrote *Pure Ketchup: A History of America's National Condiment, With Recipes*, Heinz bought five thousand copies. For

Peanuts: The Illustrious History of the Goober Pea, he found a peanut lovers' association with forty-one thousand members.

Say whether you have a built-in strategy to reach potential readers, such as targeting customers at your restaurant or students in your cooking classes, or creating a newsletter or website dedicated to potential readers. Describe any strong contacts or connections in the culinary field or media who might help promote your book.

Establish that your topic interests the media. Perhaps magazines or television shows have covered the subject recently. Knowing your reader base will help you choose which publications, websites, television shows, and other media might have articles or content that applies.

Identifying your target audience will make your book more focused. The more you know about your readers, the more you know what they desire, what they need to know, or what will benefit them. When you write your sample chapters or recipes, you will be able to visualize your readers sitting across the desk from you. When you write directly to them, you make a connection that comes through in your book.

You might like to know who buys cookbooks. In the United States, according to Bowker Market Research in 2012, about 69 percent are women, age thirty to forty-four for the biggest group and forty-five to sixty-four for the next biggest group. Hardcover cookbooks still outsell all others at 42 percent, while ebooks are up to 22 percent of all sales. Amazon.com sells 36 percent of all cookbooks, says Nielsen Books & Consumer.

Because the number of US bookstores continues to shrink (from 11,559 in 2001 to 8,407 in 2011, according to the US Census Bureau), sales to alternative retailers matter more. Big box stores like Target, Walmart, and Costco account for almost half of all books sold in the United States, and boutique retailers like Sur La Table and Anthropologie have made single-subject cookbooks an important part of their mix.

Promotion plan. Unfortunately, you can't count on publishers to promote your book very much. Often they have paid large advances to well-known authors whose books are coming out the same time as yours, and those books get the bulk of the marketing money budget. Publishers want to know how you will help them sell the book. That means getting in front of your target audience and promoting it. While this section of your proposal will be based on a theoretical plan, it must be realistic. If you say you plan to appear on *Ellen* and then get your own television show, unless you can state how you plan to do it or demonstrate that you have made inroads, agents and editors probably won't believe you.

Write your promotion plan based on what will happen when the book is published, not based on what you are doing now. If there are events where you could promote your book, list them, and contact organizers in advance to get actual commitments. Let's say you ask your local bookstore, for example, if you could give a talk when your book comes out. If the owner expresses interest, that's more valuable than saying you plan to approach the store.

The best ways to promote your book may be on a television show, in articles you write or on your blog or website, in a cooking class, in a restaurant, or at a speaking event. If none of these apply, you'll need a platform, as discussed earlier. Hold a class on the topic of your book now. If it's successful, the venue will be more likely to commit to another event when your book comes out, and you can put that in the proposal. Do you have a website where you can promote the book? Can you write articles for publications on the subject of the book? If so, which ones? Will you do demonstrations at department stores? Will you try to get interviewed on radio stations, and if so, for which shows? Make contacts, and state them in your proposal.

You might benefit if a significant figure in the food world or media writes an endorsement (blurb) on the back cover or writes a foreword to the book. If so, it's best to ask that person to commit now, so you can say so in this section. You may be nervous about sending a letter or email asking for a commitment to read the book, but often people are honored.

Describe outlets other than bookstores, big box stores, and culinary stores that might sell your book, such as wineries, home-design stores, or specialty stores for products such as cheeses and chocolate. If you're writing a book for a restaurant or retailer, you have a special sales opportunity that will make editors' and agents' eyes light up. Publishers will sell discounted copies in bulk to companies that commit to buying say, two thousand to five thousand copies. It will make your proposal look that much more attractive, and for publishers, it boosts first printings and amortizes production costs. If you have endorsement deals with companies, put them in as well.

About the author. Here's where the agent or editor gets to know you. Don't write your life story, beginning with how you started cooking as a child. Leave out how you've always wanted to write this book, or how people keep telling you to write one. Instead, start with who you are now: the person who is qualified to write this book. Create a bio highlighting the experiences most related to your book. Many people I've worked with say they had no idea their bio could be so long until they thought it through. When you've never compiled your accomplishments in one place, it can be very satisfying to do so.

If you are already a published author, particularly if related to the subject of your book, that's your best credential. Publishers want to hire people who can write. The same is true if you can show you are an expert on the subject of your book. If you are a chef or cooking-school teacher, that is also an excellent credential. Being a blogger is appealing to many publishers, particularly if you are an expert in a certain food, or if you have a large following.

Otherwise, look deeply into your past. Publicity, experience, jobs, volunteer work, research, awards, travel, and special skills might qualify. Maybe you've had a life experience that provided a valuable lesson and material for your book. Brainstorm lots of ideas, but pare them down to the ones that apply most. Even if you are proud of all the quilts you've made and belong to a quilting group, leave this information out unless it somehow relates to your topic.

Join organizations and take classes to punch up your bio. If you become an officer of one of these associations, your bio will look even stronger. See if you can speak or do a demonstration on the topic of your book. Contact conferences or groups to see if you can be a guest speaker on the subject of your book, which will also add to your credentials, because it shows the publisher you know how to reach your intended audience.

Analysis of the competition. Choose a maximum of five books that either you or your target readers would find competitive because of the subject or approach. A book with a similar title and completely different content may still be a competitor if it would appear next to yours on the bookshelf.

Compare your book to books that are doing well. To find out, go on Amazon.com to see the book's ranking. Amazon lists millions of books, and the lower the ranking, the more popular the book. In a perfect world, you'd want to compete with books that are under 50,000 in rank. Do not compare yourself to books that are not published in your country, books that are out of print, or books that are self-published. Publishers want to see books recently published by their competitors, within the last ten years. By the same token, do not be unrealistic about your book and compare it only to the three best-selling cookbooks of last year.

List all information about each competing book, including title, author, publisher, price, whether it's a hardcover or paperback, and publication date. In a paragraph, describe each book's contents briefly and compare it to yours. End by stating how your book will be different. Do not be disrespectful. You never know whether the reader of your proposal sold that book, published it, or is best friends with the author or editor.

"Tell us why your project is different, not why it is better," advises Sydny Miner. "'Better' is a subjective judgment and ultimately the consumer is your judge. Do not tell us that there has never been anything like your book, that there is simply no competition. If that's the case, there may be a good reason. Instead, tell us that there have been successful books kind of like yours, but that yours will be different."

Sometimes you also want to mention complimentary books. For example, there may be books that are organized in an unusual way, like your book, or books that cover the subject in a different way than yours does. If so, limit them to a few books. Editors often look up sales figures, and they don't need to slog through a list of a dozen or more books.

Table of contents. I recommend creating two. The first is a short list of chapter titles that fits on one page so agents and editors can grasp the book's concept, content, and structure. That's called the Table of Contents at a Glance. On the next page, start a chapter-by-chapter description (called the Expanded Table of Contents) of the parts in more detail, from introduction to index. Write up to a one-page description of each chapter, describing what it will cover, its purpose, and how it benefits the reader. Follow with a list of all recipes if you're writing a cookbook or a book that lists recipes at the end. Include sidebar titles, if known. Other parts of the book to list might include a glossary, pantry list, resources list and buying guide, and bibliography.

Ten to twelve chapters are common. The structure usually starts with the simplest elements and flows to the more advanced aspects. Make sure the chapters flow in some logical way. For more details on cookbook organization see page 173.

Sample recipes and/or sample chapter. This section shows that you not only have a well-thought-out understanding of your book, but you can deliver. It must be substantial, and it must be your best writing. If your book is primarily recipe-based, submit up to one dozen recipes, each on a separate page. Recipes must be foolproof and flawless, showcasing the range of your skills and knowledge. You must have tested every recipe before submitting it, because agents and editors can tell whether recipes work just by reading them, and they might even test them. Each recipe should be complete. If it includes tip boxes or a sidebar, include them with the recipe. If your book is recipe-based but contains lots of narrative writing, submit a few chapter openings or other text as examples.

If your book is not a cookbook, submit at least one complete chapter. Do not submit the introduction, because much of its content is already covered in your overview. Review your table of contents, and choose a meaty chapter in the middle somewhere, one that is also not too long, perhaps six thousand words at most. Some people suggest including two chapters if you are a new author, or if you are writing a memoir.

Supporting materials. This is information that promotes your book idea or you, such as recent articles you've written on the subject.

Consult each agent or publisher's website before submitting material. For the latter, some publishers only want certain parts of the proposal, so you can cut and paste those in. For agents, look at websites to see what kind of format they want. Fortunately, most of the time you'll be emailing your proposal, so you can link to all online material whenever it comes up in the proposal, and create a separate PDF of other print material, if absolutely necessary. If you have video clips, such as of you in a cooking show or on television, put it on a website like YouTube so you can link to it.

If you must print it to send to an agent, you need a separate stack of feature articles, website content, blog postings, and other material relevant to your book idea. Start the section with a list of the supporting materials in the order readers will see them. Choose pieces that appeared in prestigious publications or on well-known websites, show the variety of your work (if appropriate), and are samples of your best writing. Include any stories written about you and a video clip if you appeared on television.

Format. Double-space your proposal with one- to one-and-a-half-inch margins all around. Include page numbers, beginning with the table of contents, along with either the title of the book or your name on each page.

This is not a design project. Do not make the proposal hard to read by using all caps, which looks like shouting, or a script font. Do not use colors or other gimmicks that detract from the substance of your text. Boldface and italics are acceptable for headings. Clean text in one font and size lets readers see the quality of your writing. Bulleted lists are easy on the eyes. Do not print on both sides of a page. Do not bind the proposal in any way. You may staple a set of supporting materials together if you have many.

If you are photogenic, you may include a head shot at the top of the bio page or on the front page of the proposal. Make sure it is your best photo and will impress the reader. Do not include other photos, such as of finished dishes, in your proposal, unless you plan to take your own photos or are proposing partnering with a professional photographer and showing examples of his or her photography and your dishes.

Cover letter. Whether you're writing fiction or nonfiction, introduce your proposal or sample fiction chapters with a short cover letter written specifically to your target editor or agent.

Overall. No typos, punctuation, or grammatical errors. For cover letters, spell the person's name and their company correctly. Get the title right. I cannot overstate the importance of proofreading, proofreading, and proofreading again. You are selling yourself. Copy with errors reduces your credibility, even if there are just a few typos. Print out your proposal, and read it several times. Have other people read it for mistakes you did not catch. You may have to do this a half dozen times. It's worth it.

• •

HELPFUL BOOKS FOR GETTING PUBLISHED

While there's only so much I can say in one chapter, these books are devoted entirely to getting published. I recommend them highly and bring most of them to classes when I teach food writing:

- *Be Your Own Literary Agent: The Ultimate Insider's Guide to Getting Published*, by Martin P. Levin. If you want to do it on your own, try this book.
- *The Fast Track Course on How to Write a Nonfiction Book Proposal*, by Stephen Blake Mettee. Here is a short but well-focused book from a seasoned editor. It includes a sample proposal, sample contract, and glossary.
- *How to Write a Book Proposal*, by Michael Larsen. A clear, thorough, nuts-and-bolts guide from an agent dedicated to helping writers succeed.
- *Jeff Herman's Guide to Book Publishers, Editors & Literary Agents*, by Jeff Herman. This is an exhaustive directory that's updated every year, with helpful essays at the start.
- *Literary Agents: What They Do, How They Do It, and How to Find and Work with the Right One for You*, by Michael Larsen. How to launch your career as a writer, with an unexpected plus: it helps deal with rejection.
- *Nonfiction Book Proposals Anyone Can Write: How to Get a Contract and Advance Before Writing Your Book*, by Elizabeth Lyon. A solid, detailed book with a proposal template and models for success.
- *The Shortest Distance Between You and a Published Book: 20 Steps to Success*, by Susan Page. She gives you advice and strategies all the way from goals for the book to getting a contract to writing it to dealing with doubt and procrastination.
- *Thinking Like Your Editor: How to Write Great Serious Nonfiction and Get It Published*, by Susan Rabiner and Alfred Fortunato. An agent and her husband, a freelance editor and writer, offer useful advice on how books succeed and why.

• •

Do You Need an Agent?

If you want to be traditionally published, you probably need an agent if you intend to go after the biggest trade publishers. If you plan to pursue small publishers, such as university presses and regional presses, you can probably submit your proposal directly, and most agents will not be interested because the amount of money you will receive, called the "advance," is usually much lower. In this section, we'll look at the pros and cons of getting an agent. Later, you'll learn about the smaller publishing houses to which you can submit directly, without an agent.

Your chances of being published are exponentially better with a good agent. *Writer's Market*, which lists information on book publishers every year, provides listings that give the percentage of books a publisher accepts from agents versus authors. You'll notice that:

- The number of books publishers accept from agents (versus unrepresented authors) is usually higher, frequently much higher.
- Typically, the larger the publisher, the more books it publishes from agents. Many of the biggest publishing houses will not read book proposals unless they come from a literary agent.
- The smaller the advance ($10,000 and under), the more writers the publisher accepts directly. Rutgers University Press accepts 70 percent of its books from authors without agents and offers a $1,000–$10,000 advance.

If you're thinking you just want to get published and you don't care about the advance or quality of the publisher, snap out of it. You will "live, sleep, and breathe that subject, 24/7, for two or more years, and it will take money away from your other jobs," says literary agent Carole Bidnick. So it's in your best interests to find a good fit.

With a great proposal, you deserve a good publisher. Aim high with a good agent who will be your advocate and guide. Author Mark Bittman once wrote in a newsletter, "An agent will change your career. If your idea is a good one and you're capable of delivering on it, an agent can recognize that and convince an editor you're worth a gamble. Yes, you might be able to do it yourself, but the process will work better, faster, and more profitably with an agent. Most experienced authors agree that doing it yourself is a complete waste of time and money."

"An agent allows the author/editor relationship to be about the work, not the business or money, and an agent is there for contingency purposes," explains Harriet Bell, a publishing consultant. "If anything goes wrong, authors need someone on their side to navigate the waters." She's talking about after you get the contract. Contrary to what people believe, agents do lots more than just get you in the door.

The Agent's Job

Agents understand the industry and can evaluate your book's chances. If they take you on as a client, they should review your proposal and give suggestions on how to improve it. You will sign a contract in which you agree that the agent receives a 15 percent commission of all money due you. You may also be charged for office expenses relevant to your proposal, such as phone calls and shipping. Beware, however, of agents who charge an initial reading fee. Agents will target the most appropriate trade publishers for your book and send out your proposal with a cover letter. Right there, you've got a huge advantage. Editors drown in proposals and query letters. They pay attention to cover letters from agents, often giving them preference.

Many publishers put unsolicited, unagented queries, proposals, and manuscripts into what's called the "slush pile," unless they are rejected outright for lack of representation. It's a derisive moniker for low-priority reading. That shows you how much editors rely on referrals, authors they've already published, and agents. On the other hand, all proposals accepted by a publisher get read.

If you've managed to work with an agent who specializes in cookbooks and food-based books, you'll be in good shape. Agent Doe Coover explains, "We have a more intimate relationship with editors because editors, like agents, specialize. It's our job to know the editors' tastes, what they're looking for, and what's on their lists [which books they publish]."

Not only do agents know editors' tastes, they often know the editors personally, keeping track of who just had a baby, who got married, and who got promoted. Some agents have memorized editors' phone numbers. Most agents arrange to see editors regularly, regardless of where the editor or agent lives, meeting to gauge interest in upcoming authors and books they represent.

When it's time to send out the proposal, agents decide whether to send it to just one editor or make multiple submissions. Sometimes they think a certain editor would love your book and call that one editor first. Or they might send the proposal to ten or twelve editors and wait for replies.

Some agents spend up to three years trying to sell a book, but it usually takes less time. If every appropriate editor turns it down, that's the end. If editors say they would buy your book if it were different, you and the agent will decide whether to change it. If an editor makes an offer, the agent evaluates it and negotiates it on your behalf. This is another advantage, as contracts are often ponderous documents with small type and obscure language. Agents know the terminology and which items to pursue. "An agent is your buffer, but also your advocate, always looking for more: more advance money, more public relations and marketing, more design input, more photographs, and so on. Your agent is also your reality check as to what's reasonable and possible," says literary agent Lisa Ekus.

Finding and Getting an Agent

Agents can be elusive. Since they reject almost all book ideas and authors in their in-boxes, many limit their visibility. At the same time, they sincerely want to discover fresh talent, so many others have websites and attend writers' conferences. To contact them, avoid a phone call, unless you've been referred and know they want to have a conversation. If they don't know you, go through traditional channels by sending them queries and proposals.

You'll have lots of competition. Like editors, agents also drown in queries and proposals, and most represent all kinds of nonfiction, not just cookbooks and food-based books. Coover says she gets twenty-five to thirty cookbook proposals per month, not counting other kinds of nonfiction. Jane Dystel of Dystel & Goderich Literary Management says she sees around forty proposals per month, with food-based books making up only 10 percent of the books her agency represents.

Like editors, agents want to be contacted a certain way. Some like email, while some want regular mail; some want just the query, but some want the whole proposal. Look at their websites to find out how and what to submit before doing so.

All agents say they want new writers and new voices, but most don't take on writers who will attract low advances. Because they get 15 percent of the advance, it's not worth their time. When Lisa Ekus started her agenting business, she dedicated half of her list to first-time writers. "I felt it was critical to give new voices a platform," she says. "Publishers are more resistant to an unknown first-time writer. I sold about 80 percent. Almost all are working on a second and sometimes a third book." Today, however, her business has matured, and she will turn down writers with good credentials and book ideas if she feels she can't give them the time they deserve. Ekus also has businesses that teach media training and offer public relations services to writers.

To find agents, try these tactics:

Look in the acknowledgments section of a book. When authors like their agents, they thank them in the acknowledgments section.

Join the International Association of Culinary Professionals. If you are a member of the food industry, cooking teacher, restaurateur, or published food writer, membership entitles you to go to the annual conference that some agents attend and to review the online directory, which contains contact listings for agents who specialize in food-based books (iacp.com). Even better, you'll meet published authors, and if you get to know them, you might ask for information about their agents.

Join other food-based associations. Agents might be members or attend events. Members might know agents and be willing to help you. Associations include:

- The American Culinary Federation: acfchefs.org
- The American Institute of Wine & Food: aiwf.org
- Les Dames d'Escoffier: ldei.org
- Slow Food: slowfood.com
- Women Chefs and Restaurateurs: womenchefs.org

Go to writing conferences. Agents often speak at conferences, teach classes, lurk in the audience, and sign up for pitch meetings that are like speed dating. Sometimes you can pay extra and have an agent evaluate a few pages of your proposal.

Take a writing class, or join a writing group. The instructor might know an agent and refer you, or someone in the group might know an agent.

Someone you know, or a friend of a friend, must have written a book. That person might have an agent—ask.

Research online databases. At PublishersMarketplace.com, look under agents who specialize in cookbooks, or type in an agent's name to get instructions on how to submit a proposal. LiteraryMarketplace.com lists agents in alphabetical order by name, and you can buy a reduced membership to get the information you need. AgentQuery.com is a newer database that also lists agents.

When you find an agent who wants to represent you, make sure you have good chemistry and that you trust the agent. You want an agent who returns your calls, someone who is truly excited about your book.

When You Don't Need an Agent

Not everyone needs one, particularly if you're targeting academic, regional, or smaller publishers. Smaller publishers will read your query letter or proposal regardless of whether you have an agent.

Agents may not be interested in your book anyway because the advances are much lower than from traditional publishers, and the 15 percent of your royalty will not be worth their time. That's fine. Andrew F. Smith, a prolific author of food history books, says he's been successful by networking and getting to know editors at small publishers without the help of an agent.

Here's the breakdown of publishers that don't require agents:

- Academic presses such as the University of California Press, Berg, and Routledge, which publish reference and historical books, specialized studies, essay collections, and readers
- Small publishers like Agate, Harvard Common Press, Robert Rose, Sasquatch, and Storey, which publish lots of cookbooks
- Specialty presses like Prospects and Applewood, which publish historic reprints and general food writing
- Reference publishers such as Greenwood and AltaMira, which publish encyclopedias, food series, and all kinds of food books

Before you send off your proposal, do your homework. Find out which publishers would be most likely to publish a book like yours by looking for similar books in the library or bookstore. Don't send a proposal on regional foods of Kentucky to a national publisher, for example.

Most publishers have websites with submissions guidelines. Read them before submitting your query or proposal, and submit what they ask for. If all they want is a table of contents, don't send the whole proposal.

If you want to target particular editors, find out how each likes to be approached by calling a junior person (such as an editorial assistant) in the editorial department of that publishing house. Some editors want an email query first, some only want proposals, and some want snail-mailed query letters. Do not send a generic letter that says, "Dear Editor."

If an editor expresses interest in your book, you might want an agent to negotiate for you and deal with the contract. Agents often take a reduced commission or a project fee for this work. If not, hire an attorney who specializes in publishing to review the contract. Don't have an attorney who specializes in trusts or tax law review the contract. Their unfamiliarity with standard publishing practices will drive your editor crazy.

Reasons for Rejection

When you've compiled your list of agents or editors, send out your proposals or queries all at once, and follow up if you don't hear back. Unless you have a connection, waiting for a response takes forever because agents and editors take weeks, often months, to answer. Be prepared for rejection, but also realize that it only takes one agent or editor to like your book idea. Agents and editors reject projects for several reasons, not necessarily because they don't like you or your book idea. Here are some examples:

- An agent has already sold a similar book, or it conflicts with a current project in the pipeline at a publishing house.
- They are not interested in the subject.
- They think the idea is too narrow and will attract too few readers.
- The subject has been done to death.

- The trend has already passed. (Publishers can take two years from first contact to publication, so trend-based books can be risky. Smaller publishers can sometimes turn around a book more quickly.)
- Your idea is too trendy or not substantive or interesting enough for a whole book. It might be best for a magazine article instead.
- They don't like your writing.
- They don't think you are qualified to write the book or have a sufficient platform.

Most often, however, agents reject queries and proposals because the author has not done a professional job. Most of the time, they haven't done the homework required to write an effective proposal. Ekus says, "Often I receive proposals that are incomplete, poorly researched, about a subject that's been done to death, or even illiterate."

Sometimes publishers think your book has the germ of an idea and may suggest how they'd like to see it. Lori Longbotham wanted to write an unillustrated cookbook of lemon recipes, both savory and sweet. Chronicle recast it as a book on lemon desserts, with only sixty recipes and beautiful photography. It was so successful that Chronicle had Longbotham follow with *Luscious Chocolate Desserts*, *Luscious Berry Desserts*, and *Luscious Coconut Desserts*.

The Contract

Regardless of whether you go it alone or use an agent, you'll receive a publishing contract once you and your editor agree on the sale. Contracts vary in size and complexity, but all cover the main issues you will negotiate.

The advance. An advance is a loan against royalties, but you do not have to pay back this loan. You will not earn any further income until after book sales reach the amount of the advance. Typically, advances for first-time authors range from $5,000 to $25,000 with a trade publisher, less for academic and specialty publishers.

The royalties. Let's say an editor offers you a $10,000 advance, with the cover price of the paperback book estimated at $20. Typically, royalties are 10 to 15 percent of the price of a hardcover, and 7.5 percent of the price of a paperback. At 7.5 percent, your take is $1.50 per book. Once the publisher has sold 6,667 books, equal to your $10,000 advance, you will begin receiving royalties if more books sell. A typical ebook royalty rate is 25 percent of net sales. Some publishers, particularly small houses, pay royalties on a percentage of net sales rather than on retail price.

Sometimes publishers pay the photographer, and sometimes you do. If you are on the hook, your advance should be large enough to cover the cost.

Agents try for the biggest advance they can get because most books do not earn past their advance. Regardless of whether you use an agent, you may have to use the funds from your advance to pay for travel, recipe ingredients, researchers, and testers. Publishers usually charge the cost of indexing against royalties.

You won't get all your money at once. Publishers will divide up the advance into multiple payments (depending on the size of the total advance), such as when you sign the contract, when you turn in the manuscript, and when the book comes out. If you have lots of upfront costs, you may find the timing challenging.

Rights. Standard contracts vary, but most publishers buy world rights, all languages and editions. That covers hardcover, paperback, and ebook rights.

Timing. The time publishers give you to write your book varies, but usually they have a date in mind and work back from it to establish a deadline. It could be nine months or three years to publication, depending on the complexity of the book and whether it will have photographs.

The publisher often chooses the season based on when they think the book will do best. For example, it makes more sense to publish a cookbook of soups and stews in the fall—when readers are looking for hearty comfort foods—than it does in the spring. And most gift books come out in the late summer or early fall, in time for the holidays.

"You want to fight for all the time you can get," advises food writer Janet Fletcher, who has authored several cookbooks. "Take your time, and do a good job." On the other hand, she has also written books quickly, within six months, when the publisher has a launch date in mind.

The fine print. The publishing industry has its own private language of bonus clauses, subsidiary rights (the rights to use the material in abridged, adapted, and condensed versions), options, and discounts you get for buying books. To fully explain the various options and legalese would take pages, but since my expertise is in writing and not contracts, refer to "Helpful Books for Getting Published," on page 256 to learn more. If you have an agent, you still have the final say on whether to accept the offer. Once you agree, it takes two to three months to get a signed contract and the first advance check.

If you've been doing the math as you've been reading, you'll see that writing a book is not much of a moneymaking proposition. If you spend one year writing a book for a $15,000 advance or less, it's not a living wage. Now that you know you're not going to make much money, what's another 15 percent of "not much money" anyway? Agents are worth it. They want you to succeed, they'll work hard to get the best deal, and they'll help you move forward with your next book.

Agents want you as a long-term investment, not a one-shot deal. "Advice, recommendations, inspiration, and consolation are also necessary components of a strong author-agent relationship," says Ekus. "I think of myself as a combination pitch woman, negotiator, and mother— which includes nurturing and nagging."

The Publishing Experience

Congratulations. You have a contract, and you've started writing your book. Here is a general outline of the publishing process.

Working with your editor. The editor who acquired your book may be your editor, but not necessarily. You may work with someone new. The editor could leave before you turn in your manuscript, and you'll get another editor. Agent Coover says one of her authors was assigned to a new editor who had rejected her book idea earlier at another publishing house!

It's your job to establish a relationship with your editor and to meet your deadlines. You may have a few preliminary conversations about the book, but then you could be on your own. While every editor is different, it seems to me that most editors spend their time on the front end, acquiring books and dealing with contracts. Then they leave you to write your book, and they engage once you've turned in your manuscript, not before. Also, your editor may be editing between ten and twenty books simultaneously, so unless you're a big author, you're not going to get the most attention.

Don't let that stop you, however, if you have questions or concerns. Tell your editor if you're having problems with the deadline, you have significant questions about the book's structure, or you're wondering whether to write a different book. Do so at the front end, not a week before the due date. "Editors are happy to hear from writers," says Fletcher. "They don't reach out, but I think they'd love to help when a writer has questions. Publishing houses are so understaffed they don't have the time they'd like to shepherd manuscripts."

She recommends giving the editor a chunk of the manuscript early, perhaps the first third of it, and getting feedback. "They may have a different idea and good suggestions and you don't want to get to the end of it and then find out," she advises. That happened to a friend of mine. He turned in a book that had taken years to research and write, only to be given a few months to rewrite it according to the editor's instructions. In the end, he won a national award for the book, but it took him years to cool down.

Manuscript deadlines. When it comes to writing the manuscript, unless you have deadlines for specific sections, it doesn't matter where you begin. Some authors start with the most difficult parts, as they take the longest. Some start at the beginning. Some write the easiest parts first, just to get going. As long as you make progress and gauge how you're doing in relation to your deadline, go in whichever order you like. Remember that you will have written a sample chapter or two for your proposal, and that should ease your mind, even if you have to revise them. Also be careful of getting waylaid by fascinating research. We food enthusiasts tend to be excited by everything we discover, and you will need discipline.

The most important thing is not to get overwhelmed by the idea of writing an entire book. Break it down into chapters, break it down into sections, and do a piece at a time, even if you tell yourself you're only going to write for fifteen minutes per day. Create a schedule, and hold yourself to it, chapter by chapter. Leave a little time at the end to review or to build in a little time away from the manuscript. If you are developing recipes for a book, gang your cooking and baking in some way, to maximize efficiency. Author Rick Rodgers says he tries to test up to six recipes a day. If you are also taking the photos for your book—wow. You must already be an expert in organization. Otherwise you might have to put your life on hold for a while. Recipe blogging can be a challenge while you're working on a cookbook.

Also build in time to have others review your chapters or test your recipes. Line up at least one trusted advisor who will read your work as you complete it and give you constructive feedback. It's good to have a reality check before the editor sees it. Some people hire editors to review their work before sending their manuscript into the publisher, just to get an extra edge of professionalism.

The editing and review process. The editor's job is to review your manuscript, edit it, and send it back for revision. You might not hear back for a week or more after turning in your magnum opus. Don't take it personally. Eventually, you'll get a call or an email. Your editor needs time to look at the big picture in what's called a developmental edit—whether material in one chapter would be better in another or combined with it, whether a section lacks focus or you've left things out, or whether you've written too much. He or she may query you on anything that seems confusing, tangential, incorrect, or poorly phrased. You may get this information in a phone call, a letter, or as questions in the text of the manuscript.

The copyediting and production process. After you make the corrections and adjustments and turn in a second draft, your manuscript goes to a copyeditor, who will edit it to fit the style of the publishing house, to improve the flow and clarity of the prose, and for consistency, punctuation, and grammar. The copyeditor will also question whatever appears to be unclear. Some of the comments might seem obtuse, such as "It seems if you want to keep the eggs, pork, etc. set off by em dashes, we should drop 'raised'—only 'produce' needs the verb." Sometimes they have opinions or questions, particularly on recipes. A good copyeditor specializing in recipes is worth her weight in gold. She will question times, doneness, ingredients, pan sizes, and what got left out, and perhaps suggest what you should add in. In the past authors got these queries as tons of tiny yellow sticky notes on a printed manuscript. More commonly now, you'll get electronic queries in a Microsoft Word file.

Photography. If your book has photographs, the process usually begins after you've turned in the manuscript, but I have worked on cookbooks that started much earlier. While you may suggest a photographer, the publisher has final say, even if the photography budget comes out of your advance. Every publishing house works a little differently, but typically, your editor makes a preliminary list of which recipes will have photos. You'll also see a layout of the book, showing where photos will appear.

You probably will not be involved in the photo shoot, which takes place in a studio. Sometimes shoots take place elsewhere, such as in the countryside or at farms, homes, restaurants, or farmer's markets. (For more on photo shoots, see pages 174–176.) The ten-day photo shoot for the first cookbook I wrote for Craig Priebe, *Grilled Pizzas & Piadinas*, took place at the New York home of the art director because he had a balcony, and we needed an outdoor location for grilling. On site were the editor, the art director, the photographer, the photographer's assistant, the prop stylist, the food stylist, and my coauthor. He was there to make the pizza crusts. Photos for our weeklong second shoot for *The United States of Pizza* took place in the photographer's studio, with Craig rushing over with the pizza crusts. A food stylist topped and finished each pizza.

The cover. The art department will probably work on a book jacket early on, because the publisher needs the image and title for the catalog and other sales and marketing materials. If your editor approves the cover design, he or she will send it to you for your input. The author usually does not have final say over the design or the title. That's up to the publisher. Typically the contract will say only that you are to be consulted. If you have a disagreement, here is where an agent can be indispensable. The agent's job is to advocate for you, so he or she can speak to the editor on your behalf. One thing to consider about the cover is whether it will look good as a small image online. Keep in mind that Amazon sells around 36 percent of all cookbooks, according to Nielsen Books & Consumer's market research.

Even if you don't have an agent, speak up if you have specific issues. Janet Fletcher recalls when a publisher came to her with a cover almost identical to that of a book by another author. "It was so close in design, type, and color, I thought this was totally dumb on their part because readers can be confused," she recalls. She contacted the author of the other book. "We both ganged up on the publisher and got them to change my cover," she says with satisfaction.

Page proofs. You will see your pages a second time, as proofs of a designed book with the photos inserted. Take care to make sure the recipes match the photos. I have reconciled a few with their respective recipes. Sometimes there were two tomato slices when the recipe called for three, for example. Salads are problematic because they wilt as soon as they are dressed, so the photographer has only a few moments to shoot. In one photo, the food stylist placed eye-dropper-size bits of creamy salad dressing on the greens, so small you couldn't see them. We changed the recipe to a vinaigrette.

When you get the proofs, take the opportunity to read every word and check every photo, caption, title, pull quote, etc. Even though your editor and copyeditor have reviewed your manuscript, and even though the book may be proofread at this stage, errors may remain, and you're the one with the most to lose if they go through. Look at each page as a whole, not just the text. I caught an error on a photo in which the photographer had used a paper sheet for a plain background, and the edge of the sheet was visible. You never know what you'll find, and you want to find every possible error.

Endorsements. Often at this point, when first pages are in hand, the book is sent to the people who have agreed to give you an endorsement or blurb. It's your job to find the contact information and give it to the publisher. Your editor might also have suggestions on who would be best to ask to endorse your book.

The final stages. From there it's on to printing. A print run of five thousand to ten thousand books is considered typical for a first-time author at a large publishing house (unless you're a big name), and maybe two thousand to three thousand at a smaller house. The number is partially based on preorders for the book. Publishers would rather print fewer books and reprint than keep thousands of books in their warehouse and pay storage charges. Most publishers depend on backlist books that continue selling long after publication. Some books stay in print decades after they were written, particularly if they don't include photos, which date the book.

You Could Also Self-Publish

While most of this chapter addresses traditional publishing, more and more people choose self-publishing. Whether it's right for you depends on your goal. If you're writing a cookbook or memoir for yourself or your family, and you have no intention of selling it, self-publishing is a great idea. It also depends what you mean by "self-published." In the broadest sense, self-publishers are authors who pay the full cost of publishing their books. If you print your word processed document on eight-and-a-half-by-eleven-inch paper, make twenty copies, and put each in a binder, that's self-publishing. If you want to produce a bound book that looks professional, you have a few choices: subsidy publishing, print it yourself, or hire a custom cookbook publisher.

Subsidy publishing. In this case, you write your book and pay a publisher to produce it. Typically, printing is on a digital press, also called POD (print-on-demand). This means that books are printed in response to orders as they come in, as few as one at a time.

Most books subsidy presses publish are trade paperbacks (six by nine inches) or mass markets (typically five and a half by eight and a half inches) with four-color covers. A few publishers offer hardcover, full-color books with color photography, but they're expensive to produce. I have seen self-published hardcover books with color photography that cost the author as much as $50. The publisher usually sets the retail price, but they may also just charge a flat rate, so you have to figure out how to charge enough at the retail level to cover costs and eventually make a profit.

At this stage, hardcover, full-color books are often still too expensive for you to resell at a profit. If you are just creating a few for gifts, however, that's different.

Subsidy publishing has advantages. The company mails the book to each purchaser and processes the funds. You don't store the books. The publisher pays you royalties when copies are sold, often much higher than what traditional publishers pay. You can make revisions by submitting new copy and printing a new edition.

On the other hand, many bookstores will not stock self-published books, and you need a special distributor like Ingram Spark to get your book into the Ingram database, the largest book database in the United States, so bookstores can order it. If you publish your book through Amazon's CreateSpace, most bookstores won't sell it. Many other subsidy publishers will arrange to put your book in online bookstores like Amazon, and some offer public relations and marketing services for additional fees.

Publish it yourself. In this case you would find a printer who will print whatever amount of books you want and ship them to you (or you can choose to work with a printer and distributor like Ingram Spark). You will hire all the same people a publisher works with to produce a book, including a copyeditor, a graphic designer to design the book and create the cover, and a proofreader to proofread the book after layout. You will choose the size and paper stock, and decide on whether to include photographs or illustrations, and then work with a photographer or illustrator.

Before you do it all, however, you might want to evaluate bids from printers first. If you find out, for example, that it costs $15,000 to get the photos you want into the book, and then $40 per book to print each copy, you may want to rethink the scope. At the end, you take receipt of your published books and store them. Then you sell them.

In short, writing the book is just the first step. You make decisions on all aspects of design and production. This is a great way to go if you want to control every aspect of your book's production, down to the paper stock and typeface.

Hire a custom publisher that specializes in cookbooks. If you don't want to publish your cookbook yourself, some publishers print customized high-quality cookbooks for food companies, community groups, and nonprofits such as Junior Leagues. Services include editing, marketing, and distributing your book.

Custom publishers specializing in cookbooks include:

- Cookbook Publishers (CookbookPublishers.com): minimum order is five thousand books.
- Favorite Recipes Press (FRPBooks.com): minimum order is four thousand books.
- Fundcraft (Fundcraft.com): minimum order is two hundred books.
- Heritage Cookbook (HeritageCookbook.com): minimum order is four books.
- Morris Press Cookbooks (MorrisCookbooks.com): minimum order is one hundred books.
- Wimmer Cookbook Distribution (WimmerCo.com): minimum order of one thousand books for its standard cookbook template, three thousand for its custom cookbooks.

Several good reasons exist to self-publish. See if any of these are right for you:

- You have a huge social media presence on your blog or website where you can drive sales online. Melissa Joulwan, author of *Well Fed* and a follow-up cookbook, has sold more than one hundred thousand cookbooks through her blog.
- Profits go directly to you. You pay the expenses up front, and profits go to you. Subsidy publishers typically offer higher royalties than traditional publishers.
- Get into print faster than traditional publishing. Traditional publishing typically takes between eighteen months and two years from the time you submit your manuscript to the time you hold a finished book in your hands. Self-publishing is often faster.
- You can keep the copyrights and subsidiary rights to your work. It is possible to keep the copyright with a traditional publisher, but difficult to keep the subsidiary rights, which include foreign rights and first and second serial, audio, and theatrical rights.

- You establish a track record to sell to a traditional publisher, if you are a first-time author. "If someone came to me with high sales, such as ten thousand copies in a year, and had a track record of public speaking and demonstrations, I would consider them," says agent Bidnick. If you're committed enough to have someone design, print, and sell your book one copy at a time, you'll impress agents and editors as a go-getter.

- You want to control every aspect of the entire process, from editorial to design to marketing. If you are the type who doesn't want anyone telling you what to do, self-publishing is a better fit for you. You don't have to hire an editor to judge your sentences, content, or structure, but I still recommend it. You can design the cover, even if it's by using templates from the subsidy publisher's site. You decide on the book's size, paper quality, and typeface. Some people relish this new learning experience.

- You can print a small number of copies. If you don't have much money, don't want stacks of books in your garage, and don't want to process and ship each order, POD makes sense.

••

WRITING A FAMILY COOKBOOK

"It all started because a favorite aunt was dying at the same time my daughter-in-law was expecting her first grandchild," says Judy Kancigor, author of *Melting Pot Memories: The Rabinowitz Family Cookbook and Nostalgic History.* "I wanted to preserve history of the family. I told everyone, 'If you're related by blood or marriage, you can be in the book.'"

She wrote a letter to all her relatives, suggesting the kinds of recipes she wanted. Some responded right away, while others had to be nagged. "My cousin's husband copied my aunt's entire handwritten recipe book, because she was the primary cook in the family," she recalls. "She was close to ninety—she remembered everything. We went through her book page by page, and she told me which recipes to put in."

At first, Kancigor was overwhelmed by the task, but eventually she worked on it full-time. "If you can get people to help you, delegate," she advises. Three years later, she had a cookbook with 850 recipes about her family's Jewish heritage and foods. Working with a custom publisher of cookbooks, she sent in handwritten recipes on separate pages. A typist keyed them into Microsoft Word files. Kancigor made "this huge leap" and ordered five hundred copies, with three hundred earmarked for friends and family. The other two hundred sold. She made revisions and ordered more. "Another five hundred were gone in six weeks," she says.

"My cookbook was very expensive," admits Kancigor. "I wanted the photos a certain way, and I wanted heavier stock and dividers." In total, she published eleven thousand copies and sold them all. She did so by speaking to Jewish women's groups, putting a coupon in the back of the book for ordering, and getting the book into Judaica shops, cookbook stores, and temple gift shops. She put it on Amazon. Even so, her book was not much of a moneymaker. She jokes that her dad used to say, "You lose money on every sale but make it up in volume."

Kancigor writes terrific, funny recipes. Here's a sample: "If doubling the recipe, don't put it all in the food processor at the same time, because it overflows from the bottom. This I learned from personal experience. In my daughter-in-law's kitchen yet." As she says, "The writing is what I enjoy more than the cooking. I crack myself up. I sit there, enjoying me."

"My kids are still scratching their heads and saying, 'How come people are reading about our family?'" she says. "People bought the book because they have photos like that, or they see their own family. The immigrant story is universal. People bought the book for a daughter-in-law who's not Jewish and coming into their family, or for bridal showers." Kancigor promoted the book all over the country.

At an International Association of Culinary Professionals annual conference, editors approached her when she spoke on a panel with Ruth Reichl. Later that year, she signed a contract. Workman Publishing published *Cooking Jewish*, with a first printing of thirty-five thousand books. She rewrote the book at her editor's urging. "They taught me how to write a recipe," she said. "I didn't have pan sizes, serving sizes, and Workman is very precise." They sent her on a twenty-four-city book tour, put her on TV, set up four radio tours where interviewers called her for four days by phone, plus she continued doing her own publicity.

Reasons to Hesitate

Before you get all excited and rush to self-publish, there are just as many reasons not to do it, if you want a commercial success. The biggest is that, as with traditionally published cookbooks, you need a marketing system or platform. I hope you already teach cooking classes, own a restaurant, own a retail store, host a television show, have a heavily trafficked website, distribute a newsletter seen by thousands of people, or have a big network of people who follow you online.

In each case, your book will appear in front of targeted readers who could buy it. Carol Fenster self-published a book on dietary restrictions and sold it through the lecture circuit. "She had the numbers, database, touring, and platform within her area of expertise," says her agent, Lisa Ekus, who sold Fenster's self-published book to Putnam/Penguin in a two-book deal.

One of the writers I've worked with, Melissa Guerra, had a PBS television show called *The Texas Provincial Kitchen*. She self-published five thousand professionally designed color paperback cookbooks and sold them at the end of each show for $19.95, then reprinted another eight thousand when those were gone. Her book sold around twelve thousand copies before the show went off the air.

While her cost per book was around $5, she says she broke even and wouldn't have done so if she did not have free storage. (Do the math: thirteen thousand books at $5 each equals a $65,000 initial cash investment.) "The worst thing a novice writer can do is not listen when people tell you how the book industry functions," says Guerra. "Writing for a publishing house is definitely the way to go." Her query letter for a second book, written with my help, attracted the interest of eight agents. Wiley published *Dishes from the Wild Horse Desert*.

The second issue is that when you self-publish, you write a lot of checks. You figure out how to publish the book, and most often, you sell it yourself, unless you can get a distributor who specializes in self-published books. And third, it's a challenge to get into bookstores and other retail stores with a self-published book.

Here's my list of more reasons to hesitate:

- You believe your book will sell a million copies and you're going to get rich. This is not a good reason to publish anything, no matter how it's produced. It's too hard to write a book if money is your only motive.
- Your book will have less credibility than a traditionally published book. The stamp of a traditional publisher means that someone in the business thought your work was worthwhile. It has more status.
- You might have to store several thousand books, if you agree to a minimum printing. "I didn't realize it," says Judy Kancigor, author of *Melting Pot Memories* (see page 273). "They come to your house. In your garage, you have to get them up on top of something in case your washing machine

overflows." She stored her books in clear plastic cartons, raised off the floor.

- If you sell one at a time, it will take forever. Most stores buy from distributors, and most traditional distributors (except for Ingram, via its subsidiary Ingram Spark) don't take self-published books. Some self-publishing companies offer more distribution than others, so be sure to research this aspect. Your book needs to sell in other places besides online.
- If you don't like the idea of promoting yourself, it's going to be awfully hard to sell all those books.
- You have to become an expert on many aspects of publishing, including editing, design, paper stock, production, and printing. If you just want to write, these responsibilities can be overwhelming.
- Unless you work with a subsidy publisher or a distributor, fulfillment is your responsibility. That's a fancy word for processing the order: cashing checks and taking credit cards, boxing up books and mailing them out, one by one.
- You want a full-color, hardcover, coffee-table book. Forget it, unless you are very wealthy and want a book for yourself or a few copies for friends and family.
- Self-publishing can be astonishingly expensive. You pay all up-front costs, and you may get stuck with the leftover inventory.

What Should You Budget If You Self-Publish?

There is no one answer. It depends on how many copies you order; whether you want hardcover, paperback, or ebook (or multiple formats); how many recipes you include; and whether there are photos. A few self-published authors on my blog have given numbers. Marcy Goldman, said it cost her about $5,000 to publish a hard copy of her book and a Kindle version. Nancy Baggett said it cost her $800 to publish her ebook, and most of that was for nutritional analysis software. Melissa Joulwan said that she first published through CreateSpace, where she made a profit of $5 per copy. Once she changed to an offset printer, her profit went up $10. This is not a direct comparison, as CreateSpace offers distribution, while a printer doesn't.

If you're not planning to sell your self-published book, you might consider custom software programs, which let you store and organize recipes, then print them ready for binding. The best known and regarded are Living Cookbook, Cook'n Recipe Organizer, and Mastercook. Some generate meal plans, grocery lists, and nutritional analysis. (But if you land a publishing deal, you'll end up doing lots of retyping and reformatting, because publishers want a standard Microsoft Word file.)

What About Ebooks?

Many authors have published e-cookbooks, but so far sales are disappointing compared to print books. Most readers still want to purchase a print cookbook. There is the added complication of having to submit a different file for each device, which can require special coding. And these cookbooks sell for considerably less than regular cookbooks, often pricing out at around $2.99 per copy. I just don't think it's worth the trouble, at least, not yet. Of course, if you have a huge audience waiting to buy your self-published ebook, you'll do well.

On the other hand, ebook readers like the Kindle and the iPad are a good place for self-published essays of about five thousand words. Again, you can expect to do all the marketing. For ebooks, that means it will be online. It doesn't work to appear at writing festivals or speaking engagements with an ebook. There's nothing to show.

• •

SELECTED RESOURCES FOR SELF-PUBLISHING

These online and print sources provide lots more information, should you wish to pursue this type of publishing. Self-publishing experts include Dan Poynter, at parapublishing.com, author of *The Self-Publishing Manual: How to Write, Print and Sell Your Own Book*, and Guy Kawasaki and Shawn Welch, authors of *APE: Author, Publisher, Entrepreneur—How to Publish a Book*. Here are some subsidy publishers to explore:

- AuthorHouse.com
- CreateSpace.com
- iUniverse.com

- Lulu.com
- SmashWords.com
- Xlibris.com

Writing Exercises

1. If you're looking for an agent, make a list of ten who are good fits for your book. Research each so you can find something personal to say in your cover letter, such as a particular book they agented that resonates for you, or something about an article you read about them online. If you're going directly to a smaller publisher, make a list of five that might be interested in your book, and research their online submission processes.

2. Start your book proposal by making an outline and then filling in each section. Start with the easiest one, the bio.

3. If you want to self-publish, find three authors who created books you admire. Search for background material about how they did it. Many bloggers offer posts on their process or extensive announcements about their product. You can also read about these authors and their process in the self-publishing category on my blog at diannej.com/b.

12: BRINGING HOME THE BACON

Maybe you started writing about food for fun and pleasure. As you put more effort into it, you decided you want to get paid for your time. Whether you'd like pocket change, a full-time job, or a new career working for yourself, this new chapter looks at several ways to create an income.

I decided to add this chapter in this new edition because so many food bloggers are wondering how to make a living from their blogs. While for the most part being paid well for food writing is challenging, for the ambitious, the self-motivated, and those with ingenuity, it is possible. Of course, there are all the traditional ways of making an income that I have addressed in previous chapters, particularly Chapter 5 on freelance writing and Chapter 7 on writing cookbooks.

But there is more, so much more, and you will be amazed by what you read here, not only by the variety of work you can try, but by the successes of some of our fellow writers, some of whom are making mid-six-figure incomes. As with anything else, just as many have tried things that haven't worked, or what they tried took more work than they thought. I can't guarantee that all these jobs and entrepreneurial businesses will result in great fortune for you, but maybe they'll spark an idea, and some might be a great fit.

This chapter looks at traditional ways to make money as a food writer, work that comes from being a food writer, how to generate income as a food blogger, and how some food writers have become mega-businesspeople. You'll also get a short primer on tax deductions, so start saving your receipts now.

The Old-School Approach

Let's look first at the traditional ways to make money as a food writer, in full-time or part-time jobs, in print or online:

Newspaper or magazine writer. Full-time writing jobs at newspapers and magazines are difficult to get because of slimmed-down staffs. But it can be done. Melissa Clark became a full-time writer for the *New York Times* after freelancing for the paper and coauthoring cookbooks with several high-profile chefs. It's more possible to work for them as a freelance writer, someone who pitches stories. That's always a good way in. Some publications have test kitchens, where you might be able to work your way into writing opportunities from there. A journalism, English, or culinary degree is the best background.

Website writer. Typically, the full-time jobs at food-based websites go to editors who also write articles. Sites to consider are *Eater*, *Serious Eats*, and *Tasting Table*. Magazines and newspapers also need writers for their web content, including blogs at alternative weeklies that have a robust food section. Faith Durand came to the popular website TheKitchn.com as a reader, then a commenter, then a writer, and now she is the managing editor.

Columnist. Many food writers pen a weekly column that is syndicated to appear in several newspapers or websites. For more, see page 128.

Public relations person. You might work for a food company itself or for a public relations company that represents food companies, housewares, or culinary personalities. This involves writing press releases and web copy, creating events, working with media people to get coverage, and running the social media strategy for the company.

Copywriter. You write promotional content for websites, catalogs, brochures, or ads. You might be asked to craft a brand voice and tone, to articulate key messages, to write scripts for television ads, to come up with names for new products, and to help launch them. You could also write copy that appears on the product itself, such as on the label on a bottle of artisan vinegar.

Recipe developer. Particularly if you have a background as a dietician or a degree in the culinary arts, you could be a professional recipe developer for food companies who want to publicize recipes based on their products. These recipes would appear on their websites, on labels, and even in books. Other entities that hire recipe writers are agricultural commodity boards formed to support farmers and producers. Cookbook authors and bloggers are particularly attractive to these boards. Amy Sherman started out with a blog called Cooking with Amy in 2003, and has since developed recipes for the American Lamb Board, Copper River Marketing, Dannon Yogurt, and the Wisconsin Milk Marketing Board.

Editor. Food-based websites and publications need full-time editors to assign stories, manage freelance writers, and edit writing. Editors usually get to write too. You might also be asked to develop an editorial calendar, curate and promote top food content, edit the newsletters, manage social media, and oversee content creation.

Ghost writer or collaborator on cookbooks. If you can put your ego on the side and write a book for a chef or a celebrity, in their voice, these can be lucrative gigs. Read more about this field on page 170.

Work That Comes from Food Writing

Many people who start out as food writers launch into related fields that are still about food, but not about writing. Here's a sample:

Cooking-class teacher. If you are an accomplished home cook who has taken many cooking classes, and you are a good teacher, this might be a good fit for you. Many cooking schools let you assist so you can see what goes on in a kitchen and get a reduced price on the class. From there you can try teaching at a community center or small cooking school. Cookbook authors and bloggers have good credentials for this job.

Food stylist. Bloggers are accustomed to styling their own dishes, and some cookbook authors get to do the same during a photo shoot. Some decide to make this into a career, contracting themselves out to photographers, public relations firms, product and appliance manufacturers, and television producers. Your job may involve shopping, cooking, and organizing the kitchen. Culinary school or extensive cooking class experience is a plus.

Culinary tour guide. Many cookbook authors, including Joanne Weir, David Lebovitz, and Giuliano Hazan, take groups on culinary food tours abroad, either in their own country or elsewhere. You don't need to leave home to lead a tour. Some food writers supplement their income by doing local culinary tours. Here in the San Francisco Bay Area, freelance writers including Sarah Henry, Karen Solomon, and Anna Mindess and blogger Sean Timberlake lead tours through a company called Edible Excursions.

Retail worker at a food store. It can be dangerous if you spend your whole paycheck in the store, but I do know a few bloggers who work at a wine store and at Williams-Sonoma on the side. Hey, if you like to cook and drink, why not get a discount?

Retailer. Maybe you get obsessed with a particular idea for a product. Linda Lau Anusasananan started a business with her husband to produce a line of high-quality Asian sauces while she was a full-time food writer and editor at *Sunset* magazine. Since leaving the magazine in 2005, she began a blog at JadeSauce.com to provide new recipes and lists of sales outlets. Heidi Swanson of 101Cookbooks.com opened a pop-up store that evolved into an online purveyor called Quitokeeto.com. And Michael Ruhlman sells kitchenware he codesigned on his website (shop.Ruhlman.com/collections).

Teacher of food writing. People all over the United States teach food writing in their towns (and they use this book as a resource, bless them). If you like to teach and believe you can inspire people to write, this may be a good side opportunity for you.

Speaker. It's rare to get paid to speak, but there is payment in kind, plus the thrill of travel. Most of the time companies will pay for your travel expenses and hotel, or they'll give you a budget toward travel (though it's unlikely you'll get paid on top of that). I do a lot of appearances because I love to speak, I love to travel, and doing so keeps me and my book in the limelight.

Radio show host. Some writers find out that they are especially good at radio, as either a host or a scriptwriter. It's a great opportunity if you are a restaurant critic and love to talk about new places or answer questions for best places to go. Some people also interview cookbook authors and chefs.

CRAFTING A CAREER IN RADIO

NANCY LESON learned much of what she knows about food during her first career, as a waitress. For fifteen years, she was the *Seattle Times* restaurant critic and food writer, winning many awards. Now she has a varied career as a radio host, speaker, and tour guide. Here's Nancy on how her radio personality evolved:

"People familiar with my byline would often say, 'You sound just like you write!' In 2006, Seattle NPR-affiliate KPLU gave me the chance to put their money where my mouth was. Paid $100 each week to speak into the mic, I began a long-standing radio gig, jiving with one of the station's jazz hosts on a four-minute segment dubbed 'Food for Thought.'

"It takes about an hour of my time to prep and tape each weekly segment, and it replays three times. The show helped promote my *Seattle Times* columns, and better still, allowed me to laugh and kvetch about anything and everything related to food.

"Though I'd long been acknowledged as the 'voice of food' for the *Seattle Times*, within several years, more people recognized me as the voice of food for KPLU than for the daily paper. This fun radio gig increased my currency as a public speaker and—perhaps most importantly—provided me with a continued platform and steady paycheck when I chose to 'pretire' in 2014 to work freelance.

"Thanks to my continued involvement with the station, my career has blossomed in ways I couldn't have imagined. As a radio personality, I've performed in a station-sponsored stage show, entertained donors at a private dinner, and hosted a trip to Europe as part of KPLU's partnership with a local travel company. That work earned me an additional $2,000 in 2014. Now I have to find time to write my novel."

Freelance cookbook editors. Some cookbook writers learn how editors work and get freelance assignments from cookbook editors to edit manuscripts. Some food writers discover that they're really good at copyediting, which leads to work from cookbook publishers as well.

Brand manager or social media specialist. If you've become an expert in social media, you might qualify for a full-time job or consulting work. Your job could include running a company's website and social media strategy. You could be in charge of creating content, such as writing blog posts and website or brochure copy, and hiring writers. You would represent the company at events aimed at influencers or media. If this is a consulting position, make clear that you will avoid conflict of interest content with your own blog, or else clearly mark it as sponsored.

Food industry consultant. If you have an expertise in a particular cuisine or technique, you might be able to earn good money consulting for food manufacturers or restaurants.

· ·
WHAT I LEARNED AS A FOOD CONSULTANT

ANDREA NGUYEN is a five-time cookbook author, freelance writer, cooking teacher, and consultant. She's worked with local eateries and large companies like Nestlé food, and shares her experience about taking on projects:

"I started consulting in 1996, after earning a master's degree in communication management. Soon I applied what I learned to the food industry. This work is not my main source of income (fortunately, writing cookbooks keeps me busy). Most clients find me via my cookbooks, website, and even LinkedIn. I bring my expertise in Asian foodways as well as strategic communication.

"For example, a local restaurant asked me to help them with their pho noodle soup. I met them on site to consult with the owner and line cook. We conducted our conversation in Spanglish. The owner reported that after implementing my suggestions, the number of new Asian customers increased.

"An international food company wanted to explore Asian dumplings and invited me to teach their research and development team. I also had to conduct a lunchtime tasting for sixty people at their corporate headquarters. I'd never done that before, but why not? I just needed to be organized and deployed my background as a cooking teacher and public speaker.

"A small Italian pasta company had problems with producing dumplings for a private-label project. We discussed target markets' expectations, competing dumplings, and product name. The president and upper-level management asked me to not only improve their filling but also decipher how to work a dumpling-making machine purchased from Taiwan. I traveled to their factory in Connecticut, worked with the R&D chef and helped the machinists troubleshoot. I also persuaded two entrenched Eastern European workers to alter their techniques, which were similar but slightly different from the raviolis that they'd made at the factory and the pierogies that they grew up eating.

"In negotiating contracts, friends who'd done similar work clued me in on the process and terms such as 'gold standard,' which defines what you as a consultant deem the ideal goal for the client. I've also learned how to clarify objectives, roles, timelines, and fees on paper. To avoid a conflict of interest, I tell clients what I can do—advise, collaborate, and serve as a brand ambassador—and what I cannot do—function as a PR contact or send out press releases."

· ·

Spokesperson. In this situation, you are representing the product and whatever talking points the client has identified. You might be asked to write editorials that will be placed in newspapers or on a wire service, host a radio show, be available for media interviews, or host a webinar. Make sure you can live with whatever you've been asked to say and that you feel comfortable promoting the product. You might be paid a flat fee with a limit on the time and number of appearances, or you might be paid a day rate for appearances. Some writers use an agent to get in the door, and some do the work themselves.

In 2011 Tess Masters of BlenderGirl.com partnered with Vitamix as the face of its technique and recipe videos. More recently Ten Speed Press released her mobile app on smoothies. She also signed a two-book deal.

Television host. The poster woman for this accomplishment is Ree Drummond, the Pioneer Woman, who was offered a Food Network show based on the popularity of her blog and subsequent cookbooks. That's not going to happen for everyone, but it is an awesome career move that blossomed from food writing.

Start an online magazine. Chuck Reece and his partners, a graphic designer and a social media person, started BitterSoutherner.com as a way to tell stories about the South, including through food. Along with a graphic designer and a social media person, they worked together without pay to launch the publication. More recently they campaigned for donations, with merchandise rewards, and raised thousands of dollars. Reese estimates that within a year, they will have enough income for full-time salaries.

Generating an Income with Ads

Whether you start a blog or a food-content-focused website, there are money-making opportunities. In this section, we'll start with the best-known ways and then branch out to new ideas entrepreneurs have figured out that may surprise you.

The best-known and most traditional way to make an income on your blog is with ads. Some people feel uncomfortable with this idea. That's fine. Not everyone wants to make money from their site. I don't see anything wrong with it, as long as the ads are appropriate and don't overwhelm the page. For one thing, blogs are a lot of work, and I have nothing against getting compensation for all the hours we bloggers put in.

You read magazines that have advertising, right? Does it detract from the editorial content? No. I think of myself as the publisher of my blog, not just the writer, and one of my jobs as the publisher is to make an income. When I worked in magazines, I was the head of editorial, and several writers produced the content. On my blog, I am the publisher, the manager of tech support, the writer, the designer, the photographer, the head of advertising, and the marketing department. "We've got to wear more hats now, be versatile, be good businesspeople," says Michael Ruhlman, whose website sells products he designed and apps he develops with his wife, Donna Turner Ruhlman.

David Lebovitz also thinks that many food bloggers are uneasy with the idea of taking advertising, and even with the idea of making money. He said to me in an email, "Talking about money can make people uncomfortable when it comes to blogging. Part of it is that it's often thought of as a hobby ('recipes are meant to be shared!'), and there is that mentality that blogs shouldn't be about making money. For so many people, it's not possible to really make enough money at it—just some pocket change. Which is fine, but I think it makes some feel bad when they read about people making 6-figure incomes.

"Yes, it seems many of the kerfuffles in the food blogging community have to do with jealousy over something, which usually involves money. I never talk about it because it's like saying how much you make writing cookbooks. I'll discuss it with friends on a professional level, or with people who want to write cookbooks to some extent, but it's not the primary reason I blog (or write cookbooks). And some of the bloggers I see who are raking it in have blogs that don't interest me at all, such as too many Pinterest-ready pictures."

Lebovitz makes a decent income from ads on his site, which is the most established way to generate money from an online site. The amount you make is based on the number of page views your site gets. If you get, say, a hundred thousand page views per month at a cost per thousand of $2, that equates to only $180. And apparently $2 is high. Of course, you can choose to have more than one ad, but you have to balance them with the space available on the page. Some bloggers have contracts with more than one advertising network and show ads on the right (the standard column, it seems, for ads), within a post, and in banners at the top and bottom of their blogs.

Ad networks reserve a space on your blog and fill it with changing ads, mostly from national advertisers. Some include sound and animated video, while others temporarily blot out your content to display the ad. Some ad networks require you to apply. They analyze the numbers of visitors to your site and your blog niche to see if you are an acceptable fit. Some of these networks include:

- BlogHer
- Federated Media
- Mode Media
- Martha's Circle

Once you look more closely at these networks, decide whether you like the advertisers and how they display products. Do you want ads for peanut butter, laundry detergent, or wrinkle creams? How about an animated dog running across your screen? They're not for everyone. "So far, we've declined more than 50 percent of all incoming ad requests just because we didn't feel comfortable running them," said Nicky Stich of DeliciousDays.com. A former client of mine who has a raw food site with big numbers says she can't find a network that has appropriate ads.

That said, choose an ad network that lets you customize which ads appear on your site, and reject ads you don't want. "Like it or not," says Elise Bauer of SimplyRecipes.com, "your readers will associate you with the ads on your site, especially the graphical [nontext] ads."

Some ad networks have requirements about placement, such as "above the fold," a newspaper term that means the top half of the page. On a website it's above the point where a reader would have to scroll. Some ask that you do not have any other ads on the page.

Besides an ad network, you could start your own ad agency and sell ads one by one, but most people find that notion too time-consuming. Shauna James Ahern uses this model on her blog, GlutenFreeGirl.com, but it has taken lots of work to line up advertisers for gluten-free products and keep them. Some bloggers use PassionFruitAds.com, which lets them sell ad space For most of us, it's more realistic to go through channels designed for the web, such as advertising networks and Google AdSense.

Google AdSense, the box ads with clickable links, are free, and you don't need high traffic to get started. You choose from a set of keywords relevant to your site, such as "low fat healthy." Google reads those words and puts up relevant ads. You're paid on a formula based on price per click. At first, you might make a few cents a day. Over time, as you build the content on your website and increase traffic, the amount can increase. Most publishers (the name Google uses for bloggers and website owners) don't make much from AdSense, however, unless they have big numbers. Finally, some bloggers have partnered with Ahalogy (ahalogy. com/publishers) to boost Pinterest traffic to their blogs and consequently drive up ad revenue.

Other Income That Comes from a Blog

If you're not interested in ads, there are other ways to generate bucks. But just like ads, most of them are dependent on the amount of traffic you generate. There are generally two kinds of traffic: Google (search) traffic and regular readership (organic) traffic. Ideally, bloggers want organic traffic above all else, since they are not beholden to Google for their numbers.

As for search engine optimization (SEO), if you look up how to increase traffic to your blog, most experts advise you to have accessible, quality content and a regular posting schedule. So in that sense, you are doing the right thing by reading this book and increasing the quality of your content! Here are a few more ideas about making money as a blogger:

Become an affiliate. Join programs where you get paid a percentage if a reader clicks through to another website and makes a purchase. These days you can choose from dozens of affiliates. Select them based on which products your readers might like. There are manufacturers like Vitamix, retail stores like Williams-Sonoma, plus web hosts and other online vendors. Setting up an Amazon store is popular.

Some bloggers who create ebooks include affiliate programs, where they count on other bloggers to sell their products. The software program E-Junkie makes it easy to do so. You may have to put embedded links in your post to receive a percentage of money spent. If so, you must disclose in your post that it contains affiliate links. Some bloggers have used affiliate programs to great effect to increase their income.

Become a brand ambassador or write sponsored posts. Many food product companies (called "brands" by bloggers) offer ambassador programs in which you are paid to promote the company and its products, either in person at conferences, in the media, or in your blog posts over a certain timeline. It might be as simple as creating a recipe using the company's product and then promoting your post on social media. These are called "sponsored posts," and you need to disclose in the blog post itself that you are being paid to write about a product or service.

There are many ways to get gigs like this. Some bloggers develop a relationship with public relations people who pitch them. Some meet company employees at blogging conferences and follow up. Some just send a pitch cold with a story idea and price for the post. Some follow companies they're interested in on social media and form a relationship. They may want to know numbers for your blog readership and your social media readership, and may base their decision to hire you partly on that.

If you want a gig like this, think about products that you enjoy using, rather than taking a job to promote a product you don't really care about. Readers can smell insincerity, and you don't want to have to rely on promotional language because you can't come up with your own copy.

As for what to charge, there is no industry standard. I know bloggers who've been paid anywhere from $250 to $3,000 for a recipe post promoting a product. To figure out what you should charge, consider your time to develop a recipe, shop for ingredients, the cost of those ingredients and any essential equipment, whether you will make a dish more than once, and how long it takes to style and shoot it, write the post, and promote it.

Also think about your value. Maybe it will take you only a few hours, but you think you're worth more than an hourly rate. Think of your post as an advertisement, and label it clearly, preferably at the top of the post. You may be legally obligated to do the work a certain way. Some companies will ask you to sign a contract. Some contracts say you can't work with competing brands for several months. Some companies want to review your post beforehand. Some want you to embed their own video or link to a company promotion. Charge more if so. You control your content on your own post, so guard it. And some contracts can be in your best interest. The point is to read them carefully.

* *

TIPS FOR WRITING SPONSORED POSTS

I'm not much of a fan of sponsored posts, because most bloggers don't do them well. They go overboard and write promotional material instead of their usual post. Most of the time they're not paid enough to make writing them worthwhile, but amazingly, it takes very little to get a blogger to gush about a product on a blog. Here are some tips for writing responsible sponsored content:

TELL A STORY, JUST AS YOU WOULD DO SO NORMALLY. You want your post to look as much like one of your normal blog posts as possible. Write in everyday text. Don't put the product name in all caps or use the TM symbol after a product name.

DON'T GUSH. Your readers are your first priority, not your client. They want to trust you when you endorse a product. Write in your usual style, and don't write hype, like "this is the greatest thing ever." Don't lapse into advertising terms, such as "accept no substitutes."

DON'T GIVE AWAY THE SPACE ON YOUR BLOG. Your expertise and reach are crucial, and that's why a company is interested in you. You don't need to embed its video if you are not getting paid to do so, for example. Nor do you have to use the company's language if it doesn't sound like yours.

DISCLOSE. If you live in the United States, you are required by law to disclose that you are being paid to write the post. Create a header that says "sponsored post" and place it prominently. If disclosing makes you uncomfortable, don't write sponsored posts.

Some companies want much more than just a post. They want you to host parties for your blogger friends, serve their foods, and then promote the event on social media with videos and photos, for example. Charge accordingly for your time and influence, if this kind of work interests you. In this case, you must disclose on social media that you were paid, since you will be endorsing a product directly.

There's no one way to disclose on social media. Some people put "#ad" or "#sponsored" in their Tweets and posts. The key is to be transparent with your readers.

* *

Pay for sponsored giveaways. Some bloggers charge to write a post about a product and then give it away to a lucky reader. I'm not a big fan of the idea because people don't always understand that the blogger is being paid to endorse the product. This is another kind of sponsored post, and you must disclose it. You won't be writing an objective review, of course. Ask the company to give you professional photos of the product and to ship the product to the winner.

Opportunities from blogger networks. These are networks that offer you opportunities to promote products for pay, such as BlogHer and Mode Media. Make sure that you're excited about the products they offer for compensation and that they're paying a reasonable amount of money (over $200). And do these promotions sparingly. You don't want to publish post after post where you're pushing products for pay, because readers will stop trusting your content.

Advertising income through YouTube. John Mitzewich, a former cooking teacher and chef, started Food Wishes, a video-based blog. Then he put his videos on YouTube and became an advertising partner. His videos became so successful that Allrecipes.com purchased his channel and video library for six figures and hired him to stay on as a consultant.

Donations. I'm not kidding. If you are a starving artist type who blogs for love, you might have patrons willing to give you a donation, even recurring donations (a subscription). PayPal and Patreon software have buttons and boxes you can install. Patreon lets you offer rewards to your supporters, such as a thank-you on Twitter, merchandise, or an "exclusive update" seen only by them, such as a podcast sent one week before you release it.

Making Money Outside Your Food Blog

Up to now I've been listing ways to make money directly on your blog. But after you blog for a while, you realize you have certain skills that qualify you for new kinds of work, or qualify you to charge for your time. Here's a whole new list of possibilities. Most of these are not going to add up to a full-time job, but if you're looking for regular income they might be worth a shot:

Become a corporate blogger. Find the websites for products you love, and find a blog with content written by freelance writers. This may be difficult if writers don't get a byline, of course, but some food websites include blogs that feature original content, and they pay well. If the company wants photographs, videos, or slideshows, negotiate a higher price.

Write for popular websites. Some consumer food blogs hire bloggers to write for them, too, such as the *Kitchn* and *Serious Eats*. Read Chapter 5 on freelancing for general information.

Before you pitch, read the website, become a commenter, and become a subscriber to learn exactly what kinds of stories they like. Find the submission guidelines, and adhere to them religiously. Editors don't want to work with someone who can't follow instructions. If you do get a piece published, share it with your social media followers.

For a regular column on *Serious Eats*, a client and I brainstormed until we came up with a missing category. As a chef, she could write about any food and felt confident about this one. She pitched the category and wrote regular posts for a long time. The pay is around $100 and it's a good way to build up your writing portfolio.

. . . .

IF YOU WANT TO WORK WITH BRANDS

As an online community manager, Annelies Zijderveld travels to many food blogging conferences with the goal of meeting the right bloggers to hire. While there, she keeps her customer demographics in mind and listen for key words that make her light up with ideas like Pavlov's dogs to a bell. If you want to work with a food company, here are her suggestions from the perspective of someone who hires and manages bloggers:

DO YOUR RESEARCH. Before you hit send on an email introduction or query, visit the company website and social profiles. This may seem obvious, but your expertise needs to align with a company, so figure out their main points, and try to get an idea of their customers. Also, keep your own readers in mind, and be choosy. Ask yourself if working with the nineteen-ingredient nutrition bar company would match the minimally processed food content your readers expect. Consider your threshold of how many brands you can actually work with before your blog begins to look like a billboard, losing the long-earned trust you've gained from readers.

START WITH AN INTRODUCTION. As an ardent fan of the food company, send a note to someone in marketing, letting them know how you have used their food or product in your everyday life. Ask whether you can connect about ideas you have to broaden the reach of the brand through a recipe, blog post, or social media campaign. In the first communication, hold off on making a pitch. Instead, think of the long-term possibilities, and cultivate a relationship. Have your list of ideas ready when the brand person circles back to you, after checking out your presence online. **BRAND SUCCESS IS YOUR SUCCESS.** When I developed an influencer program for a cereal company, a few of our writers stood out. They sent in their articles in advance and then went above and beyond what we had discussed as their monthly work. They understood that if the brand succeeded, they succeeded. These ambassadors saw themselves as part of our team and invested accordingly. Their articles posted to the company blog, and they promoted their work to their readership just as if they had published it in a glossy magazine. They were the ones I knew I could count on over the long term, and they pitched new ideas for us to work together.

Working with brands can be gratifying for the blogger who sees an opportunity to creatively engage with products they already consume while broadening the scope of that company's audience.

Host social media events for clients. Dr. Jean Layton, who started the blog GlutenFreeDoctor.com in 2006, fell in love with Google+ and has been teaching how to use it since 2012. She has produced hangouts for clients such as Bob's Red Mill, in which each week a panel of bloggers discussed a particular grain. For each event, she charges between $400 and $600. She discovered that she understands the intricacies of social media better than many companies, and has started a consulting business devoted to helping companies and individuals manage their social media platforms effectively. She's also teaching classes at community colleges.

Become a professional photographer. Several food bloggers have made transitions to this field as a natural result of their blogs. Matt Armendariz of MattBites.com, Hélène Dujardin of Tarteletteblog.com, and Todd Porter and Diane Cu of WhiteonRiceCouple.com are just a few who have branched out successfully, photographing cookbooks for authors and creating images for corporate clients including Whole Foods, Nestlé, and Jordan Winery. Armendariz published the book *Food Photography for Bloggers*, while Dujardin published *Palate to Pixel*. Oxmoor House tapped her to become a full-time senior photographer.

Porter and Cu learned video and have made many book trailers for cookbook authors and corporate clients such as Tourism Australia. All teach photograph workshops as well, and some teach online on Creative Live.com, which charges students $100 to take a class.

Go on a trip. Some bloggers charge a day rate if they are invited to go on a trip to visit a food company, particularly if they are expected to be active on social media the whole time and write a post about their experience. The bigger bloggers actually have talent agents who negotiate these trips for them.

Write an ebook. This isn't a way to repurpose your blog content. The ebooks that sell have new content, because no one wants to pay for content that is already available for free. Ebooks are typically shorter than cookbooks and cost less. Specific topics are best.

Food blogger Lindsay Ostrom of PinchofYum.com taught herself how to use her dSLR camera and how to edit in Photoshop and Lightroom. Her blog readership soared with Pinterest. She created an ebook that discusses technical tips, props, composition, lighting, and other subjects of interest to food bloggers, and made an extensive web page that listed the book's table of contents, showed example pages and video tutorials, and included testimonials. As a result she has sold around five thousand copies. She also created an affiliate program so other bloggers could sell her book for a commission. And she's created more ebooks, this time about cooking.

License your photos. If you're an amazing photographer, charge to have someone use your photos on a website or for commercial purposes such as in an ad or packaging. You can sell your photography online at sites such as ZenFolio.com, SmugMug.com, iStockPhoto.com, and countless other photography sites. They don't promote your work, though, so you need to know how to mark up your images to appear in the searches of site users, or have some other way to reach companies willing to pay for your work.

Develop an app. Some bloggers partner with a company or programmer to release these software programs for mobile devices. David Lebovitz, for example, created a Paris Pastry Guide that sells for $3.99, and cookbook author Andrea Nguyen partnered with Chronicle Books to create the Asian Market Shopper App for several mobile device platforms.

Michael Ruhlman wrote an app, Schmaltz for the iPad, which became a book he sold to Little, Brown. He also has an app based on his book *Ratio* and another on bread baking. When I asked him what defines a good app, he said, "Something that's useful, encourages people to cook, and makes cooking easier and more fun. It does something no other device can do in the kitchen. It does more than just show you videos—which you can watch on TV—or show you a recipe—which you can see in a cookbook."

On what skills food bloggers need to develop, he said, "They need an imagination and an understanding of digital devices and what they're capable of doing, and how to make them do new things. Otherwise it's all the same stuff. People who know how to cook, have culinary knowledge, and cook well and have valuable info to give need to be very creative in new ways to use the technology."

Sell blog merchandise. Create aprons, T-shirts, cards, mugs, canvas bags, and photo cards with your blog's logo or with photos from your blog.

Kickstart a project. Maybe there's something new that you want to do yourself, but you don't want to take out a bank loan. Try Kickstarter.com, Indiegogo.com, or a similar crowdfunding website. Blogger Shauna James Ahern (GlutenFreeGirl.com) started a Kickstarter campaign to launch her own brand of gluten-free flour mix. Blogger Jerry James Stone (Cooking Stoned.com) Kickstarted his first cookbook, which fans fully funded in just three days. It earned almost three times its original goal number by the end of the campaign. Herbalist Dini Falconi and illustrator Wendy Hollender wrote *Foraging and Feasting* and raised around $100,000 to send people a $38 signed hardcover book. Their original budget was $25,000.

"Wendy and I worked for no pay on this book for the last three years," she said when I interviewed Falconi for my blog. "We put a low number on Kickstarter to reduce our risk. You need a low enough amount because if you don't make it, you don't get anything at all. The $25,000 is not the cost of the book, but a starting point. We're still working on the actual budget. Even when we receive the money, we're going to use it for printing and production, and we probably won't pay ourselves anything."

Become a restaurateur. Okay, it's not for everyone, but food blogger Pim Techamuanvivit (ChezPim.com) did so, as did blogger Molly Wizenberg (Orangette.blogspot.com). Both have significant others who are chefs (and one is a distinguished restaurateur), which must have helped.

Start a monthly club. Kirstin Jackson of the food blog ItsNotYouItsBrie. com started a cheese club that sends three kinds of cheese to readers every month, followed by a newsletter with more information and recipes. There is a three-month membership, and those who sign up for a year get a complimentary signed copy of her book.

Consult on a television sitcom. Gabi Moskowitz, who writes at Broke AssGourmet.com, consulted on a television sitcom called *Young and Hungry*, based on her life and writing. She also was involved in a web series in which she cooked with the cast. An agent at Creative Artists Agency emailed her to ask if she had ever considered making her blog into a sitcom. She interviewed writers, consulted on the script, and the sitcom premiered on ABC Family.

Partner with a food retailer. Michele Tam of NomNomPaleo.com partnered with Whole Foods to curate a selection of "Nom Nom Picks" at forty Whole Foods markets in Northern California and Reno. She created a flyer, "Michelle Tam's Hand-Picked Favorites," based on products in the store. On the shelves, tags (called "shouter tags") announced her product picks. The stores also sell her cookbook.

Become a coach. Katie Farrell of DashingDish.com is a registered nurse in addition to a food blogger. On her blog you can find four- and eight-week health coaching programs, including one for getting in shape for weddings, called the Bridal Bootcamp.

The Big Money

So far most of these strategies might make you a few bucks, maybe a few hundred, depending on your traffic or how hard you work at these things. Next you'll read about people who have done very well online, and they've worked hard for it. I've discovered that some food writers bring in incredible income online while sitting at their desks. Of course, they are not just food writers but brilliant marketers who understand the technical opportunities to deliver original content, sometimes to a paying audience. These opportunities are evolving, limited only by the imaginations of the food writers who invent them.

By "big money," I mean that some of the people I'm mentioning here have a business that supports more than just themselves. Some of them bring in mid-six-figure gross incomes.

One more qualification for being mentioned in this section: these people are driven, competitive, super-talented writers as well as excellent marketers, fast learners, and tech-savvy social media mavens who tend to work way too many hours. Keep that in mind. Here's what's happening now online:

Create a website based on searchable content, not a blog. Some food writers have started sites based on content they don't write. These sites have sustained the founders and created enough opportunities for them to hire others at market rates.

LeitesCulinaria.com began in 1999 as a place for food writer David Leite to post writing clips as a way to attract editors. From there he developed it into a recipe-based searchable website, fueled by recipes from cookbooks that are tested and reviewed by a group of professional and home cooks. All the revenue from his site comes from advertising, which pays him and a group of contractors. A steady stream of cookbook giveaways augments the site's traffic.

When I asked David for advice he would give to food writers who want to start a successful site, he said, "Find out what you do that's different from others. In our case, we feature food writing. We have the testing section, which has more than 150 testers. We're also extremely responsive to readers on the site as well as on all social media platforms. We choose recipes from cookbooks as a way for readers to test drive them." On a personal note, he says, "Be relentless. I'm at this sixty to seventy hours a week. Renee Schettler Rossi, our editor in chief, is at it about the same amount of time. And don't compromise your values. You can never get them back."

Another example of success is Food52.com. Founded in 2009 by former *New York Times* food writer Amanda Hesser and her partner,

Merrill Stubbs, a chef and food writer, Food52 is a crowd-sourced website that began as a platform for cooks whom they encouraged to share their recipes to win prizes. Food52 recently raised $9 million from venture capitalists. The founders grew their network to thirty thousand recipes, 70 percent contributed for free. More recently they launched an online shop, Provisions, which now accounts for two-thirds of Food52's revenue, with the rest from ads. They had 3.8 million unique visitors per month in 2014.

Don't expect to make a huge income right away. These sites are all based on attracting views, which takes a few years to build. Other sites that have made it big over the years are *Serious Eats* and *Chow*, which bought the forum-based site Chowhound.

Launch a subscription service. Jenny McGruther switched to a traditional foods diet in 2006 and started a blog on the subject in 2007, called NourishedKitchen.com. Based on the amount of interest in her blog and newsletter, she created an online business of teaching people to cook traditional foods (nutrient-dense, unrefined foods including organ meats and foods that are fermented, sprouted, and raw).

She charges by the month and by the class for her online cooking classes and healthy meal plans. Hundreds of people have signed up, enabling her to quit her day job as an office manager.

Her website sells meal plans and recipes and multimedia cooking classes. For the first plan, readers pay monthly for food plans, a weekly shopping list, access to a recipe database, and bonus recipes every week. The multimedia series Get Cultured! features over fifty video tutorials, twelve ebooks with more than one hundred recipes, tutorials, articles, and fact sheets devoted to fermented foods.

When I interviewed her for my blog, McGruther said she built her content working with "several other bloggers to promote each other's premium content, which helps us all reach a broader audience. We also share suggestions, tips, and technical advice."

She prepares lots of text to describe each product, which leads to more purchases. When I asked about these long entreaties, she said, "I determined what I would like to see before I purchase something. With a physical product, you can see it. With digital information, it's a little more challenging. I did my best to make sure it was very clear to see exactly what people were getting. That helps me create informed buyers who are not confused about the product."

When I asked how other food writers could build a business like this, she said, "They need to build a devoted audience based on their specialized knowledge. Once they have a way to convey that knowledge to their readers, they need to make it very clear about what the product will do for their readers. If they outline it directly and hit a price point that provides substantial value, they'll be in a good position."

Melissa Lanz of TheFresh20.com created a meal-planning service in 2010, employing twenty fresh seasonal ingredients per week. A former Internet marketing executive, she has since published a cookbook and now employs a staff. Customers can buy an annual plan for $54, a three-month subscription, specialty plans, or ebooks. A fundraising program for schools and charities lets them sell the plans and keep 40 percent of the revenue. According to the *New York Times*, in 2012 Fresh20 had more than thirty-five thousand subscribers, each of whom paid $5 per month. Lanz said her company was projected to earn $860,000 that year.

Aviva Goldfarb, founder of the Six O'Clock Scramble (TheScramble .com), another online meal subscription service, said in the same 2012 article that she had about six thousand subscribers who pay $3 to $7 per month. That's a minimum of $18,000 per month.

Slightly different is chef "Meathead" Goldwyn, who started a Pit-master Club at AmazingRibs.com. For $9.95 per month, customers get a temperature guide magnet, live video seminars with top pitmasters, access to a forum, and entry into a giveaway. He also sells barbecue products with Amazon affiliate links.

I couldn't close this section without talking about PinchofYum.com and FoodBloggerPro.com. Lindsay Olstrom created Pinch of Yum, a food blog, in 2010. Her husband, Bjork, a techie, took charge of the tech issues and business. Soon, in response to queries about how to succeed as a food blogger, Bjork launched Food Blogger Pro, a subscription site for food bloggers, for $25 per month. He's closing in on seven hundred subscribers as of this writing. You do the math. (Disclosure: I recently became an affiliate.)

For the last three years, Olstrom has listed the monthly income from both sites in detail on the Pinch of Yum blog, so anyone can see how they're making money. Of course, having two million unique views a month doesn't hurt, but on top of significant revenue from ads, they generate income from affiliate programs, both as affiliates and as content producers who offer affiliate sales to others. As affiliates, their site includes links to hosting services and other software. As content producers, they offer affiliate programs to other bloggers who want to sell their products for a small commission. Check the Pinch of Yum blog under "Income" to see the monthly reports. As this book went to production, they were making as much as $20,000 per month.

Both have recently become self-employed full-time. It was a hard road to get there. "Lindsay was a fourth grade teacher until June [2014]," explains Olstrom. "Before, she got up at five a.m. and wrote a post before school, three times a week, until seven thirty a.m. When she came home around three P.M., she tried new recipes. She did photography on weekends for two to three recipes."

When I asked him how they got the bandwidth to start new projects, Olstrom said, "I like the idea of 1 percent infinity, the idea that you're not writing an ebook this month—you're just dedicating 1 percent of your day to improving. You can't do much each day for fifteen minutes, but you can do a lot in a year. It's about goals and how to start them today. You're not going to hit a home run or even a single, but you're going to hit the ball every day and get somewhere and win in the long run. The hard thing is starting."

Create a program using emails. Jadah Sellner and Jen Hansard cashed in on a trend a few years ago when they launched SimpleGreenSmoothies .com. They began with a free weekly email with recipes, shopping lists, and tips. From there, they lobbied customers to purchase a twenty-one-day cleanse. For $59, customers get a meal plan, recipe guide, weekly shopping list, and access to an online support group. In about a year and a half, Sellner grew her Simple Green Smoothies community to two hundred thousand subscribers, with more than ten million page views. Like other people mentioned here, these two entrepreneurs now support a staff.

As a side business, Sellner now does consulting for others. At this writing, her one-on-one Mentorshop Lab costs $1,500 per person. She also conducts a Business + Soul Mastermind Retreat. "People come to me when they're ready to grow their communities into a meaningful, world-changing movement," she says on her website.

Get your own franchise on About.com. About.com reaches eighty-seven million unique visitors per month just in the United States, and partners with experts who write about food and cooking. The writer creates a website that's similar to a blog, but About.com is in charge of promoting it. I've heard that some experts make an income similar to a full-time job, if they create a robust website. That means the harder you work, the more your site grows, the more people you reach. You get paid per article and per every thousand page views. As traffic increases, so does the amount paid.

Eric Handlesman, About.com's general manager of Food, says an experts' monthly compensation ranges from $600 to $700 per month to "two or three food writers who have made in excess of $100,000 in a year, depending on the whims of Google. We do have one writer who consistently makes in excess of $100,000 per year."

How to Create a Professional Business

By now you might be all fired up to get your new business going. That's great! Some people jump in without much preamble, but others want to be more deliberate. If you're the type who likes vision boards and planning, this section is for you. Here are a few ideas about how to get a professional business started. Even if you've been a freelancer for years, there are probably things in this section that you haven't done yet:

Write a business plan. This is a document that outlines the goals of your business. You'll want to think about how much time you can devote to it and how much money you'd like to make. Decide how many conferences you plan to attend each year, or how many projects you plan to take on. You don't have to make this too formal unless you're the type who enjoys doing so.

After eighteen years of self-employment, I don't prepare a formal yearly plan, but I do look ahead to figure out what I want to do next year, and I regularly imagine what I'd like to be doing a few years out. I put one big new task in front of myself, like teaching internationally or creating private one-day workshops. This year, I got back to writing personal essays, and one was published. Soon I hope to start teaching an online class.

I love the variety and the challenges of setting these new goals that push me forward, and as a result, I'm rarely bored.

A good plan can keep you organized and on track too. You can look back on it regularly to see how you're doing or to change direction. Some things to consider for your business plan:

- What is your niche or specialty?
- Who is your target audience, and how will you reach them?
- Who is on your team?
- Who are your competitors?
- Whom do you admire?
- Which publications would be most interested in your story ideas?
- Which conferences would help you network and grow?
- What is your plan for self-promotion?
- What skills do you most need to improve?
- What new computer skill do you need to learn?
- What sort of outside help will you need, such as a designer or web developer, and what is your budget?
- How will you know when you have succeeded?

You might benefit from asking "What if?" questions. What you think of as impossible might just be doable, say Alexander Osterwalder and Yves Pigneur, authors of the book *Business Model Generation: A Handbook for Visionaries, Game Changers, and Challengers*. "What if" questions should "provoke us and challenge our thinking," they said. "They should disturb us as intriguing, difficult-to execute propositions."

Jaden Hair of SteamyKitchen.com is a big fan of vision boards, a visual representation of what you want from your life or career. They're collages you create on poster board from magazine photos and cutouts of meaningful words. The idea is to add clarity to your goals and desires, and show them visually. Hair framed hers and hung it somewhere where she could see it, to keep the inspiration going. Get a poster board, a big stack of magazines, and glue, and ask yourself what you want. Some people know exactly what they want, some create a board of possibilities, and some create a board with a theme.

Create your personal brand statement. I used to think these kinds of things were hokey, but they have value. A branding statement clarifies who you are and what you do, both for you and your potential clients. It defines three things:

- what you are best at
- whom you serve
- how you do it uniquely.

Your goal is to make it memorable, punchy, and solution oriented. It will appear on your website, and it's something to memorize for when people ask what you do. To create it, start with a list of your career highlights and business skills and focus on which create your unique selling proposition (USP).

Spend lots of time on this point. Lots of people develop recipes, for example. What's unique about the way you do it? What do you want to be known for? Define why you want to do what you do. Why are you called to it?

Marketing guru Seth Godin advises that your unique selling point is not for everyone. A niche gives you a competitive advantage that lets you avoid trying to please everyone. Your USP is about differentiation: what you do that your competitors do not. Describe your skills in terms of your client's benefit and traits worth remembering. Be specific. If you are a freelancer who specializes in clean copy and making deadlines, editors will want to work with you.

Write the brand statement for potential clients. If you're not sure who they are, brainstorm and make a list of their possible titles or situations. Write it in plain, punchy language, not market-speak. Some people like to write about themselves in third person ("she"), but I'm a fan of writing in first person ("I"), since it's coming from me. Keep your statement short, the length of one breath.

Your goal is to have readers understand right away what you do. Tantalize them with specific information that leaves them wanting more. If you're serious about this, you might want help from a copywriter or a branding consultant. Next is more advice from two branding experts.

"Build your brand fire on a solid base of reality (no corporate-speak, but also no dear-diary, please, either) and who you are. The work you do will create the kind of glow that attracts others, but can also sustain you if you aren't afraid to talk about your expertise, how you get hired, and what people can expect from you, once they gather 'round your fire," Tara Street advised me in an email. She cofounded BraidCreative.com, a branding and business visioning consultancy for working creatives.

"One thing I've learned during my many years of marketing is how powerful it is to put a face and personality to the people I'm marketing and selling to," wrote Lia Huber, founder of NourishNetwork.com and a branding consultant. "When I'm selling to a vague 'audience,' I feel pushy and insecure, and I shrink back from stepping boldly into my calling. But when I focus on the people in my audience—developing a persona for my ideal customer—then I see clearly how excited they are to have found me, and how much they really need what I have to offer." Huber offers a free three-part video on defining your brand at Building-AuthenticBrands.com.

Create a professional website. Once you've written your branding statement, put it on a website that sells your services or products. You'll want to review the site regularly and make sure it's still accurate. It's always going to be a work in progress.

People who might hire you will visit your site and find out more about you. If you have a food blog, your "About" page might not cover your services and products in this level of detail. For this reason, many successful bloggers have created more formal websites for potential clients. This is especially true if they form a new business, such as photography or social media consulting.

This website doesn't have to be enormous. It should link to your blog and look similar to it in design. The point is to include a bio that lists your accomplishments, samples of your work, and perhaps some testimonials. Some people integrate their professional information into their blogs, and some people integrate their blogs into their professional websites. There's no one way to do it. Here's what you might put on your site:

- An "About" page. Connect with potential clients on a personal level. Share your story so they want to work with you because of who you are, your accomplishments, and your background. List degrees if they are relevant. Three or four paragraphs are enough.

- A professional head shot. Readers want to see who's talking to them.
- A list of your books or links to articles you've written. Make it easy for editors or others to find samples of your work quickly, if that is your goal.
- A list of upcoming classes or events. If you want to be hired as a speaker, it helps to have examples of current events or lists of past speaking engagements. Because I speak and teach so often, I have one page for events and another aimed at people who might invite me to a conference.
- A press or media page with links to mentions or profiles. Make these readable. Links to the actual articles are best, versus creating tiny images of the articles that no one can read.
- A newsletter sign-up. Your target readers are your most valuable resource. While social media followers come and go, your newsletter subscribers choose to hear from you and want to hear from you. So if you can, send them a monthly newsletter, even a short one, to give them valuable free information they can't find elsewhere. Sneak in a few advertisements for yourself or your products.

Create a media kit and rate sheet. Write an introduction to help your potential client connect with you. It should describe the theme of your blog briefly. If you want advertising or sponsorship on your blog, describe your target readers. List monthly page views and unique page views, and social media stats. You may want to date them as a reminder to refresh them regularly. State the sizes and costs of ad space, and say where they will appear. If you charge fees for giveaways and sponsored posts, list them. Some of this could sound quite dry, so imagine your target reader, and speak directly to him or her. Include a few of your best photos to break up the text. You may want to make this a downloadable PDF, or you may want people to contact you directly to receive it. Put a call to action at the end, such as asking them to email you to begin working together.

Some websites offer templates and more advice. For a free media kit template aimed at food bloggers, see recipetineats.com/blogger-resources /free-media-kit-template.

Network. Find people who are already doing what you want to do, and research them. Don't call up and say you would like the same job they have, and ask how you could get it. They will see you as a potential threat, and your strategy could backfire. Instead, find someone doing complementary work. If she's doing a meal plan subscription for gluten-free people, and you want to do one for Orthodox Jews, you can ask her whom she worked with and how she organizes her products, without her feeling like you're going to take her business.

Join a networking group. Many food bloggers, for example, have begun private networking groups to help each other grow a business. They also join closed groups on Facebook such as Food Blogger Friends and the Food Blogger Network as places to ask questions and gain insights. You can join regional and national groups, such as Austin Food Blog Alliance (austinfoodbloggers.org/) and the Food Bloggers of Canada (foodbloggers ofcanada.com).

Join a professional organization or two. I've benefited from being a member of the International Association of Culinary Professionals, the San Francisco Professional Food Society, the Baker's Dozen, and the Association of Food Journalists. I've attended meetings and conferences to meet people I admire, to network, and to learn. Some of the members have hired me and become repeat clients. Oh, and I've also made some lifelong friends.

Go to a food blogging conference. There are more food blogger conferences than ever these days, not to mention smaller classes on such subjects as food photography and styling. I've listed the biggest ones in the Appendix.

••

FIVE REASONS TO ATTEND A BLOGGING CONFERENCE

Some find it overwhelming to attend a conference, and some are good at jumping in and enjoying themselves. Set a goal for yourself before you leave: What are you going to learn? Who would you like to meet? Have specific goals to meet a certain number of people or hand out at least twenty cards. And then just have a good time:

- Meet other people, including those you admire, whom you've only read online.
- Get the latest information on social media, food trends, book publishing, search engine optimization (SEO), and photography.
- Get inspired and motivated. You'll find ideas on how to improve your blog, photography, business, and social media prowess.
- Network with companies, big bloggers, publishers, even literary agents.

- Have fun! Choose a city you've never been to, go to parties and restaurants with groups, and enjoy yourself. Take time off to explore, and get in a little breather outside the conference.

Learn to negotiate. I saved one of the most important skills for last. If you're negotiating with a client to do work, you have a few choices on how to price yourself. You can do one of the following:

- Base the project amount on your hourly rate. If you think the job is worth $25 per hour, then you just add up the amount of hours you think it will take you. Add everything you can think of: testing a product, photographing it, developing and testing a recipe, grocery shopping, editing photos, social media, etc. Add 50 percent more (because you always forget something), and present your total.
- Provide a project fee. I like this idea because you will be paid better. I know a food blogger who, when approached to write a recipe post with a photo for her blog, said the fee was $3,000. She based her fee on her value, not her hourly rate. Not only did she get the job, but the company became a repeat client.
- Determine what you want to make per year and how many hours you want to work. Let's say you want to make $52,000 (for easy division) per year. That's $1,000 per week. Now how many hours? Ten, you say? That's $100 per hour. The rate is not outrageous for many jobs. The challenge is working an average of ten hours every single week.

You can also ask, "What's your budget?" and wait for an answer. Some negotiators believe there's a disadvantage to speaking first. No matter what number you receive, say, "That seems a little low." You have nothing to lose, and with food bloggers, it's usually true.

HOW TO NEGOTIATE AS A FOOD BLOGGER

JADEN HAIR of SteamyKitchen.com has years of negotiation skills under her belt. She runs a blog, has written three cookbooks, and is cofounder of FoodBlogForum.

More recently, she launched KitchenTableMastery.com with business tips for food bloggers. Here are some of her best tips:

YOUR CLIENT IS IN THE BUSINESS OF MAKING MONEY. If a brand has the budget to hire a PR agency, it has the money to pay you fairly for your services.

KNOW WHAT YOU WANT. Before talking with a potential client, figure out what it might look like to work together. How would you feel when you post, and how would your readers and your client feel about the post?

What is your target dollar amount, the minimum you will accept? Know these numbers before you negotiate. Include detailed hours and an hourly rate so potential clients can see exactly what it takes to deliver a top-notch result.

BE WILLING TO WALK AWAY. Sometimes it's better to graciously say, "No, thank you," instead of trying to force a bad deal down. Saying no is powerful. It means you have defined what is most important to you and you are willing to protect your priorities.

NEVER NEGOTIATE ON EMAIL. Negotiation in person is best, so you can catch subtle facial expressions, tone, and the body language that helps you understand what the other side is thinking. Next best is Google Hangouts or Skype. If video isn't viable, use the phone, preferably a landline for a good quality connection.

I DON'T NEGOTIATE DIRECTLY WITH A BRAND. I prefer the buffer of a public relations or marketing agency. The agency's job is to work with the client on promotions, to budget and track programs, to deeply understand what the client wants, needs, and desires. Also, agencies understand the online space better. If you do a good job, they might have other clients to work with in the future.

IF THEY WANT A REDUCED FEE, DON'T CUT YOUR RATE. Instead, reduce the deliverables. If you cut your rate, you won't be able to work for the original rate if they hire you again.

DON'T WORK FOR FREE IF YOU PLAN TO WORK FOR A COMPANY AGAIN. I do plenty of free work for tiny companies who cannot afford advertising or a PR agency. I don't expect them to pay me, and I don't expect them to ever hire me in the future. That's okay! It's my gift to them. Otherwise, once a brand knows they can get free work, they'll keep finding ways to support that habit.

· ·

Now That You Have a Business, What Can You Write Off Your Taxes?

As a food writer, can you now write off all meals, research, and travel? Probably not, unless you can meet certain criteria.

The first test is how much time you spend on food writing. In the United States, according to the IRS, if you put in at least five hundred hours per year, you have a business. If it's less than that, you have a hobby.

The IRS allows no deductions for hobbies unless your hobby makes a profit. In that case, you can deduct expenses up to the same amount as your hobby's expenses. If you took a loss, for example, in which food writing earned you $2,750, but you spent $3,500 on food, travel, classes, and office expenses, you could deduct only $750 of the expenses. These expenses constitute a miscellaneous deduction and may be subject to further restrictions.

If you have a food writing business that takes up more than five hundred hours per year, you may qualify for some tax deductions. Here are test questions the IRS might ask to determine whether your business qualifies:

Do you keep records documenting your writing and research? Doing so would indicate you have a serious business. Let's say you wrote about a restaurant meal, or that consuming it influenced you to write a recipe inspired by it. You need more than the credit card receipt to show as evidence. Keep notes on the meal, a sample menu, a map, a parking receipt, a sample draft, and any photos. For recipe development, keep versions of each recipe, with notes on how you worked.

For meetings, research, and so forth, keep a mileage record of how far you drove, for what purpose, and on what date.

Do you have a business with income, and have you taken classes to help you in developing your expertise? If so, you may write off whatever expenses are ordinary and necessary for performance of your business. Let's say you took a weeklong cooking class in Venice. You received a syllabus, kept notes, took photographs, and researched restaurants, markets, and food purveyors, thus establishing a true business purpose for your trip: your desire to increase your knowledge and expertise of Italian food, thereby improving your marketability.

Is it reasonable to expect a profit? The more you can show you are in business to make a profit, the more legitimate your write-offs become. Here are a few examples:

- You want to travel to Turkey and write articles about your food explorations there. Querying editors before you leave indicates you are looking for profit-generating opportunities.

Querying editors afterward might indicate you are looking for ways to write off your vacation. It doesn't matter if the editors reject the articles. What matters is your intent and record-keeping prowess.

- Let's say a newspaper paid you $75 for three recipes. The cost of groceries came to $100. While you didn't make a profit, expenses are deductible, as is the mileage to and from the grocery store.
- You want to write a cookbook based on using kitchen appliances like rice cookers and food processors. Your purchase of kitchen equipment might be deductible if you can show that you also bought similar books for research purposes, wrote a book proposal, interviewed kitchen-shop retailers, and looked for an agent. Even so, since they are capital expenses, the deduction might occur over the life of the equipment as opposed to a full deduction on the year of the purchase.

Once you meet the above criteria for a business, you qualify for the right to deduct ordinary and necessary expenses for a self-employed business person, such as telephone bills, office supplies, and membership fees. Keep detailed files of your work-related papers, including copies of your notes, plus all bills and receipts.

Many food writers also cater, develop recipes, do food styling for photographs, act as spokespeople for brands, consult for industry, and teach cooking classes. The good news is these pursuits are interrelated and can be considered one business. Therefore the Venice cooking class may make you a better caterer and recipe developer, in addition to increasing your knowledge as a food writer.

This is a cursory discussion only. For more details, consult a professional tax preparer. And remember, you must have income in order to write things off against it.

In the End

From this book's first chapter, my goal has been to help you write about food, whether for yourself or for publication, for a hobby or for income. I hope you have found the tools you need to express your ideas, thoughts, and opinions in words. Now it's up to you. Believe in yourself and your ideas, and believe that you can move forward. Keep writing and rewriting, even if it's only for fifteen minutes per day.

At least half of the path to publication is about not giving up. Just remember that even Julia Child was rejected the first time an editor saw her manuscript. Imagine how much we would have lost if she gave up right then. As publishing veteran Harriett Bell told me, "Every successful cookbook author was once someone who just had an idea." Discovering a promising new writer is one of the things editors and agents love most about their jobs. Give them the opportunity to find you.

ACKNOWLEDGMENTS

This book would not have been possible without the generous responses of the knowledgeable food writers, bloggers, editors, and agents I interviewed. Almost everyone, no matter how well known, gave me their time and came up with thoughtful responses. They read emails and took calls at the office, at home, on the road, on vacation, and after retirement. I am grateful for the time they spent educating me, sharing their sagacity, and giving advice so beneficial to my readers.

Several colleagues and former clients gave me useful information for this edition, including new essays from Robyn Eckhardt, Jaden Hair, Nancy Leson, Marge Perry, Molly Stevens, Stephanie Stiavetti, and Annalies Zijderveld. Josh Greenbaum came up with the witty title.

My husband, Owen Rubin, provided a sense of humor, technical support, and wizardry with Microsoft Word.

Agent Carole Bidnick encouraged me from the first mention of this idea and championed the third edition of this book.

I'm grateful to all readers of my blog, also called Will Write for Food (diannej.com), who provided thoughtful comments relevant to the third edition of this book, and to all those I interviewed and who wrote guest posts from which I cribbed information for this edition. I thank my clients and students, from whom I have learned so much. I am indebted to other authors of books and websites for resource material on good writing, blogging, freelancing, proposal writing, self-publishing, and finding agents.

Thanks to the team at Da Capo for skillfully handling the third edition: Renée Sedliar, executive editor; Beth Wright of Trio Bookworks, copyeditor extraordinaire; and Jonathan Sainsbury, who designed my fun new cover.

Thanks to all those who've kept my skills sharp by hiring me to edit articles, proposals, manuscripts, and recipes, and to those who've encouraged me as a writer.

BIBLIOGRAPHY

Abu-Jaber, Diana. *Crescent*. New York: Norton, 2003.

Ackerman, Diane. *A Natural History of the Senses*. New York: Random House, 1990.

Allen, Gary. *The Resource Guide for Food Writers*. Oxford: Routledge, 1999.

Allen, Moira Anderson. *Starting Your Career as a Freelance Writer*. New York: Allworth, 2003.

Allende, Isabel. *Aphrodite: A Memoir of the Senses*. New York: Perennial, 1999.

Allison, Karen Hubert. *How I Gave My Heart to the Restaurant Business: A Novel*. New York: Ecco, 1997.

Almond, Steve. *Candyfreak: A Journey Through the Chocolate Underbelly of America*. Chapel Hill, NC: Algonquin, 2004.

Annual Directory of Syndicated Services. New York: New York Editor & Publisher, annual.

Armendariz, Matt. *Focus on Food Photography for Bloggers*. Burlington, MA: Focal, 2013.

The Asia Society. *Asia in the San Francisco Bay Area: A Cultural Travel Guide*. New York: Avalon Travel, 2004.

Avakian, Arlene Voski, ed. *Through the Kitchen Window: Women Writers Explore the Intimate Meanings of Food and Cooking*. Boston: Beacon, 1997.

Baggett, Nancy. *The All-American Cookie Book*. Boston: Houghton Mifflin, 2001.

Beard, James. *Delights and Prejudices*. Philadelphia: Running, 2002.

Beinhart, Larry. *How to Write a Mystery*. New York: Ballantine, 1996.

Bellingham, Linda. *Food Styling for Photographers: A Guide to Creating Your Own Appetizing Art*. Burlington, MA: Focal, 2008.

Bemelmans, Ludwig. *Hotel Bemelmans*. New York: Overlook, 2004.

Beranbaum, Rose Levy. *The Bread Bible*. New York: W. W. Norton, 2003.

Bittman, Mark. *How to Cook Everything: Simple Recipes for Great Food*. New York: Wiley, 1998.

Boorstin, Sharon. *Cooking for Love: A Novel with Recipes*. Lincoln: iUniverse, 2004.

Bourdain, Anthony. *Bone in the Throat*. New York: Bloomsbury USA, 2000.

———. *A Cook's Tour: In Search of the Perfect Meal*. Waterville, ME: Thorndike, 2002.

———. *Gone Bamboo*. New York: Bloomsbury USA, 2000.

———. *Kitchen Confidential: Adventures in the Culinary Underbelly*. New York: Ecco, 2001.

Brillat-Savarin, Jean Anthelme. *The Physiology of Taste: Or Meditations on Transcendental Gastronomy*. Translated by M. F. K. Fisher. New York: North Point, 1986. Originally published in 1825.

Brite, Poppy Z. *Liquor: A Novel*. Three Rivers, MI: Three Rivers, 2004.

Brown, Marcia. *Stone Soup*. New York: Aladdin Picture Books, 1997.

Bruni, Frank. *Born Round: The Secret History of a Full-time Eater*. New York: Penguin, 2009.

Buford, Bill. *Heat: An Amateur Cook's Adventures as a Kitchen Slave, Line Cook, Pasta Maker, and Apprentice to a Dante-Quoting Butcher in Tuscany*. New York: Random House, 2004.

Byrn, Anne. *The Cake Mix Doctor*. New York: Workman, 1999.

———. *Chocolate from the Cake Mix Doctor*. New York: Workman, 2001.

———. *The Dinner Doctor*. New York: Workman, 2003.

Capalbo, Carla. *The Food and Wine Lover's Companion to Tuscany*. San Francisco: Chronicle, 2002.

Capella, Anthony. *The Food of Love*. New York: Viking, 2004.

Carl, Joanna. *The Chocolate Frog Frame-Up*. New York: Signet, 2003.

Child, Julia. *Mastering the Art of French Cooking*. Reprint edition. New York: Knopf, 2001.

Clark, Robert. *James Beard: A Biography*. New York: HarperCollins, 1993.

———. *The Solace of Food: A Life of James Beard*. New York: Steerforth, 1998.

Colwin, Laurie. *Home Cooking: A Writer in the Kitchen.* New York: Perennial, 2000.

———. *More Home Cooking: A Writer Returns to the Kitchen.* New York: Perennial, 2000.

Corriher, Shirley O. *BakeWise: The Hows and Whys of Successful Baking with Over 200 Magnificent Recipes.* New York: Scribner 2008.

———. *CookWise: The Hows and Whys of Successful Cooking.* New York: Morrow Cookbooks, 1997.

Counihan, Carole, and Penny Van Esterik, eds. *Food and Culture: A Reader.* Oxford: Routledge, 1997.

Coyle, Cleo. *On What Grounds: A Coffeehouse Mystery.* New York: Berkley, 2003.

———. *Through the Grinder: A Coffeehouse Mystery.* New York: Prime Crime, 2004.

Crawford, Isis. *A Catered Murder.* New York: Kensington, 2003.

Cunningham, Marion. *Lost Recipes: Meals to Share with Friends and Family.* New York: Knopf, 2003.

Daheim, Mary. *Just Desserts: A Bed and Breakfast Mystery.* New York: Avon, 1999.

———. *Legs Benedict: A Bed and Breakfast Mystery.* New York: Avon, 1999.

———. *Nutty as a Fruitcake: A Bed and Breakfast Mystery.* New York: Avon, 1996.

David, Elizabeth. *A Book of Mediterranean Food.* New York: New York Review, 2002.

———. *An Omelet and a Glass of Wine.* Guilford, CT: Lyons, 1997.

———. *South Wind Through the Kitchen: The Best of Elizabeth David.* New York: North Point, 1999.

Davidson, Alan, ed. *The Oxford Companion to Food.* New York: Oxford University Press, 1999.

———, ed. *The Wilder Shores of Gastronomy: Twenty Years of the Best Food Writing from the Journal "Petits Propos Culinaires."* Berkeley: Ten Speed, 2002.

Davidson, Diane Mott. *Catering to Nobody: A Culinary Mystery.* New York: Bantam, 2002.

———. *Dying for Chocolate: A Culinary Mystery.* New York: Crimeline, 1993.

————. *Killer Pancake: A Culinary Mystery*. New York: Crimeline, 1996.

————. *The Last Suppers: A Culinary Mystery*. New York: Crimeline, 1995.

De Angeli, Marguerite. *Henner's Lydia*. Scottdale, PA: Herald, 1998.

De Groot, Roy Andries. *Auberge of the Flowering Hearth*. New York: Ecco, 1996.

————. *Feasts for All Seasons*. New York: Random House, 2000.

————. *In Search of the Perfect Meal: A Collection of the Food Writing of Roy Andries de Groot*. New York: St. Martin's, 1986.

Dujardin, Hélène. *Plate to Pixel: Digital Food Photography & Styling*. Indianapolis: Wiley, 2011.

Edge, John, T. *Southern Belly: The Ultimate Food Lover's Guide to the South*. Athens, GA: Hill Street, 2002.

Ehlert, Lois. *Eating the Alphabet*. New York: Red Wagon, 1996.

Ephron, Nora. *Heartburn*. New York: Vintage, 1996.

Escoffier, Auguste. *The Complete Guide to the Art of Modern Cooking*. New York: Wiley, 1983.

Esquivel, Laura. *Like Water for Chocolate: A Novel in Monthly Installments with Recipes, Romances and Home Remedies*. New York: Anchor, 1994.

Falconi, Dini, and Wendy Hollender. *Foraging and Feasting: A Field Guide and Wild Food Cookbook*. 2nd ed. Accord, NY: Botanical Arts, 2013.

Fenster, Carol. *Wheat-Free Recipes and Menus*. New York: Avery, 1997.

Field, Carol. *In Nonna's Kitchen: Recipes and Traditions from Italy's Grandmothers*. New York: HarperCollins, 1997.

Fielding, Henry. *The History of Tom Jones, A Foundling*. 1749. Reprint, New York: Oxford University Press, 1998.

Fisher, M. F. K. *Among Friends*. New York: Knopf, 1971.

————. *The Art of Eating*. New York: Vintage, 1976.

————. *As They Were*. New York: Knopf, 1982.

————. *Consider the Oyster*. New York: Duell, Sloan & Pearce, 1941.

————. *A Considerable Town*. New York: Knopf, 1978.

————. *The Gastronomical Me*. New York: Duell, Sloan & Pearce, 1943.

————. *How to Cook a Wolf*. New York: Duell, Sloan & Pearce, 1942.

———. *The Measure of Her Powers: An M. F. K. Fisher Reader.* New York: Counterpoint, 1999.

———. *Sister Age.* New York: Knopf, 1983.

Fitzgerald, F. Scott. *The Great Gatsby.* 1920. Reprint, New York: Scribner, 1995.

Fluke, Joanne. *Blueberry Muffin Murder: A Hannah Swensen Mystery with Recipes.* New York: Kensington, 2003.

———. *Chocolate Chip Cookie Murder: A Hannah Swensen Mystery with Recipes.* New York: Kensington, 2001.

———. *Lemon Meringue Pie Murder: A Hannah Swensen Mystery with Recipes.* New York: Kensington, 2004.

———. *Strawberry Shortcake Murder: A Hannah Swensen Mystery with Recipes.* New York: Kensington, 2002.

———. *Sugar Cookie Murder: A Hannah Swensen Mystery with Recipes.* New York: Kensington, 2004.

Frey, James. *How to Write a Damn Good Novel: A Step-by-Step No Nonsense Guide to Dramatic Storytelling.* New York: St. Martin's, 1987.

Fussell, Betty. *Story of Corn.* Albuquerque: University of New Mexico Press, 2004.

Gabaccia, Donna R. *We Are What We Eat: Ethnic Food and the Making of Americans.* Cambridge, MA: Harvard University Press, 2000.

Gage, Fran. *Bread and Chocolate: My Food Life in and Around San Francisco.* Seattle: Sasquatch, 1999.

Gardner, John. *The Art of Fiction: Notes on Craft for Young Writers.* New York: Vintage, 1985.

Garten, Ina. *The Barefoot Contessa Cookbook.* New York: Clarkson Potter, 1999.

Gold, Jonathan. *Counter Intelligence: Where to Eat in the Real Los Angeles.* Los Angeles: L.A. Weekly Books, 2000.

Goldberg, Natalie. *Old Friend from Far Away: How to Write a Memoir.* Audio book. Louisville, CO: Sounds True, 2002.

———. *Writing Down the Bones.* Boston: Shambhala, 1986.

Gordon, Nadia. *Death by the Glass: A Sunny McCoskey Napa Valley Mystery.* San Francisco: Chronicle, 2003.

Grimes, William. *Eating Your Words: 2000 Words to Tease Your Taste Buds.* New York: Oxford University Press, 2004.

Guerra, Melissa. *Dishes from the Wild Horse Desert*. Hoboken, NJ: Wiley, 2006.

———. *The Texas Provincial Kitchen Cookbook*. Linn: The Provincial Texas Kitchen, 1997.

Hamilton, Gabrielle. *Blood, Bones, & Butter: The Inadvertent Education of a Reluctant Chef*. New York: Random House, 2011.

Harris, Joanne. *Chocolat*. New York: Penguin, 2000.

———. *Five Quarters of the Orange*. New York: Perennial, 2002.

Hemingway, Ernest. *The Garden of Eden*. 1986. Reprint, New York: Scribner, 1995.

Henderson, Fergus. *The Whole Beast: Nose to Tail Eating*. New York: Ecco, 2004.

Herbst, Sharon Tyler. *The New Food Lover's Companion: Comprehensive Definitions of Nearly 6,000 Food, Drink, and Culinary Terms*. Hauppauge, NY: Barron's Educational Series, 2001.

Herman, Jeff. *Jeff Herman's Guide to Book Publishers, Editors & Literary Agents*. Novato, CA: New World Library, 2014.

Hesser, Amanda. *The Cook and the Gardener: A Year of Recipes and Writings from the French Countryside*. New York: W. W. Norton, 2000.

———. *Cooking for Mr. Latte: A Food Lover's Courtship, with Recipes*. New York: W. W. Norton, 2003.

Hoberman, Mary Ann. *The Seven Silly Eaters*. San Diego: Voyager, 2000.

Holman, Sheri. *The Mammoth Cheese: A Novel*. New York: Atlantic Monthly Press, 2003.

The Huffington Post Complete Guide to Blogging. New York: Simon & Schuster, 2008.

Hughes, Holly, editor. The Best Food Writing Anthologies. New York: Marlowe, annual.

Jackson, Kirstin. *It's Not You, It's Brie: Unwrapping America's Unique Culture of Cheese*. New York: Penguin, 2012.

Joachim, David. *Food Substitutions Bible: More Than 5,000 Substitutions for Ingredients, Equipment & Techniques*. Toronto: R. Rose, 2005.

———. *A Man, a Can, a Plan: 50 Tasty Meals You Can Nuke in No Time*. Emmaus, PA: Rodale, 2002.

Jones, Evan. *Epicurean Delight: The Life and Times of James Beard*. New York: Knopf, 1990.

Jones, Idwal. *High Bonnet: A Novel of Epicurean Adventures*. New York: Modern Library, 2001.

Joulwan, Melissa. *Well Fed: Paleo Recipes for People Who Love to Eat*. Austin: Smudge, 2010.

Kamp, David. *The United States of Arugula: The Sun-Dried, Cold-Pressed, Extra-Virgin Story of the American Food Revolution*. New York: Broadway, 2006.

Kancigor, Judy Bart. *Cooking Jewish: 532 Great Recipes from the Rabinowitz Family*. New York: Workman, 2007.

———. *Melting Pot Memories: The Rabinowitz Family Cookbook and Nostalgic History*. Fullerton, CA: Jan Bart, 1999.

Kasper, Lynne Rossetto. *The Splendid Table: Recipes from Emilia-Romagna, the Heartland of Northern Italian Food*. New York: Morrow Cookbooks, 1992.

Katz, Solomon H., and William Woys Weaver, eds. *Encyclopedia of Food and Culture*. Scribner Library of Daily Life. New York: Charles Scribner's Sons, 2002.

Kawasaki, Guy, and Shawn Welch. *APE: Author, Publisher, Entrepreneur—How to Publish a Book*. Nononina, 2012.

Kelly, Ian. *Cooking for Kings: The Life of Antonin Carême, the First Celebrity Chef*. New York: Walker, 2004.

Kingsolver, Barbara, with Steven L. Hopp and Camille Kingsolver. *Animal, Vegetable, Miracle: A Year of Food Life*. New York: HarperCollins, 2007.

Kiple, Kenneth, ed. *The Cambridge World History of Food*. New York: Cambridge University Press, 2000.

Kurlansky, Mark. *Cod: A Biography of the Fish That Changed the World*. New York: Penguin, 1998.

———. *Salt: A World History*. New York: Penguin, 2003.

Lamott, Anne. *Bird by Bird: Some Instructions on Writing and Life*. New York: Anchor, 1995.

Lappé, Frances Moore. *Diet for a Small Planet*. New York: Ballantine, 1971.

Larsen, Michael. *How to Write a Book Proposal*. Cincinnati, OH: Writer's Digest Books, 2004.

———. *Literary Agents: What They Do, How They Do It, and How to Find and Work with the Right One for You*. New York: Wiley, 1996.

Laudan, Rachel. *The Food of Paradise: Exploring Hawaii's Culinary Heritage*. Honolulu: University of Hawaii Press, 1996.

Levin, Martin P. *Be Your Own Literary Agent: The Ultimate Insider's Guide to Getting Published*. Berkeley: Ten Speed, 2002.

Levine, Ed. *New York Eats: The Food Shopper's Guide to the Freshest Ingredients, the Best Take Out and Baked Goods, & The Most Unusual Marketplaces in All of New York*. New York: St. Martin's Griffin, 1997.

Levy, Paul, ed. *The Penguin Book of Food and Drink*. New York: Penguin USA, 1998.

Lewis, Edna. *The Edna Lewis Cookbook*. New York: Ecco, 1983.

———. *In Pursuit of Flavor*. Charlottesville, VA: University Press of Virginia, 2000.

———. *The Taste of Country Cooking*. New York: Knopf, 1976.

Liebling, A. J. *Between Meals: An Appetite for Paris*. New York: North Point, 2004.

Lin, Grace. *Dim Sum for Everyone*. New York: Knopf Books for Young Readers, 2001.

Longbotham, Lori. *Luscious Berry Desserts*. San Francisco: Chronicle, 2006.

———. *Luscious Chocolate Desserts*. San Francisco: Chronicle, 2004.

———. *Luscious Coconut Desserts*. San Francisco: Chronicle, 2010.

———. *Luscious Lemon Desserts*. San Francisco: Chronicle, 2001.

Lyon, Elizabeth. *Nonfiction Book Proposals Anyone Can Write: How to Get a Contract and Advance Before Writing Your Book*. New York: Perigree, 2002.

Lyons, Nan. *Someone Is Killing the Great Chefs of Europe*. New York: Harcourt, 1990.

Madison, Deborah. *The Greens Cookbook: Extraordinary Vegetarian Cuisine from the Celebrated Restaurant*. New York: Bantam, 1987.

———. *The Savory Way*. New York: Broadway, 1998.

———. *Vegetarian Cooking for Everyone*. New York: Broadway, 1997.

Malladi, Amulya. *Serving Crazy with Curry*. New York: Ballantine, 2004.

Manna, Lou. *Digital Food Photography*. Florence, KY: Course Technology PTR, 2005.

Marken, Bill. *How to Fix (Just About) Everything: More than 550 Step-by-Step Instructions for Everything from Fixing a Faucet to Removing Mystery Stains to Curing a Hangover*. New York: Free Press, 2002.

Marranca, Bonnie, ed. *A Slice of Life: Contemporary Writers on Food.* New York: Overlook, 2003.

Mayes, Frances. *Under the Tuscan Sun.* New York: Broadway, 1997.

McCloskey, Robert. *Blueberries for Sal.* New York: Puffin, 1976.

McGee, Harold. *On Food and Cooking: The Science and Lore of the Kitchen.* New York: Scribner, 2004.

McGrath, Mike. *Kitchen Garden A to Z: Growing, Harvest, Buying, Storing.* New York: Harry N. Abrams, 2004.

McLagan, Jennifer. *Bitter: A Taste of the World's Most Dangerous Flavor, with Recipes.* Berkeley: Ten Speed, 2014.

McNair, James. *Cold Pasta.* San Francisco: Chronicle, 1985.

Medrich, Alice. *Bittersweet: Recipes and Tales from a Life in Chocolate.* New York: Artisan, 2003.

Melville, Herman. *Moby Dick.* 1851. Reprint, New York: Bantam Classics, 1981.

Mendelson, Anne. *Stand Facing the Stove: The Story of the Women Who Gave America the Joy of Cooking.* New York: Henry Holt, 1996.

Mesnier, Roland. *Dessert University: More than 300 Spectacular Recipes and Essential Lessons from White House Pastry Chef Roland Mesnier.* New York: Simon & Schuster, 2004.

Mettee, Stephen Blake. *The Fast Track Course on How to Write a Nonfiction Book Proposal.* New York: Quill Driver, 2001.

Murdock, Maureen. *Unreliable Truth: On Memoir and Memory.* New York: Seal, 2003.

Myers, Tamar. *Eat, Drink and Be Wary.* New York: Signet, 1998.

———. *Parsley, Sage, Rosemary and Crime.* New York: Signet, 1997.

———. *Too Many Crooks Spoil the Broth: A Pennsylvania Dutch Mystery with Recipes.* New York: Signet, 1995.

Narayan, Shoba. *Monsoon Diary: A Memoir with Recipes.* New York: Villard, 2003.

Nathan, Joan. *Foods of Israel Today.* New York: Knopf, 2001.

Nestle, Marion. *Food Politics: How the Food Industry Influences Nutrition and Health.* Berkeley: University of California Press, 2003.

Orwell, George. *Down and Out in Paris and London.* New York: Harvest/HBJ, 1972.

Oseland, James, ed. *A Fork in the Road: Tales of Food, Pleasure & Discovery on the Road.* Footscray, Victoria, Australia: Lonely Planet, 2013.

Osterwalder, Alexander, and Yves Pigneur. *Business Model Generation: A Handbook for Visionaries, Game Changers, and Challengers.* Hoboken, NJ: Wiley, 2010.

Ostmann, Barbara Gibbs, and Jane Baker. *The Recipe Writer's Handbook.* New York: Wiley, 2001.

Ozeki, Ruth L. *My Year of Meats.* New York: Penguin, 1999.

Page, Susan. *The Shortest Distance Between You and a Published Book: 20 Steps to Success.* New York: Broadway, 1997.

Parson, Russ. *How to Read a French Fry, and Other Stories of Intriguing Kitchen Science.* Boston: Houghton Mifflin, 2003.

Patent, Greg. *Baking in America: Contemporary and Traditional Favorites from the Past 200 Years.* Boston: Houghton Mifflin, 2002.

Pellegrini, Angelo. *The Unprejudiced Palate: Classic Thoughts on Food and the Good Life.* Guilford, CT: Lyons, 1992.

Pépin, Jacques. *The Apprentice: My Life in the Kitchen.* Boston: Houghton Mifflin, 2003.

Peterson, Joan, and David Peterson. *Eat Smart in Poland: How to Decipher the Menu, Know the Market Foods & Embark on a Tasting Adventure.* Madison, WI: Gingko, 2000.

Pillsbury, Richard. *No Foreign Food: The American Diet in Time and Place.* Geographies of the Imagination. Boulder: Westview, 1998.

Pollan, Michael. *Food Rules: An Eater's Manual.* New York: Penguin, 2009.

———. *In Defense of Food: An Eater's Manifesto.* New York: Penguin, 2008.

———. *The Omnivore's Dilemma: A Natural History of Four Meals.* New York: Penguin, 2006.

Pomaine, Édouard de. *Cooking with Pomaine.* Washington, DC: Serif, 1993.

Pottker, Janice. *Crisis in Candyland: Melting the Chocolate Shell of the Mars Family Empire.* Palo Alto, CA: National Press Books, 1995.

Prior, Lily. *La Cucina: A Novel of Rapture.* New York: Ecco, 2001.

Proust, Marcel. *Swann's Way.* Translated by Lydia Davis. New York: Viking, 2003. Originally published in French in 1913.

Rabiner, Susan, and Alfred Fortunato. *Thinking Like Your Editor—How to Write Great Serious Nonfiction and Get It Published.* New York: W. W. Norton, 2003.

Raichlen, Steven. *The Barbecue Bible*. New York: Workman, 1998.

Rawles, Nancy. *Crawfish Dreams: A Novel*. New York: Doubleday, 2003.

Rayner, Jay. *Eating Crow*. New York: Simon & Schuster, 2004.

Reader's Guide to Periodical Literature. New York: H. W. Wilson, annual.

Reichl, Ruth. *Comfort Me with Apples: More Adventures at the Table*. New York: Random House, 2002.

———, ed. *Endless Feasts: Sixty Years of Writing from Gourmet*. New York: Modern Library, 2002.

———. *Garlic and Sapphires: The Secret Life of a Critic in Disguise*. New York: Penguin, 2005.

———. *Tender at the Bone: Growing Up at the Table*. New York: Broadway, 1999.

Richman, Alan. *Fork It Over: The Intrepid Adventures of a Professional Eater*. New York: HarperCollins, 2004.

Richman, Phyllis. *Murder on the Gravy Train*. New York: Avon, 2000.

———. *The Butter Did It: A Gastronomic Tale of Love and Murder*. New York: HarperTorch, 1998.

———. *Who's Afraid of Virginia Ham?* New York: Avon, 2002.

Robertson, Laurel. *Laurel's Kitchen*. Abridged edition. Berkeley: Ten Speed, 1993.

Rocklin, Joanne. *Strudel Stories*. New York: Delacorte, 1999.

Roden, Claudia. *The Book of Jewish Food: An Odyssey from Samarkand to New York*. New York: Knopf, 1996.

Rombauer, Irma S., and Marion Rombauer Becker. *The Joy of Cooking*. New York: Scribner, 1985. Original version published in 1931.

Roorbach, Bill. *Writing Life Stories*. Cincinnati: Story, 1998.

Root, Waverly, and Richard de Rochemont. *Eating in America: A History*. New York: Ecco, 2004.

Rosso, Julee, and Sheila Lukins. *The Silver Palate Cookbook*. New York: Workman, 1982.

Ruhlman, Michael. *The Making of a Chef: Mastering Heat at the Culinary Institute*. New York: Owl, 1999.

Sahni, Julie. *Classic Indian Cooking*. New York: Morrow Cookbooks, 1980.

Sanger, Amy Wilson. *A Little Bit of Soul Food*. World Snacks series. Berkeley: Tricycle, 2004.

Schlosser, Eric. *Fast Food Nation: The Dark Side of the All-American Meal.* New York: Perennial, 2002.

Schott, Ben. *Schott's Food & Drink Miscellany.* New York: Bloomsbury, 2004.

Sendak, Maurice. *Chicken Soup with Rice: A Book of Months.* New York: HarperTrophy, 1991.

————. *In the Night Kitchen.* New York: HarperCollins, 1996.

Shapiro, Anna, ed. *Feast of Words: For Lovers of Food and Fiction.* New York: W. W. Norton, 1996.

Shapiro, Laura. *Julia Child.* New York: Lipper/Viking, 2007.

————. *Perfection Salad: Women and Cooking at the Turn of the Century.* New York: Modern Library, 2001.

————. *Something from the Oven: Reinventing Dinner in 1950s America.* New York: Viking, 2004.

Sheraton, Mimi. *Eating My Words: An Appetite for Life.* New York: Morrow Cookbooks, 2004.

Sinclair, Upton. *The Jungle.* New York: Bantam, 1981. Originally published in 1906.

Slater, Nigel. *Toast: The Story of a Boy's Hunger.* New York: Gotham, 2004.

Smalls, Alexander. *Grace the Table: Stories & Recipes From My Southern Revival.* New York: Harlem Moon, 2004.

Smith, Andrew F. *The Oxford Encyclopedia of Food and Drink in America.* New York: Oxford University Press, 2004.

————. *Peanuts: The Illustrious History of the Goober Pea.* Champaign: University of Illinois Press, 2002.

————. *Pure Ketchup: A History of America's National Condiment, with Recipes.* Washington, DC: Smithsonian Books, 2001.

————. *The Tomato in America: Early History, Culture, and Cookery.* Columbia, SC: University of South Carolina Press, 1994.

Stein, Sol. *Stein on Writing: A Master Editor of Some of the Most Successful Writers of Our Century Shares His Craft Techniques and Strategies.* New York: St. Martin's, 2000.

Steingarten, Jeffrey. *The Man Who Ate Everything.* New York: Vintage, 1998.

Stern, Jane, and Michael Stern. *Roadfood: The Coast-to-Coast Guide to 500 of the Best Barbeque Joints, Lobster Shacks, Ice Cream Parlors, Highway Diners, and Much More.* New York: Broadway, 2002.

Stone, Jerry James. *Holidazed: A Cocktail Cookbook for Getting Lit on Christmas*. San Francisco: Cooking Stoned, 2013.

Strunk Jr., William, and E. B. White. *The Elements of Style*. 4th edition. New York: Longman, 2000.

Taxel, Laura. *Cleveland Ethnic Eats 2004: The Guide to Authentic Ethnic Eats in Northeastern Ohio*. Cleveland: Gray, 2003.

Theophano, Janet. *Eat My Words: Reading Women's Lives through the Cookbooks They Wrote*. New York: Palgrave Macmillan, 2002.

Todhunter, Andrew. *A Meal Observed*. New York: Knopf, 2004.

Tolstoy, Leo. *Anna Karenina*. New York: Modern Library, 2000.

Trillin, Calvin. *American Fried: Adventures of a Happy Eater*. New York: Vintage, 1979.

———. *The Tummy Trilogy*. New York: Farrar, Straus & Giroux, 1994.

2015 Writer's Market. Edited by Robert Lee Brewer. Blue Ash, OH: Writer's Digest Books, 2014.

Unterman, Patricia. *Patricia Unterman's Food Lover's Guide to San Francisco*. Berkeley: Ten Speed, 2003.

Various. Skinny series of cookbooks. Chicago: Surrey, 1993–1996.

Villas, James. *Stalking the Green Fairy: And Other Fantastic Adventures in Food and Drink*. New York: Wiley, 2004.

Visser, Margaret. *Much Depends on Dinner: The Extraordinary History and Mythology, Allure and Obsessions, Perils and Taboo, of an Ordinary Meal*. New York: Grove, 1999.

Vivaldo, Denise, with Cindie Flannigan. *The Food Stylist's Handbook*. Layton, UT: Gibbs Smith, 2010.

Volland, Susan. *Love and Meatballs*. New York: New American Library, 2004.

Wechsberg, Joseph. *Blue Trout and Black Truffles: The Peregrinations of an Epicure*. Chicago: Academy Chicago Publishers, 1985.

Wells, Patricia. *A Food Lover's Guide to Paris*. New York: Workman, 1999.

Werlin, Laura. *The All American Cheese and Wine Book*. New York: Stewart, Tabori & Chang, 2003.

———. *New American Cheese*. New York: Stewart, Tabori & Chang, 2000.

Wharton, Edith. *The Age of Innocence*. 1920. Reprint, New York: Modern Library, 1999.

Wheat, Carolyn. *How to Write Killer Fiction: The Funhouse of Mystery & the Roller Coaster of Suspense*. Palo Alto, CA: Perseverance, 2003.

Whitman, Joan, and Dolores Simon. *Recipes into Type: A Handbook for Cookbook Writers and Editors*. Newton, MA: Biscuit, 1993.

The Wiggles. *Yummy, Yummy Fruit Salad*. New York: Grosset & Dunlap, 2003.

Winston, Lolly. *Good Grief*. New York: Warner, 2004.

Wood, Monica. *Description*. The Elements of Fiction Writing. Cincinnati: Writer's Digest Books, 1999.

Wyler, Susan. *Great Books for Cooks*. New York: Ballantine, 1999.

Young, Grace. *Wisdom of the Chinese Kitchen*. New York: Simon & Schuster, 1999.

Young, Nicole S. *Food Photography: From Snapshots to Great Shots*. San Francisco: Peachpit, 2012.

Zinsser, William, ed. *Inventing the Truth: The Art and Craft of Memoir*. Rev. and exp. ed. Boston: Mariner, 1998.

———. *On Writing Well: The Classic Guide to Writing Nonfiction*. New York: HarperResource, 2001.

———. *Writing About Your Life: A Journey into the Past*. New York: Marlowe, 2004.

APPENDIX:
SELECTED RESOURCES
FOR FOOD WRITERS

National Magazines That Take Freelance Writing:

- Alimentum
- Art of Eating
- Better Homes & Gardens
- Bon Appétit
- Cherry Bombe
- Clean Eating
- Condé Nast Traveler
- Cooking Light
- Cook's Illustrated
- Eating Well
- Edible Communities publications
- Esquire
- Everyday Food
- Every Day with Rachael Ray
- Family Circle
- Fine Cooking
- Food & Wine
- Food Network
- Food Traveler
- Fool
- Garden & Gun
- Gather Journal
- GQ
- Health
- Kinfolk
- Lucky Peach
- Martha Stewart Living
- Meatpaper
- Modern Farmer
- National Geographic Traveler
- Natural Foods Merchandiser
- New Yorker
- O, The Oprah Magazine
- Plate

- *Prevention*
- *Put an Egg on It*
- *Real Simple*
- *Relish*
- *Remedy*
- *Saveur*
- *Seafood Business*
- *Southern Living*
- *Sunset: Life in the West*
- *Swallow*
- *Sweet Paul*
- *Travel & Leisure*
- *Vegetarian Times*
- *Where*
- *Woman's Day*
- *Yoga Journal*

Websites That Take Freelance Writing

Check the websites of your city magazine, alternative weekly, television and radio stations, and other local media to see if they take freelance writing as well.

- FoodNetwork.com (recipes and cooking)
- Forbes.com (the occasional food story, such as "Who's Really Cooking Your Celebrity Chef Meal?")
- Grist.org (environmental news and green living advice)
- iVillage.com/food (recipes, bulletin boards)
- TheKitchn.com
- On.AOL.com/channel/food (recipe ideas, menus, drinks, and entertaining)
- Salon.com
- SeriousEats.com
- Slate.com (runs the odd food story, usually trend-based opinion pieces)

More Websites for the Food Obsessed

- Allrecipes.com
- Chow.com (recipes, cooking tips, resources, and stories for people who love food)
- Epicurious.com (recipes from *Bon Appétit* and *Gourmet*)

- Foodista.com (recipes, cooking tips, and food news)
- Forums.eGullet.org (discussion on cooking, dining, and cookbooks)
- ZesterDaily.com (stories on food, wine, and travel)
- Food52.com (recipes, stories, and contests)

Websites About Book Publishing

- AgentQuery.com (database of literary agents)
- LiteraryMarketplace.com (lists literary agents alphabetically by name)
- PublishersMarketplace.com (web pages for writers and agents to promote themselves)

Food Blogging Conferences
in the United States and Canada

- The Big Potluck—thebigpotluck.com
- Blended Conference—blendedconference.com
- BlogHer and BlogHer Food—blogher.com
- Camp Blogaway—campblogaway.com
- Chopped Conference—choppedcon.com
- Eat, Write, Retreat—eatwriteretreat.com
- Food Blog Forum—foodblogforum.com
- Food Blogger Connect—foodbloggerconnect.com
- Food Bloggers of Canada Conference—foodbloggersofcanada.com
- Food Media South—southernfoodways.org/events/food-media-south
- The International Food Blogger Conference (IFBC)—foodista.com/ifbc
- Mixed—mixedcon.com
- Okanagan Food and Wine Writers' Workshop—okanaganfoodandwinewritersworkshop.com

- Techmunch—techmunchconf.com
- Vida Vegan Con—vidavegancon.com

Food, Cooking, and Writing Classes

- Book Passage—bookpassage.com (I teach classes on general food writing and on cookbook writing at this San Francisco Bay Area bookstore)
- Gotham Writers' Workshop and Writing Classes—writing classes.com (New York–based and online classes in nonfiction writing, including food writing)
- The International Culinary Center—internationalculinary center.com/courses/food-writing-and-blogging-intensive (offers class on food writing taught by Alan Richman and others in New York)
- The International Culinary Institute—recreational.ice.edu /Home/FoodMedia (offers a variety of classes on food writing and blogging in New York)
- Media Bistro—mediabistro.com/courses (classes on food writing, freelance writing, proposal writing, etc.)
- Shaw Guides—shawguides.com (writing and cooking classes around the country)
- Writer's Digest—writersdigest.com (online classes, conferences)
- Writers who teach food writing: Monica Bhide (online), Kathleen Flinn (Seattle, WA), Diane Morgan (Portland, OR)
- Writing Salon—writingsalons.com (I teach classes at this school in San Francisco and Berkeley; you'll also find classes on freelancing and essay writing)

Associations and Nonprofits

- American Institute of Wine & Food—aiwf.org (a nonprofit devoted to improving appreciation, understanding, and accessibility of food and drink)

- Association for the Study of Food and Society—food-culture. org (international organization dedicated to academic study of food, culture, and society)
- Les Dames d'Escoffier—ldei.org (women's organization for food industry professionals, food writers, and researchers)
- International Association of Culinary Professionals—iacp .com
- Slow Food—slowfood.com (studies effects of fast food on society and life)
- Women Chefs and Restaurateurs—womenchefs.org (promotes the education and advancement of women in the restaurant industry)

Food Studies

- The American University of Rome Graduate School, master of arts in food studies—aur.edu/gradschool/graduate-programs /food-studies/introduction
- Benedictine University (online, US-based), master of science in nutrition and wellness—online.ben.edu/msnw/masters-in -nutrition-wellness
- Boston University's Culinary Arts, certificate and master of liberal arts in gastronomy program—bu.edu/met/programs /graduate/gastronomy/
- Le Cordon Bleu Graduate Program in Gastronomy at the University of Adelaide, Australia—gastronomy.adelaide.edu .au
- New York University Graduate program in food studies and food management—education.nyu.edu/nutrition

For a more extensive list, see food-culture.org/food-studies-programs.

INDEX